The Complete
Canadian
Home Astrologer

The Complete
Canadian
Home Astrologer

Gwyn Turner

NELSON/CANADA

Special thanks is given to my son, John-Barry Turner for help in the systemisation of this book.

By the same author, *Human Destiny - The Psychology of Astrology*

Nelson Canada Limited, 1980
Copyright © Gwyn Turner 1977
First published by Thomas Nelson Australia Pty Ltd. 1977

0-17-600787-3

Printed and bound in Canada

1 2 3 4 5 6 7 8 9 0   BP   8 9 8 7 6 5 4 3 2 1 0

Cover Art by LORRAINE AGLIALORO Studio 2 Graphics

Contents

1
INTRODUCTION

What this book can do for you

If you know your month of birth, you already know your Zodiac Sun Sign. Many people who follow 'The Stars' in newspapers and magazines think this is all there is to Astrology.

This is far from the case. Your Sun Sign only represents your individual or inner nature, and this is only a small fraction of the full story.

Sun Sign readings only scratch the surface of the information that a complete Astrological analysis can give, when based on a proper Horoscope Chart marked with the birth positions of the planets and all the other factors.

Just by adding one additional factor - your Ascendant Sign, (the Sign rising at the time of birth), it describes your temperament and outer expression, i.e. how you appear to others, which may be quite different to how you feel within. You can read yours on page **22-23**.

It is important to know how other people see you. It can be used to good effect in your daily life. Likewise, you will be able to gain an insight into the way others think, feel and behave. In fact there is no limit to what true Astrology can do for you.

Until now the complicated process of analysing your Astrological potentials needed the skill of a highly experienced Astrologer. However, with this book in hand, you are now your own Astrologer and can do anyone's Horoscope. There is no limit to the number of Horoscopes you can do with this book; as there are no two alike.

Understandably, some people will have difficulty ascertaining their birth time, but included in Section 5, there is an easy method of finding it.

Today, Horoscope Chart production has been revolutionised by the advent of Astrological computer calculating services which handle the time consuming task of Chart mechanics. In keeping with this new era of Astrology, this book presents a new and unique method on how to obtain and read a Horoscope Chart.

A Horoscope Chart is a map of the heavens at the time of birth. It shows the position of the planets and zodiacal signs in relation to the earth. From this pattern, formed by the planets at the time of birth, this method allows you to compile a full Astrological reading showing the capacity and potential of the individual in relation to each department of life.

Each planet in the Chart has a different influence and effect on human activity.

The Sun identifies the basic character. This represents the individual's willpower and capacities, often referred to in the press as 'Your Zodiacal Sign'. For instance, if you are born between July 24 and August 23 your Sun would be in Leo.

The Moon reflects the type of personality and how you express yourself. Mercury defines the type of intellect while Venus expresses the emotional nature.

These four qualities can work independently but all correlate to make up the character of the individual.

Mars gives energy and drive. Jupiter is responsible for expansion and optimism. Saturn contracts and restricts, making for patience and cautiousness. Uranus gives an advanced intellect with inventiveness and originality while Neptune stimulates the imagination and is responsible for that touch of genius.

Pluto is responsible for group activity and the deep-seated forces of nature.

The Ascendant Sign on the Eastern Horizon at the time of birth is also a significant point. It identifies the individual's temperament and appearance. The Zenith of the Chart, called the MC point, is another important factor as it represents the peak of the ambitions.

The Signs of the Zodiac give colouring to the planets, while each of the twelve segments of the Horoscope wheel, called Houses, define the various Departments of life.

The Interpretations given in this book have been designed by the author to combine all these influences to give an in-depth Astrological analysis of the whole life.

As the planetary system, from the time of birth, moves forward at the same pace as the growth of the individual, man's growth remains locked in this celestial relationship throughout life. Thus the Horoscope Chart becomes a clock face of life and can be read for any time ahead, presented in this book by ascertaining the individual's future Moon Cycles.

These Moon Cycles by Sign and House, each lasting some two and a half years, bring a change of outlook and therefore a change of activity. In addition, the day to day movement of the transiting planets is used to pinpoint current events.

The Interpretations of these Progressions and Transits in Section 3 have been written in such a manner that when combined they will give an insight into the nature and timing of future prospects and can be of great value in forward planning.

Advanced Astrological students will be interested to know that although the example Chart in this book is set up for the Tropical Zodiac and Placidus House system, this book can be used to interpret all other Zodiacal systems using Houses.

Compatibility between the sexes is an additional department which can be read in Section 4. By comparing the nature of either the Sun or Ascendant Signs compatibility factors can easily be discovered. Certain Signs have a common element, some mix well, others not so well.

Another way to check on compatibility is shown by comparing the individual Horoscope Charts of two people, as the exchange of the Ascendant, Sun, Moon, Venus and Mars in their Zodiacal Signs reveals factors that can attract and make for harmony.

If you have a partner and wish to know how they will affect your life, the way is shown how a more detailed analysis can be made by transposing their Planets into your own Chart and reading the Interpretations in that light. Such an analysis will point out the strengths or weaknesses that your partner will bring to your relationship and therefore will allow you to develop a greater understanding, as even the most difficult planetary combinations can be turned into positive forces.

How to use this book

To obtain a full Astrological reading for any person, it is first necessary to obtain an individual Horoscope Chart showing the position of the Signs and Planets at birth.

This Horoscope Chart can be compiled by your own calculations from instructions given in Section 6 of this book.

However, plotting an individual Horoscope Chart takes time, especially if you are a beginner. The quickest and most accurate method is to order a computer-plotted Chart. You can obtain one for any person's birth data, fully calculated, at a nominal fee.

There are a number of Astrological calculating services available. Details are given on the last page of this book.

Just write out your order as in the form below.

how to order a computer chart

Write out an order form like this or make a photocopy of it and then fill it in. Mail to a computer company as listed at the end of this book.

computer chart order form

> To Computer Manager,
> Please send me a Computer Calculated Astronomical Natal Chart for the following birth data -
> *Time of Birth . . . . . hrs . . . . . mins am/pm (If unsure, see Section 5 'How to Find your Time of Birth')
>
> Date of Birth: Date . . . . . Month . . . . Year . . . . . .
>
> Place of Birth: City . . . . Prov. . . . . . . Country . . . .
>
> Please send my Chart to:—
>
> Mr/Ms . . . .
> Address . . . .
> City . . . . Prov . . . .
> Post Code . . . . Country . . . .
>
> *Note - If Daylight Saving Time, when clocks are advanced, applied on your birth date the Computer Company will deduct this advance from the birth time given before they start calculating, so just give the time shown by the clock at birth.

The horoscope chart and its symbols

To assist you to recognise what makes up a Horoscope Chart, here are the main factors.

The circular Chart is divided into 12 sections like a cartwheel. On this are marked the exact positions of the Planets and the Signs of the Zodiac at the time of birth.

The 12 sections are called 'HOUSES' and these are fixed. The first House always starts at the left horizon of the Chart, called the 'Ascendant', and the Houses are numbered counter-clockwise.

The 12 SIGNS of the Zodiac are placed around the Chart, but do not necessarily match the House divisions. Usually a Sign will cover part of one House and part of the next, but sometimes extends to cover a third House due to the angular view from the birth latitude. Each Sign represents 30 degrees of the Zodiac, (the 12 making a total of 360 degrees). The dividing line of each House is marked with the degree of the Zodiac Sign at that point, often called the House Cusp.

Next, the ten PLANETS are placed into their correct 'positions' in the Zodiac Sign and House.

the signs	the houses	the planets

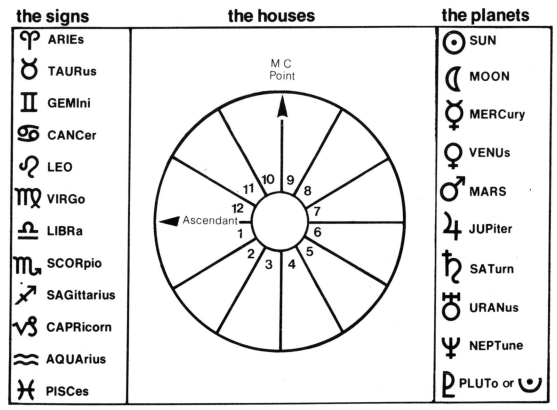

the signs	the planets
♈ ARIEs	☉ SUN
♉ TAURus	☽ MOON
♊ GEMIni	☿ MERCury
♋ CANCer	♀ VENUs
♌ LEO	♂ MARS
♍ VIRGo	♃ JUPiter
♎ LIBRa	♄ SATurn
♏ SCORpio	♅ URANus
♐ SAGittarius	♆ NEPTune
♑ CAPRicorn	♇ PLUTo or ⯓
♒ AQUArius	
♓ PISCes	

The first letters of the above Signs and Planets shown in CAPITALS are the abbreviated form as used in Computer Horoscope Charts.

However, the following abbreviations or symbols, which are sometimes included in Charts, are *not Planets,* but merely technical points that can be disregarded; PARF, PARS, PT FORTUNE, ⊕, ⊗, NODE, HEAD, TAIL, MOON NODE, ☊, ☋ .

How to read a horoscope chart

In this book you will find an Interpretation heading for each Department of life. The top of each double page spread shows what combination to look for in the Chart.

listing

As each Horoscope is different, it is a good idea to first list all the read-ups of each Chart on the handy Horoscope Reader, (see page **15**). This remains a permanent record of each Chart you do.

Because a life consists of many facets, it is important that the Interpretation for each Department of life is carefully tabulated on this list to agree with each planetary position in the Chart. These Interpretations are then read together, which automatically give you the complete life story.

To help you follow this listing procedure, a sample Horoscope Reader has been filled in on the next pages for 'Mr John Doe'. You will see how it relates to the combinations in his Computer Chart.

concentrations

In reading the Interpretations of a listed Horoscope, you may find that there is more than one read-up for a particular Department of life. This is because more than one planet falls in one particular House or section of the Horoscope Chart.

Such a concentration of planets would signify that the person will find his most vital experiences in these affairs. Although these read-ups may sometimes appear to have a different theme or even conflict, each influence will be felt at some period of the life, either having passed or to be experienced in the future.

For example, if you check John Doe's list, you'll notice a concentration in his departments of 'Financial benefits through others' and also in his 'Travel and study'. This is because both the 8th and 9th Houses of his Chart hold more than one planet.

missed departments

You will notice that in reading a complete listed Horoscope, there could be some Department headings with no read-ups allocated to them. This is due to there being no planet in the related House or section - there are only ten planets to cover twelve Houses.

However, any missed Department is automatically covered by another heading that relates to the same facets of life.

For instance, John Doe's missed read-up on 'Romance' is covered by 'Courtships', 'Marriage' and 'Friendships'.

If it is absolutely vital that you find out more information about a missed Department, due to there being no planet in a House, there is a method outside the automatic listing procedure. However, such an Interpretation is not as strong as if a planet were actually in the House but the read-up can throw a little further light on the Department concerned.

To do this you first note the *Sign* (at the spoke) on the start of the House that contains no planet and then ascertain the *Ruling Planet* of *this Sign,* (from Rulers given at the top of pages **26-27**). Next, read this *Planet* under the *appropriate Department heading* as if it was contained in the House.

For example, if we wanted more information on John Doe's missed 'Romance' we would note from the Horoscope Reader that this Department is covered by the 5th House and as the Sign (at the spoke) on its start is GEMI, and ascertaining its Ruling Planet is MERC, we would read MERC under the heading, 'Romance and matters close to the heart'.

negative and positive aspects

Each Interpretation contains both the negative and positive facets of the situation to embrace the effect of planetary aspects.

When the negative side is active, greater personal effort will be needed to counteract any undesirable effects. However when the positive or harmonious side is active, things will fall into place with little effort. A 'Square' aspect is negative and disruptive, a 'Trine' is positive and creative, a 'Conjunction' is intensifying and an 'Opposition' is stressful.

fate or freewill

While your complete Birth Horoscope indicates all your life's prospects and remains your key to future action, the Horoscope readings are not the *'voice of fate'* - they are a guide to wiser living. They tell you, what *you* are prone to think and do and, what *others* are prone to think and do - *to you!*

In other words they will advise you, what is *best* for you and, what is *not best* for you!

If action is called for, your 'Future' cycles will be a guide and tell you, *when!*

Should any statements appear conflicting at first, a careful weighing will show how far each is true in its own particular sphere. It lies with you, to adjust the balance between these warring influences, by strengthening the weaker points of your character, so that harmony may be restored.

All fate, good or evil, is made originally by our own thoughts and actions and has its roots in our character - thus *character becomes destiny.*

A careful study of your Horoscope readings will serve as a guide through life by pointing out the direction in which you are best fitted to express your particular qualifications and where lies the greatest amount of success and subsequent happiness.

To know ourselves is to become *wise* and thus to *master fate.*

Example Horoscope Chart

For Mr John Doe, obtained from an Astrological Computer Calculating Service.
(This Chart from A.B.I. PO Box 251, Wethersfield, Connecticut 06109, USA)

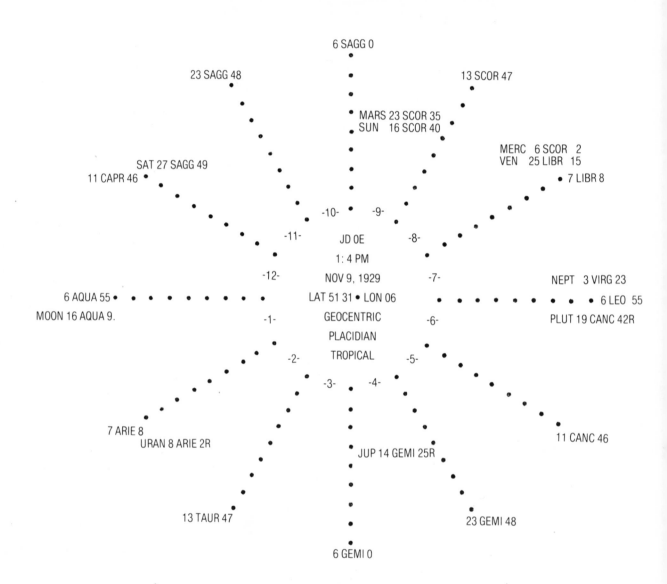

In finding the Planets *in HOUSES* they are seen as follows: 1st House = MOON;
2nd House = URAN;   3rd House = nil;   4th House = JUP;   5th House = nil;
6th House = PLUT;   7th House = NEPT;   8th House = MERC & VEN;   9th House = MARS
& SUN;   10th House = nil;   11th House = SAT;   12th House = nil.

Horoscope reader

example filled in for the chart of Mr John Doe

YOUR INDIVIDUAL NATURE	SUN IN .... *SCOR* .... SIGN
YOUR PHYSICAL TEMPERAMENT	ASCENDANT SIGN .... *AQUA* ....
YOUR SPECIAL CHARACTERISTICS	PLANETS *MOON* IN ASCENDANT SIGN
YOUR IDEAL CHANNEL OF EXPRESSION	RULER IN ...... *2nd* .... HOUSE
YOUR PERSONALITY	MOON IN ...... *AQUA* .... SIGN
IDEAL EXPRESSION OF PERSONALITY	MOON IN ...... *1st* .... HOUSE
MENTAL QUALIFICATIONS	MERCURY IN .. *SCOR* .... SIGN
YOUR FINANCIAL CAPACITY	PLANETS ...... *URAN* .... IN 2nd HOUSE
FINANCIAL BENEFITS THROUGH OTHERS	PLANETS *MERC/VENU* IN 8th HOUSE
YOUR VOCATIONAL ABILITY	SUN IN .... *SCOR* .... SIGN
YOUR AMBITIONS AND CAREER	PLANETS .... IN 10th HOUSE
ROMANCE & MATTERS CLOSE TO THE HEART	PLANETS .... IN 5th HOUSE
COURTSHIPS	VENUS IN ..... *LIBRA* .... SIGN
MARRIAGE & PARTNERSHIP	PLANETS .... *NEPT* ..... IN 7th HOUSE
FRIENDSHIPS	PLANETS .... *SAT* ...... IN 11th HOUSE
YOUR GENERAL HEALTH TENDENCIES	PLANETS *PLUT* .... IN 6th HOUSE
POINTS TO WATCH REGARDING YOUR HEALTH	ASCENDANT SIGN .... *AQUA* ....
LOCAL TRAVEL & SOCIAL ACTIVITY	PLANETS .... IN 3rd HOUSE
TRAVEL & STUDY — EXPANSION OF MIND	PLANETS ... *SUN/MARS*.. IN 9th HOUSE
HOME & DOMESTIC AFFAIRS	PLANETS ... *JUP* .... IN 4th HOUSE
YOUR CHILDREN	PLANETS .... IN ♌ LEO SIGN

(Refer to Section 3 for the following)

FUTURE PROSPECTS .. *AGE 21 (NOV. 1950)* ... Year	PROGRESSED MOON IN *SCOR* .. SIGN
FUTURE PROSPECTS .. *AGE 21 (NOV. 1950)* .... Year	PROGRESSED MOON IN *9th* HOUSE
ADDITIONAL FUTURE PROSPECTS	
for ... *MAR* ...... Month *1981* .. Year	TRANSIT ..... *JUP* ..... IN *8th* HOUSE
for .... Month .... Year	TRANSIT ...... · .... IN .... HOUSE

In finding Planets *in SIGN,* (as required for Sun, Moon, Venu and any Planets in Leo) you list the Sign that is found in the Chart written next to each Planet, such as this example, SUN 16 SCOR 40, (i.e. SUN in *SCOR* SIGN).

In some hand-drawn Charts where the Sign is not written next to each Planet, the Planet is in the Sign nearest to it in the Chart.

(Blank) **Horoscope chart**

Put your Horoscope Chart here, that you may already have, or one plotted from Section 6, or calculated by a Computer Service, and then make a list on the 'Horoscope Reader' of the various entries that apply to this Chart. Next, turn to each Department of life and read the correct Interpretation.

Likewise, you can make a list of Interpretations in a similar manner of the Charts of your family or friends.

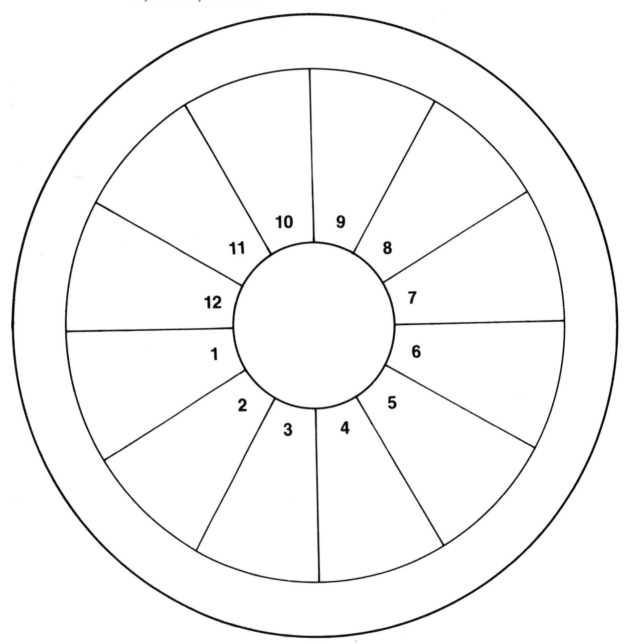

Note If you obtain a computer Horoscope where the opening page gives the Position of the House Cusps and the Position of Planets but not in circular form, you can (with the help of page **93**, Section 6) transpose this information to the circular Chart above and then read the interpretations in this book in the usual manner.

(Blank) **Horoscope reader**

YOUR INDIVIDUAL NATURE	SUN IN .... SIGN
YOUR PHYSICAL TEMPERAMENT	ASCENDANT SIGN ....
YOUR SPECIAL CHARACTERISTICS	PLANETS .... IN ASCENDANT SIGN
YOUR IDEAL CHANNEL OF EXPRESSION	RULER IN .... HOUSE
YOUR PERSONALITY	MOON IN .... SIGN
IDEAL EXPRESSION OF PERSONALITY	MOON IN .... HOUSE
MENTAL QUALIFICATIONS	MERCURY IN .... SIGN
YOUR FINANCIAL CAPACITY	PLANETS .... IN 2nd HOUSE
FINANCIAL BENEFITS THROUGH OTHERS	PLANETS .... IN 8th HOUSE
YOUR VOCATIONAL ABILITY	SUN IN .... SIGN
YOUR AMBITIONS AND CAREER	PLANETS .... IN 10th HOUSE
ROMANCE & MATTERS CLOSE TO YOUR HEART	PLANETS .... IN 5th HOUSE
COURTSHIPS	VENUS IN .... SIGN
MARRIAGE & PARTNERSHIP	PLANETS .... IN 7th HOUSE
FRIENDSHIPS	PLANETS .... IN 11th HOUSE
YOUR GENERAL HEALTH TENDENCIES	PLANETS .... IN 6th HOUSE
POINTS TO WATCH REGARDING YOUR HEALTH	ASCENDANT SIGN ....
LOCAL TRAVEL & SOCIAL ACTIVITY	PLANETS .... IN 3rd HOUSE
TRAVEL & STUDY — EXPANSION OF MIND	PLANETS .... IN 9th HOUSE
HOME & DOMESTIC AFFAIRS	PLANETS .... IN 4th HOUSE
YOUR CHILDREN	PLANETS ....IN ♌ LEO SIGN

(Refer to Section 3 for the following)

FUTURE PROSPECTS .... Year	PROGRESSED MOON IN .... SIGN
FUTURE PROSPECTS .... Year	PROGRESSED MOON IN .... HOUSE
ADDITIONAL FUTURE PROSPECTS	
for .... Month .... Year	TRANSIT .... IN .... HOUSE
for .... Month .... Year	TRANSIT .... IN .... HOUSE

How to synthesise a horoscope

In the Horoscope Reader it will be noticed that Departments of life are grouped by related headings covering character, vocation, romance, health, travel, domestic and children's affairs.

When reading a listed Horoscope, the Interpretations of related Departments may appear to generalise, but by using the art of synthesis you can narrow these down to the main issue. This is an easy procedure that gives you the extra personal touch of a good Astrologer.

To do this it will be necessary to examine the listed Interpretations that have a bearing on the Departments concerned and upon comparing these read-ups it will become obvious that one particular condition or activity will stand out above others.

Say we wish to examine the love and marriage prospects of the John Doe example, in reading his 'Courtships' (VENU in LIBR) we see that 'during courtships he will have a rival, who could cause some opposition to arise' and in his 'Marriage' read-up (NEPT) we read that 'long expected happiness could meet with disappointment at the last moment, due to deception on the part of another'.

These extracts obviously show a broken engagement but as the Interpretations also promise some happiness, there is every indication that he could have greater success in future love affairs, providing that he can learn to judge character and not be 'misled by personal magnetism'.

Alternatively, if health was the issue, we would read under 'General health tendencies' (PLUT) that for John Doe, 'Some diseases can result from self-poisoning, due to the absorption of toxins from the system' and in the other health Interpretation, 'Points to watch regarding health' (AQUA) that 'care will be necessary to always keep the blood and system in good order'.

It is quite evident that blood-poisoning is a condition that John Doe needs to guard against.

If the financial prospects of John Doe were in question, we would first read his 'Financial capacity' (URAN) which shows 'sudden changes in fortune' matched by 'sudden gains'.

Next, in reading his 'Financial benefits through others' (MERC & VENU) we note that at some period of life he could expect to gain through a legacy, emphasised by being repeated in this double read-up.

Further, it is remarkable to read in another of his listed Departments 'Home and domestic affairs' (JUP) of 'gain through inheritance' leaving no doubt that this is a prospect that is spelled out to come at some time in the future.

Likewise, in the same manner as these three examples, you can, by combining the salient points of the read-ups, obtain a greater insight into the vital issues of each Department of life, giving at the same time, a clue for forward planning.

Turning to Section 3 on 'Future', you will see how to find the period when a particular activity will eventuate.

How to check a chart by simple rectification

Rectifying a Horoscope Chart is an extra skill that you may wish to try, enabling you to check your own and other people's Charts, and by mastering this technique it will place you in the class of the better analytical Astrologer.

As given birth times are quite often not absolutely correct, a check can be made on an existing Chart in regard to its Ascendant Sign, as this is directly related to the birth time and in turn sets the orientation of the whole Chart and the dispersal of the Planets into the various Houses.

By turning to Section 5, and analysing the Ascendant Sign descriptions it will help to clarify whether the one given on a person's Chart matches them, as it should do. However, if it did not match and it was found that the description of the neighbouring Ascendant Sign to the one given was a better 'fit', then this means that the birth time given was marginally out and the original Chart needs rectifying. To do this the same Chart can still be used by merely twisting it around to bring the new Sign chosen as the Ascendant to its proper position and by renumbering the Houses, starting number 1 after this new Ascendant Sign, the Horoscope can then be read in the usual way.

Twisting of the Chart in this way will of course throw the Planets into different Houses, and this creates a further check, as by reading the whole new Horoscope it can be seen if the various Department read-ups fit the case.

For example, if in the original Chart the beneficial Planet Jupiter was in the 7th House of Marriage and Partnerships (the read-up of which promises success in this Department) and yet the subject had reached middle age without experiencing such a partnership or marriage. Then by twisting the Chart, in accord with the new Ascendant Sign, it throws Jupiter into the 8th House (which promises financial benefits through others) and the person had in fact already received substantial bequests, then it would be obvious that the new Chart's orientation 'fits the case' and confirms that the change of the Ascendant Sign was warranted.

2
INDIVIDUAL READINGS FOR ALL HOROSCOPE CHARTS

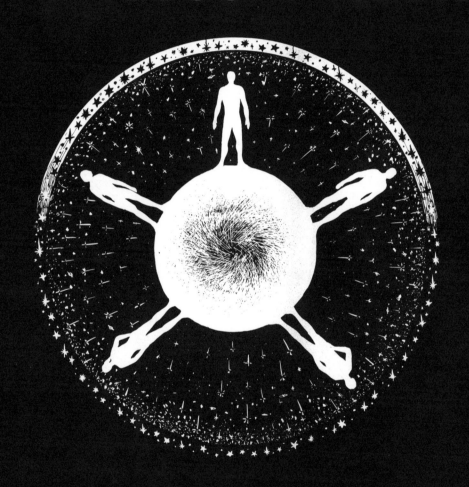

THE PAGES THAT FOLLOW COVER
TWENTY-ONE DEPARTMENTS OF LIFE
GIVING YOU 228 INTERPRETATIONS ON ALL
THE SIGNS, PLANETS AND HOUSES WHICH
ENABLE YOU TO COMPILE AS MANY
DIFFERENT HOROSCOPES AS YOU WISH

Your individual nature

♈ arie March 21 to April 20

The Sun in Aries endows you with a pioneering and reformative nature, desiring always to be at the head of things, and consequently you will be fitted for some position of authority or responsibility whether in a large or small way.

You are enthusiastic, impulsive, self-willed, independent and headstrong, and it will be necessary to curb these traits of character otherwise you will become indiscreet, hasty in speech, and perhaps a little too positive in manner.

There is a great love of change, travelling and exploring, and you will always have plenty of energy, activity and self-confidence, although at times you are inclined to go to extremes and over-estimate.

You are a good organiser but will do better in directing others than by carrying out your own plans, because you are over-active, impatient and given to irritability and restlessness.

Your Keynote in Life is **ASSERTIVENESS.**

♉ taur April 21 to May 21

The Sun in Taurus makes you reserved, diplomatic, solid, self-possessed, practical, patient, determined, stubborn and matter-of-fact.

You form your opinions slowly and deliberately, and you do not readily change them. You are reliable, honest and careful in speech and action, and are capable of holding positions where dignity and diplomacy are necessary.

By nature you are both faithful and warm-hearted in your attachments, also patient and self-controlled, but driven too far you will break out in a most dangerous manner.

You are fond of the good things of the earth, are easy-going and not inclined to move from one place to another, being fixed in your habits and desires. Through your persistent, plodding and determined characteristics you eventually win success.

Your Keynote in Life is **DETERMINATION.**

♌ leo July 24 to Aug 23

The Sun in Leo, like the fiery Arian, endows you with an ambitious and aspiring nature which enables you to command and control. You are also capable of holding positions of responsibility and authority. Whereas the Arian is inclined to act from the head, you act from the heart, therefore having much affection and sympathy.

You are magnetic, sociable and pleasure loving, are self-confident, proud and dignified, disliking any underhand dealings.

Your feelings are very powerful and deep, and care must be taken not to allow your heart to mislead you as you are very sympathetic and generous.

You are ever seeking perfection and will be at your best when instructing, directing, and organising, as Leos are born leaders, although better suited for professions than business life. In some way children will play an important part in your life.

Your Keynote in Life is **AFFECTION.**

♍ virg Aug 24 to Sept 23

The Sun in Virgo makes you practical, analytical, discriminative, with good mental abilities which could be used to advantage where method and detail are required, such as secretarial, clerical, scientific and literary work, although you will do much better working with another, as you need advice, help or direction, lacking self-confidence.

You are inclined to be sensitive and reserved but can adapt yourself to people, being very tactful. At times you will vacillate and change your mind, but on the whole, you are evenly balanced and cool headed.

The weak points to be guarded against are selfishness and criticism. You are somewhat fastidious in food and dress and particularly interested in matters to do with health.

You will experience many changes of environment in your life and may win success through your ingenious, versatile and industrious character, but must avoid worry.

Your Keynote in Life is **DISCRIMINATION.**

♐ sagi Nov 23 to Dec 22

The Sun in Sagittarius endows you with an active, jovial, enterprising, self-reliant and independent disposition with a natural inclination towards religion, philosophy or science.

Having progressive ideas and a love of freedom, there is an inclination to be sometimes a little too outspoken and tactless, although of a kindly and sympathetic nature.

You are intuitive, a good conversationalist, have a ready wit, also an interesting way of relating experiences through the varied changes, journeys or travels that will come into your life, there being also fondness for walking, sport and outdoor exercise.

You are happy when fighting other people's battles, being particularly zealous and courageous in this regard, hence some make admirable lawyers and when philosophically inclined, your inclinations may lead towards preaching or teaching.

Your Keynote in Life is **ASPIRATION.**

♑ capr Dec 23 to Jan 20

The Sun in Capricorn will make you persevering, ambitious and practical, with ability to hold positions of responsibility through your patience and determination to succeed, for you are ever striving to climb to the top, being desirous of power and fame.

You are trustworthy and reliable, have a love of justice, very rarely impulsive, being calm and deliberate, therefore your success in life will be more through slow, careful, methodical methods, than through flashes of enthusiasm or good luck. Avoid becoming too thrifty and overcareful of your own interests.

As a rule the nature is reserved and somewhat serious and not as mirthful as some of the other Signs, therefore you must guard against despondency and loneliness by mingling with bright company.

Your feelings and emotions are more inclined to be ruled by the head than the heart, being very rarely demonstrative or fond of display.

Your Keynote in Life is **STABILITY.**

found from **sun** ⊙ in **Sign** or birth month below

(If born on the first or last day of a Sign, the adjacent Sign should also be read due to its overlapping influence)

♊ **gemi** May 22 to June 21

The Sun in Gemini inclines towards all mental activity and you have decided ability along the lines of Art, Literature or Science, but must guard against changeability and lack of concentration to make a success in any of these avenues.

In all matters to do with writing, speaking, publishing, teaching, travelling, walking etc., and where there is plenty of movement and change, you will be in your element. You are inclined to live a great deal on the mental plane and are always more or less reasoning about your feelings and emotions.

You are quick-witted although rather nervous, restless and irritable at times. Geminis make good public speakers, orators, being versatile and quick at repartee, in fact Geminis can be generally picked out by their continual flow of speech.

As this Sign is dual it will bring more than one interest at a time.

Your Keynote in Life is **VERSATILITY.**

♋ **canc** June 22 to July 23

The Sun in Cancer endows you with a rather sympathetic and sensitive nature, the feelings and emotions playing an active part in your life. At times you are inclined to be rather shy and reserved, yet desire publicity, which you may attain.

You are apt to be too receptive to the influence of those around you, unconsciously taking on their conditions, and this accounts for many of your moods that are not understood, at the same time you are very tenacious. Once having made up your mind along a certain course of action, you are able to cling where others let go. You are adaptable, cautious, economical, and your intuitions are very keen with decided psychic and occult tendencies. The sea has a decided fascination for you.

You are very attached to the home and family and will have many experiences and changes in connection with your place of residence.

Your Keynote in Life is **TENACITY.**

♎ **libr** Sept 24 to Oct 23

The Sun in Libra endows you with a refined and artistic nature, fond of pleasure, cheerful, hopeful, generous, sociable, affectionate and romantic.

You have good reasoning ability, perception and comparison, being just and sincere in seeing both sides of a subject clearly.

You will make a better success of life if you join forces with another in some way, either by friendship, partnership, or marriage, for your natural inclinations are to associate with others and you will find one in particular who will play an important part in your life.

You are enthusiastic and ardent in all you undertake, although you must cultivate patience and persistency as you are liable to drop things just as suddenly as you have taken them up.

You are idealistic and must have harmony in your surroundings to be happy.

Your Keynote in Life is **BALANCE.**

♏ **scor** Oct 24 to Nov 22

The Sun in Scorpio inclines to make you firm, determined and obstinate. You have much energy and activity, also pride and self-confidence, your mind is shrewd and penetrating with a love for delving into the secrets of nature, also problems concerning life and death.

You are forceful, passionate, have a strong temper and at times can be very jealous and know how to use sarcasm to advantage. Your capacity for work and untiring energy will help you to carry on where others would give in.

You will be strongly attracted to the opposite sex and at times will need to exercise discretion.

The strength and force of this Sun sign must have an outlet and can either be very constructive or destructive according to other indications in your Horoscope.

Your Keynote in Life is **PENETRATION.**

♒ **aqua** Jan 21 to Feb 19

The Sun in Aquarius endows you with a rather shy and retiring nature, broadminded and sympathetic, interested in humanity and the hidden forces of nature. You are very intuitive with strong inclinations towards science, music, literature and philosophy. You are sometimes brought before the public owing to your interests being universal.

You are very sensitive to the mental conditions around you and must have harmonious surroundings. You will have more success in life when associated with more than one in any movement for the upliftment of humanity.

As a rule you are constant in affection with fondness for your children. You are quiet and unassuming and inclined to keep your own counsel too much and need drawing out at times, however you gain many friends through your ability to make yourself at home with strangers.

Your Keynote in Life is **UNIVERSAL LOVE OF MANKIND.**

♓ **pisc** Feb 20 to March 20

The Sun in Pisces makes you very sensitive, receptive, sympathetic, impressionable, with varying moods and although you feel deeply you rarely express your emotions.

At times the willpower needs to be strengthened, for you would rather suffer injury than fight for your rights, and you are too inclined to be influenced by persons and circumstances. You are subject to be imposed upon and there is often hindrances to your ambitions, you are better when working with or for another than entirely by yourself.

Pisces being a dual Sign you may have two sides to your character, it being difficult at times to bring your full nature to the surface. You are dependable and can be trusted with a secret.

There is a strong religious, psychic or occult trend and also a deep sympathy for all those in need. You should avoid all tendency towards worry, despondency and over-retirement.

Your Keynote in Life is **SERVICE.**

Your physical temperament

(how others see you)

♈ arie

Aries rising on the Eastern Horizon at your birth gives an energetic, active, and forceful type of body, the temperament being enthusiastic, ambitious and adventurous, desiring change, freedom and independence.

You excel in all matters where you can guide and control but must guard against becoming too impulsive, quick-tempered and outspoken.

You are frank, generous and courageous, and always ready to take the initiative in anything that arouses your enthusiasm, even when defeated you will not take long to start a fresh enterprise, there being plenty of self-confidence and determination. However, avoid too many new projects as you do not always follow through.

You are usually recognised as a leader due to your capability for quick action and getting things done.

♉ taur

Taurus rising on the Eastern Horizon at your birth gives a vital, sensitive, and magnetic type of body, the temperament being practical, determined, reserved and steadfast, gentle while unprovoked, but stubborn when opposed.

You are loving, affectionate, fond of pleasure, with keen desires and emotions and can become very jealous at times.

Through patience, endurance and persistency you are able to bring to a successful conclusion anything you undertake but must guard against being too self-centred, unyielding, argumentative and over-prejudiced.

Being rather conservative, with fixed tastes and opinions, there will be few changes during your life.

♌ leo

Leo rising on the Eastern Horizon at your birth gives a fiery, active, energetic, although a highly strung type of body, usually noble or majestic in appearance, the temperament being cheerful, hopeful and sociable.

There is ambition, self-confidence and forcefulness which helps to make you a good leader or master, but you must guard against any tendency to become bombastic or domineering. You are inventive, intuitive, with high ideals, always generous and sincere, disliking deceit — preferring frankness at all times.

The affections are ardent, demonstrative and sympathetic, but you are rather impulsive and lavish in expenditure and must guard against being too quick tempered or too passionate.

♍ virg

Virgo rising on the Eastern Horizon at your birth gives a quick and active type of body with good endurance, the age being rarely shown.

The temperament is sensitive, retiring, modest and conservative. You are industrious, perceptive, intuitive, practical, adaptable, tactful and discriminative, and having good reasoning powers, success is shown in all mental pursuits.

You learn readily and there is fluency in speech or writing, but you must guard against over-sensitiveness, anxiety, vacillation and lack of self-confidence.

There is sympathy, but the full nature is rarely shown on the surface owing to a certain amount of reserve, therefore you are often considered cold, at times difficult to understand. Guard against becoming too unforgiving or cynical.

♐ sagi

Sagittarius rising on the Eastern Horizon at your birth gives an energetic, restless and highly strung type of body, the temperament being frank, hopeful, jovial and generous.

There is ambition, high aspirations, and keen intuitions, with a love of freedom and independence which resents any form of domination.

You are sincere, just and honourable, quick to arrive at conclusions, but must guard against impulse, and a tendency to be brusque and outspoken.

The outlook is philosophical, with the ability for higher education.

You are artistic, also love exercise, sport, travel, exploring, new enterprises, etc. but must check any tendency towards gambling.

The emotions are sympathetic and demonstrative.

♑ capr

Capricorn rising on the Eastern Horizon at your birth gives a rather weak type of body with little vitality, especially in early life, but improves and tenaciously holds on as life advances, reaching a good old age. The temperament is reserved, dignified, serious, quiet and thoughtful, with plenty of self-esteem.

There is ambition, perseverance, endurance, patience, caution, coupled with a strong will and self-reliance, therefore you are capable of holding positions needing executive and organising ability, but must guard against worry or melancholy, for this would hold you back in life.

The emotions are not demonstrative or sympathetic, and there is often a lack of humour and too much seriousness, a little colour and brightness would not go amiss.

found from the ASCENDANT SIGN (i.e. The Sign in the middle of the left-hand side of the circular Chart, the start of House number 1) (The Ascendant point is sometimes marked in Charts as ASC or A)

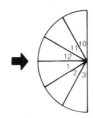

To find your Ascendant Sign without a Chart turn to page **83**

♊ gemi

Gemini rising on the Eastern Horizon at your birth gives an active, highly strung, restless and excitable type of body, the temperament being sensitive, aspiring, perceptive and imaginative.

There is a love of change and diversity, with a natural inclination to experiment, investigate and enquiry into all scientific, intellectual, educational and literary subjects.

You are clever, inventive, adaptable, having the ability for writing, speaking and thinking, with great dexterity and fluency of speech but must guard against changeability, lack of concentration, perseverance and continuity, there is also a liability to irritability and over-anxiousness.

More than one pursuit can be followed at a time.

Your feelings although sympathetic are inclined to be sacrificed to intellect.

♋ canc

Cancer rising on the Eastern Horizon at your birth gives a sensitive body, easily affected by environment and surroundings, the temperament being quiet, retiring, receptive, rather changeable, sympathetic, with a fertile imagination.

There is a love of sensation and novelty, with an attraction to psychic and occult activities.

You are industrious, diplomatic, cautious, economical, tenacious, and persevering, which will help you to acquire success in your undertakings, but must guard against moodiness, impatience, also a tendency to be reserved, mistrustful, and too exacting.

The feelings and emotions are active and strong, with plenty of sentiment and romance.

♎ libr

Libra rising on the Eastern Horizon at your birth gives a well balanced type of body, rather elegant and graceful in appearance, the temperament being refined, courteous, gentle, affectionate, and sympathetic.

There is perception, foresight, a love of comparison, justice, peace and harmony, with a fondness for beauty in nature, music, art, etc.

Being impressionable, imaginative and idealistic, environment plays an important part in your life. There is good taste and ability in all artistic pursuits but you must guard against becoming too fickle, changeable and inconstant.

You make many friends, love social activity, and will be most fortunate when associated with others.

The emotional nature is very strong and to reach its fullest expression needs companionship, partnership or marriage.

♏ scor

Scorpio rising on the Eastern Horizon at your birth gives a strong, alert, and forceful type of body, usually proud and dignified, the temperament being reserved, tenacious and secretive.

There is determination, persistency, courage, braveness and endurance, with a great deal of force, which can be used constructively or destructively.

The judgment is keen, penetrating, and critical, with a love of investigating all matters secret, curious, mystical or occult.

You are self-reliant, emphatic, aggressive, resourceful and ingenious with muscular and mechanical skill, but must guard against becoming too suspicious, sarcastic, brusque, sceptical and combative.

The opinions and habits are rather fixed but the emotions and passions are easily stirred.

♒ aqua

Aquarius rising on the Eastern Horizon at your birth gives a strong but highly strung type of body, refined and stately in appearance, the temperament being friendly, open and frank, although you are inclined to be silent and self-contained at times.

The intellect is very active, particularly along the lines of science, art, music, literature and sometimes towards occult and hidden matters.

You are persevering, patient, firm, determined, and discriminative, with a strong will and decided opinions, but must guard against being imposed upon as you attract many friends.

Although loving society and companionship, you need drawing out at times.

Avoid any tendency towards becoming too retiring and melancholy.

♓ pisc

Pisces rising on the Eastern Horizon at your birth gives a weak type of body, somewhat lacking in vitality, the temperament being sensitive, emotional, dreamy and impressionable, rather quiet and easy going.

You are idealistic, imaginative, receptive, mediumistic, loving change and variety, beauty and refinement, and all artistic pursuits such as music, singing, acting, dancing, and literature. There is also a strong occult and mystical trend. The will needs strengthening, as you are easily influenced, also inclined to be lazy, self-indulgent and fond of luxury.

The feelings and sympathies are easily appealed to, particularly by those who are dependent or incapable of helping themselves. Avoid any tendency to retire, shut yourself in, or become a recluse.

Your special characteristics

are found from your Rising Planets, which are those Planets, if any, found in the ASCENDANT SIGN. (Note – as part of the Ascendant Sign falls in the 12th House and part in the 1st House, a Rising Planet can be in either House, but remember it must be in the Ascendant SIGN, confirmed by the Sign notation.)

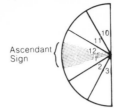

☉ sun

You derive special characteristics from the Sun, as in this position it will merge and intensify those qualities already described in 'Your individual nature' with those of 'Your physical temperament', which in turn strengthens your constitution and adds to your vitality.

This position adds a certain appearance of dignity and pride, marking you out among the crowd, and also gives you a sociable and friendly disposition through which you will easily attract people.

Generally speaking, the Sun; in this strong position, benefits the health, but should any indisposition arise, it can often be traced to over-strain, sometimes connected with your work.

The Sun rules government affairs, high offices and positions of rank and title and in this position it indicates that you are likely to concern yourself with people of this type during your life, or these tendencies may apply to the nature of your own work or profession, which is more fully described under 'Your vocational ability'.

☽ moon

You derive special characteristics from the Moon, which gives you a sensitive and imaginative nature. Also, your moods are liable to change and fluctuate from day to day and this gives you the ability to adapt yourself to a variety of subjects, for you like change and variety, both in occupation and environment.

It indicates that you will probably be happiest when dealing with the public in some way, although you will also be attached to home life and could take an interest in houses, land, property or even mining.

This influence makes you careful and economical in all things, but as your sympathies can be played upon by others, you will find that success will be more assured by saying 'No' to those who impose upon you.

The effect of the Moon on your health indicates that any indisposition can be traced to your over-sensitive nature, some facets of which are described under 'Your personality'.

☿ merc

You derive special characteristics from the planet Mercury, which makes you extremely sensitive and like quicksilver; you will be easily affected by change of atmosphere and the magnetic conditions around you. This makes the temperament rather changeable, excitable and somewhat nervous, although very adaptable; fond of moving about, chiefly short journeys.

This influence makes your mind particularly active, increasing the ability to express through writing and the fluency of speech, however, on the negative side, this often brings a lack of concentration and perseverance, with too many rapid changes of mind and often too many irons in the fire.

As Mercury rules the nervous system, it indicates that many of your physical complaints will arise from too much mental activity, talking or study, as well as from worry or inharmonious surroundings.

It indicates you are well suited for commerce and in all matters that need alertness, ingenuity and fertility of mind such as discussed under 'Your mental qualifications'.

♀ venu

You derive special characteristics from the planet Venus, which tends to increase the strength of your feelings and the affectionate side of your nature. It gives you a love of beauty and colour and you could develop artistic ability along the lines of designing, art, music, singing or decor.

It indicates that you like ease and comfort and dislike combativeness, preferring to win your way by charm and wit.

With this influence there is an appreciation of luxury, fashion clothes, perfumes, jewellery, flowers and beautiful surroundings, but very little inclination for deep study and there can be a decided lazy streak in your nature.

The effect of this planet Venus on the appearance bestows greater physical beauty and adds flesh to the body, particularly in later life.

Venus also rules the kidneys and parts of the generative system, therefore it increases the possibility that any indisposition in your health can be traced to over-indulgence of the appetite and over-doing your pleasures.

♂ mars

You derive special characteristics from the planet Mars, which adds plenty of energy, courage and endurance to your make-up and gives you a sense of enterprise and adventure.

It makes you a lover of freedom and independence, disliking restraint, confinement or delay and increases your self-confidence so that you are usually able to hold your own easily, being prompt in word and action.

It indicates you are an active and energetic worker and can accomplish much in a short time, being suited to occupations of a martial nature.

Mars generally gives a strong constitution and much physical endurance, although there is a tendency to feverishness, cuts, accidents and troubles with the eyes or head.

Although it tends to make you generous and frank, you will need to guard against being too rash and headstrong, for this influence makes you aggressive and self-willed and while you will probably rise in life through your own efforts, it would be wise to avoid giving way to impulse and acting before you think.

♃ jup

You derive special characteristics from the planet Jupiter, which is a rather fortunate influence, both for social and general prosperity. It tends to give you a good start in life, also a hopeful, buoyant and cheerful disposition, which should go far towards making you popular and gaining you many friends.

It gives executive ability, power and dignity and fits you for leading positions in social and business circles and could bring travel or overseas activities into your life.

Generally speaking, Jupiter benefits the health, but should any indisposition arise, it can generally be traced to indiscretion in diet, which results in disorders of the blood and liver, fatty degeneration and a tendency to stoutness in the course of years.

As Jupiter is the 'Good Luck' planet, its influence will protect you, and whatever adversity or pitfall that may come your way, you will find yourself invariably 'falling on your feet'.

♄ sat

You derive special characteristics from the planet Saturn, which tends to give you a disposition that is serious, grave and sober, with the qualities of self control, reserve and restraint, as well as some natural inclination to frugality, prudence and cautiousness.

Your progress and success may be slow, but you are sure to gain honour and credit as life advances, through your practical ability, persistency and continual effort, for you rarely undertake any project without planning or premeditation.

At times you may be a little lacking in buoyancy and cheerfulness, or appear too reserved and serious, but you can appreciate mirth and humour when it comes your way.

Although Saturn may be a hard task master, in appearing to limit and restrain, its influence is necessary to steady and deepen the mind, making it serious and better able to concentrate on the problems of life.

Responsibility comes early in life, probably through the loss of a parent, or the necessity to fend for yourself.

♅ uran

You derive special characteristics from the planet Uranus, which gives you a very original intellect and makes you rather independent and capable of thinking things out for yourself, for you dislike rules, restraints and conventions and frequently break or ignore them.

It also gives you a fondness for pioneer work and the investigation of unusual things, as well as the ability for higher mental studies, whether scientific, metaphysical, musical or literary. You may also take an interest in higher mechanics, aviation, electronics, radio, television, etc.

Sudden and unexpected changes with unusual experiences tend to occur in your life, either for good or ill, many like a bolt out of the blue, with very little warning.

The main faults of this Uranus influence are over-sensitiveness, impulsiveness, eccentricity and wilfulness as well as a high nervous tension, which will need the direction of your willpower to channel these characteristics into positive expression.

♆ nept

You derive special characteristics from the planet Neptune, which makes you very sensitive and receptive, subject to strong intuitions and impressions. This influence increases the feelings, emotions and senses to a high key and you are likely to have some taste for music, art or literature.

At times you will find yourself very intuitive and could develop some psychic ability, however, always be on your guard against any hypnotic suggestion.

There is always a love of comfort, ease and beautiful surroundings, and you are generally good natured and sympathetic.

As you lean towards helping those less fortunate than yourself, you must be careful against being imposed upon by others, and also careful in your choice of friends, for you are likely to meet deception from those around you.

Neptune indicates that the sea will probably have a strong attraction for you, with the probability of some enjoyable excursions and travel marked in your life.

♇ plut

You derive special characteristics from the planet Pluto, and while these will not be noticed as long as this influence remains dormant, it gives you hidden strength and force, which if used constructively, can move mountains, but, if used destructively, tends towards subversive activities.

It makes you think in terms of me and mine, your loyalty being towards that which is mine; my child; my idea; my country, and no sacrifice is too great for love and loyalty.

In your own sphere, you will like to be king of your castle and you can be blind to danger when fighting to protect your own.

It also indicates a pull towards group activities, particularly those involved with social reform.

The influence of Pluto can be treacherous and therefore you need to be beware of deep-rooted prejudices in your make-up that could manifest to your detriment.

Your ideal channel of expression

Found from the HOUSE in which your ruling planet is placed. First, from the following list find the ruling planet of your Ascendant Sign

Next, note the HOUSE (segment) in the Horoscope Chart in which your ruling planet is placed and then read that HOUSE Interpretation below

If your **Ascendant Sign** is ⟶	arie ♈	taur ♉	gemi ♊	canc ♋	leo ♌
Your **Ruling Planet** is ⟶	mars ♂	venu ♀	merc ☿	moon ☽	sun ☉

⌂ first

The position of your ruling planet would have to some extent influenced your early environment, determining conditions in your childhood home.

It adds uniqueness to the character, marking you off clearly from other types, both in physical appearance and mannerisms, depicting your personality as you appear to the world.

Depending on your recognition of this personality so can you influence others to your advantage.

This position also has a good deal to do with the physical body and its material needs and it is therefore necessary to channel your energy according to your bodily strength.

Some of these traits have already been described in the read-up for 'Your physical temperament', and possibly under 'Your special characteristics'.

⌂ second

The position of your ruling planet indicates that much of your interest will lie in your earning capacity and the acquisition of worldly goods, making money and financial matters one of the important objects of your life.

This may be due to your own interest in the accumulation of money, or on the other hand, circumstances may necessitate your doing so.

It is quite possible that you may establish your own business or work for yourself.

You will have a certain amount of anxiety concerning money matters, although generally speaking this influence is fairly fortunate and indicates ability to gain money through affairs outlined under 'Your financial capacity'.

⌂ fifth

The position of your ruling planet indicates that you will find a natural avenue of expression in social and pleasure-loving activities and will find your greatest happiness in pursuits or hobbies that entertain or give pleasure to others, such as dancing, music, art, the theatre, etc.

You should be able to extract a good deal of enjoyment from life, and where adventure or matters of enterprise are concerned you should be in your element.

Your creative capacity can vary in its mode of expression from pure mental, such as authorship, editing or educational matters, to a more physical expression such as, love affairs, children, social intercourse, amusements, speculations and entertainments, etc.

Always take care that you do not go too far in matters of pleasure.

For added information refer to 'Romance and matters close to your heart'.

⌂ sixth

The position of your ruling planet indicates that much of your interest will lie in your vocation and shows that this will be a very important department of your life as you will devote much time and energy to your work.

This position does not usually favour working on your own account, so much as working for, or with another. In other words, you make a better executive than master.

The symbol of this influence is 'Service' and whether you are in a high or low position, you will find your greatest happiness in the opportunity to serve, either individually or universally.

At certain periods of life it may be necessary for you to guard your health, especially when you overwork.

For added information refer to 'Your general health tendencies'.

⌂ ninth

The position of your ruling planet indicates that you will find a natural avenue of expression in all higher thought subjects and shows that you will find great happiness in enriching and developing the mind.

You may interest yourself in science, philosophy, law, religion, or other profound subjects, and could become proficient as a writer or publisher, as this influence has much to do with the more abstract side of the mind and its cultivation.

You could travel a good deal, or have to do with foreign affairs, the sea or shipping, and may take up permanent residence abroad.

You could be drawn towards educational pursuits or have an urge to preach or teach. The keynote of life being the desire for knowledge and wisdom.

For added information refer to 'Travel and study'.

⌂ tenth

The position of your ruling planet indicates that much of your interest will lie in all matters to do with your occupation or career, through which you will find your best channel of expression.

You are rather ambitious and enterprising and will have a desire for recognition, which will help in raising you to a position of responsibility.

It favours the influence of superiors and those well placed in the business or social world, and brings opportunity for achievement and a certain amount of power.

The influence of a parent could be strongly felt in connection with your career, or you may follow the same occupation as your father, or take after him in appearance or disposition.

For added information refer to 'Your ambitions and career'.

virg ♍	libr ♎	scor ♏	sagi ♐	capr ♑	aqua ♒	pisc ♓
merc ☿	venu ♀	plut ♇	jup ♃	sat ♄	uran ♅	nept ♆

🏠 third

The position of your ruling planet indicates that you will find a natural avenue of expression in all mental activity such as reading, writing, study and correspondence. In fact all matters connected with communication will interest you.

The intellect awakens very early in life, causing your occupation or hobbies to be more of the mind than they would otherwise be.

Your mind will absorb much of its knowledge through books and study, as well as frequent change, moving about, journeys, etc.

Neighbours, kindred, relatives and your social circle make up an important part of your life, and you will find your greatest happiness in intellectual attainments.

For added information refer to 'Local travel and social activity'.

🏠 fourth

The position of your ruling planet indicates that you will find a natural avenue of expression in all home and domestic affairs and shows that you will find your fullest expression when occupied with affairs of the home in one way or another.

During the early part of life there is generally a close link with one of the parents — probably your mother — who could exert a strong influence in your life, or in some way circumstances in your environment may hamper you or keep you tied.

You could gain through all matters to do with houses, property, mining, or the products of the land, either commercially or through inheritance.

The full significance of your ruling planet may not be felt until the latter years of life.

For added information refer to 'Home and domestic affairs'.

🏠 seventh

The position of your ruling planet indicates that you will find a natural avenue of expression in all matters to do with partnerships, friendships, union and marriage and denotes that you will usually be linked with another in most of your undertakings.

It inclines strongly towards marriage and renders it unlikely that you will remain single. You can easily attract other people to you and will be happiest when in the company of others, whether in business or domestic life.

Some of life's most important lessons are learnt through other people, and at some period, you are likely to be be brought before the public in some way.

For added information refer to 'Marriage'.

🏠 eighth

The position of your ruling planet indicates that much of your interest will centre around matters that have to do with your material assets; not so much through your individual earning capacity, as through the help or co-operation of other people.

You could derive money through wills or legacies, insurance, lotteries, or deaths, and a marriage or business partner is likely to benefit you.

This position generally brings experiences through the deeper side of life, and you could take an interest in the secrets of nature, occultism, etc. or be affected in some way through the loss of a friend or relative.

It is not the best position for health during infancy, but when this period has passed, the energy and strength of the body increases, as well as the activity and forcefulness of your nature.

For added information refer to 'Financial benefits through others'.

🏠 eleventh

The position of your ruling planet indicates that much of your interest centres around matters connected with friends and acquaintances and denotes that you will find much pleasure in mingling with others. In fact you will gain some of your chief experiences in life through friendships.

You can make friends easily and will be rather a popular person in your own sphere of life, and if you study the nature of your ruling planet, you will know the type of person that will be most congenial and helpful to you.

This influence will bring your greatest success in connection with associations, societies and groups of people, either socially or vocationally.

For added information refer to 'Friendships'.

🏠 twelfth

The position of your ruling planet indicates that much of your interest will be in matters of a hidden nature.

Your abilities may be somewhat restricted or latent, awaiting expression or you could be subject to confined or hampered conditions that may be forced upon you during some part of your life.

These temporary restrictions are sometimes necessary to bring out some special feature of your character, and you will find your best channel of expression in 'behind the scenes' work' that may need a certain amount of secrecy or seclusion, such as nursing, hospital work, laboratory research, or spend time researching and creating through art or writing.

There may also be a strong desire to investigate psychic or mystical affairs, or dabble in the secrets of nature.

Your personality

(how you express yourself)

♈ arie

The *Moon* endows you with an enthusiastic, impulsive, independent and self-reliant personality, with an inclination to be at the head of things, i.e. a leader in your own particular sphere.

The personality is definitely outstanding and attracts prominence or publicity.

There is great intellect with sharpness and shrewdness, also originality, at the same time there is a tendency to be irritable, aggressive, hasty in temper, thereby causing obstacles, unless tolerance and forethought are observed.

Owing to the desire to excel there is a tendency to overdo things, and the energy of this Sign is sometimes wasted in trying to find the right channel of expression, although a dauntless courage and persistency usually brings ultimate success.

You can be rather headstrong and like direct action, sometimes 'rushing in where angels fear to tread'.

♉ taur

The *Moon* endows you with a reserved, self-reliant and determined personality with an inclination to acquisitiveness.

The personality is kind, generous, persevering with forethought and therefore attracts the good things of this earth, at the same time however, there is a tendency to be firm or somewhat obstinate.

There is not the same desire for change as some personalities, who seek mental or scientific advancement. You, with your fixed, conservative desires, gain more through practical and worldly activities.

The personality is very pleasure-loving, the senses being easily stirred, with the ability to enjoy the material things of life.

However, because you react fairly slowly to your feelings, others may see you as lacking in animation.

♌ leo

The *Moon* endows you with a strong, self-reliant and ambitious personality, with plenty of enthusiasm and energy.

There is ability for organisation and leadership which can result in influential positions.

The personality attracts popularity through sincerity, generosity, and warm-heartedness; susceptible also to affairs of the heart, you become a favourite with the opposite sex.

Fond of pleasures and society, with much artistic taste, you must always guard against extravagance. Speculation will play an important part in your life.

You feel that life is to be enjoyed and with a strong love of luxury, this can lead to a desire for social pomp and prominence.

♍ virg

The *Moon* endows you with a reserved, quiet and unpretentious personality, disliking flattery and preferring to earn your way through merit of mental ability. The personality although reserved attracts many friends.

There is ability for occupations which draw out the analytical and weighing qualities, such as chemistry, health matters, dietetics, nursing and scientific research.

There is a strong desire to excel, but owing to modesty you rarely come into the limelight or reach positions of prominence, being more at home and fortunate in association with others or working under a head.

To achieve success, over-anxiousness and worry must be avoided.

Your desire to be in control of your feelings may lead others to see you as being too 'prim and proper'.

♐ sagi

The *Moon* endows you with an active, restless, jovial, frank, and optimistic personality, with a love of walking, riding, and outdoor exercises, but you should avoid extremes and over-exertion.

There is a love of change, travel, exploring, especially in foreign countries. There is also an inclination for the investigation of religion, philosophy, or occult sciences, with ability for law or teaching.

The nature is sincere and honourable, with a love for beauty and harmony, also a fondness for animals, especially horses and dogs.

You are a natural born adventurer and speculator, liking wide open spaces rather than the confinement of four walls, being irked by anything small.

You have a good sense of humour and can be easily recognised by your 'hail fellow well met' attitude, although care should be taken not to be too outspoken.

♑ capr

The *Moon* endows you with an ambitious, cautious, and acquisitive personality, with a desire to be at the head of things.

The personality attracts prominence, fame and publicity, or you become very well known in your own particular sphere, mostly through the indirect help of others, owing to your sensitive and retiring nature.

The feelings and emotions are somewhat subdued, and if not careful can become cold and calculating. Fear, melancholia or avariciousness would hold you back in life.

There is a tendency to pause before making up your mind as you will be assessing how your 'self-gain' stacks up.

You are a patient planner and will persist almost forever to achieve a goal.

found from **moon** ☾ in **Sign**

(As an example of Moon in say Aries, it would read on the Chart like this —
'MOON 24 ARIE 32' or '☾ 24 ♈ 32')

♊ gemi

The *Moon* endows you with a wide awake intellect and active personality with a love of study, books, scientific and literary pursuits.

The personality is dual in nature, with a desire for change and expression, thus brings much moving about. This love of change may cause irresolution or lack of perseverance until concentration is cultivated and a settled course is decided upon. Having found the right channel of expression and avoided superficialities you may become very clever, having insight and capacity.

Owing to your ability to follow more than one occupation at a time and also to adapt yourself to new surroundings, success is shown in literary occupations particularly in the Newspaper field, salesmanship, etc.

You are a good talker and can be quite interesting, providing you don't talk somebody's head off.

♋ canc

The *Moon* endows you with a sensitive, shy and reserved personality, possessing much feeling, imagination and sympathy.

Owing to the receptivity of the Cancer personality, it is coloured to a large extent by persons and surroundings, and consequently environment plays a prominent part in its expression.

There is an appeal to the feelings and emotions through all psychic activities, and there is also some ability for acting, mimicking, expressing the thoughts and emotions of others, also for music, painting, poetry and dancing.

The sea has a strong fascination and there is a decided love of change. While you are not highly active, content with whatever comes and goes, you can cling tenaciously to things that take your fancy.

♎ libr

The *Moon* endows you with a refined, just, courteous and warm-hearted personality, with the art of acquiring friends and public popularity, and you are always more successful when associated with another in undertakings.

You are fond of social pleasures, with appreciation for music and the fine arts generally, also dress, ornaments and luxury.

There is ability as a performer, with good powers of imitation.

There is also good perception and love of comparison, with excellent critical ability. However, you tend to judge and criticise rather than act.

You are a good listener rather than a talker and are always willing to fall in with other people's plans.

♏ scor

The *Moon* endows you with a forceful, energetic, courageous, self-reliant and rather aggressive personality, with a tendency to be obstinate, quick-tempered and often a little abrupt or too plain spoken.

There is capacity for hard work, with determination to carry out whatever you undertake. You will not tolerate imposition nor be coerced by threats, but are amenable to kindness.

The feelings and emotions are very active and can be expressed through the higher senses, such as occultism or the mysteries of nature, or purely through pleasures and the satisfaction of the tastes.

Intolerance and selfishness will hold you back in life, also too much secrecy.

You have a powerful magnetic personality, but as you do not show your feelings on the surface, others may find you difficult to fathom.

♒ aqua

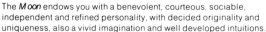

The *Moon* endows you with a benevolent, courteous, sociable, independent and refined personality, with decided originality and uniqueness, also a vivid imagination and well developed intuitions.

There is an inclination for philosophical, scientific, literary, educational, political or occult pursuits.

Being very sensitive to the mental conditions of others, you have a natural gift for reading character.

The sympathies are towards furthering any cause for the upliftment of humanity, therefore friends, associations and societies play an active part in the life.

Because your interests are more universal than personal, others see you as having a detached attitude and find you difficult to understand.

♓ pisc

The *Moon* endows you with a rather dreamy, quiet, retiring and sympathetic personality, with a tendency to be too easily influenced, therefore more determination and firmness is necessary.

The feelings and emotions are easily swayed through romance, music, dancing, and mystical subjects. There is a fondness for luxury, beauty, pleasures, comforts, and sometimes an over-indulgence in matters of the senses.

The imagination finds a congenial outlet in reading, writing or composing, there being fluency and correctness of detail.

Harmonious surroundings are necessary for your physical and mental comfort.

Because of a tendency to an inferiority complex, you sometimes put on a bigger front than you can maintain.

Ideal expression of your personality

 ## first

The position of your *Moon* shows restlessness, with a constant desire for change either in environment or occupation. This may arise from your vivid imagination and intuitiveness. It favours success in occupations which bring you in close touch with the public.

You may have a close affinity with the mother or take after her in appearance or characteristics.

The sensitive side of your nature is accentuated and you must be careful to choose congenial surroundings and suitable companionship, otherwise your health may suffer at times.

Change or roaming is probably the best medium to satisfy your curiosity and will give you the necessary experiences to gather knowledge and wisdom. Between the age of 27 and 29 you will get opportunities to make these changes.

For added information regarding the expression of your personality, also read the *Moon* under 'Your special characteristics'.

 ## second

The position of your *Moon* concentrates your energies on all financial affairs and is rather fortunate for obtaining possessions.

You would be successful in all public undertakings or where you deal with many people. At the same time there shows much fluctuation in your monetary affairs, sometimes being good, though at other times rather adverse.

You could have luck to do with liquids in some way, or indirectly through shipping or travel. But in any case, you will put most of your personality into acquiring money and possessions, even though you are liable to ups and downs. Much of your personality will find expression in the Department of life described under 'Your financial capacity'.

 ## fifth

The position of your *Moon* indicates that your happiest expression is in all matters of adventure, enterprise and speculation. Pleasures, entertainments, social gaiety and affairs of the heart all add to the zest of life for you.

You may find yourself rather changeable in your heart affairs, and then all of a sudden become very attached to one who least deserves it. Children's affairs often play an important part in your life and you should have some talent for entertaining others.

Speculation, games of chance or important enterprise are sure to interest you at some period of your life.

You have great creative capacity. Use it in conjunction with the qualities as described in 'Your personality', much of which you will be able to express in 'Romance and matters close to your heart'.

 ## sixth

The position of your *Moon* shows that the best expression of your personality will be found in your work and although you may have constant change, this will be good for you as your health may get very down from time to time through overwork and too much concentration on one job.

You will be best suited in the employment of others, rather than in business on your own, unless it be in connection with the public in some way or where you are dealing with liquids, which the *Moon* rules.

Try at all times not to be too irresolute and wavering, for you would lose opportunities in consequence. Avoid over-work and worrying, as this will distract the mind and react on the body. Servants, employees or the common mass will indirectly affect your career.

With your ambition to serve and pride in achievement your personality will expand through your work.

 ## ninth

The position of your *Moon* denotes a clear and studious mind and you will therefore find your best expression in science, philosophy and educational pursuits.

You could become proficient as a writer or publisher, and may excel in the legal profession or where higher educational ability is required.

There will be a love of travelling and oversea activities are sure to play an important part in your life. You will travel far with both pleasure and profit.

The expansion of intellect will mean more to you than purely physical and material pleasures.

Much of your personality will find expression in the Department of life described under your 'Travel and study'.

 ## tenth

The position of your *Moon* shows that you express your personality strongly in your career and vocational activities. However, circumstances are bound to bring an element of change in career activities.

You will be rather ambitious and desire fame and are sure to become well known at some period of life; for this position gives public acclaim or notoriety!

Your activities can successfully run along either business or social lines, but care must be exercised that you do not incur jealousy or enmity which would affect your career from time to time.

Much of your personality will find expression in the Department of life described under 'Your ambitions and career'.

found from **moon** 🌙 in **House**

🏠 third

The position of your *Moon* denotes a receptive intellect and an inclination to study — you will therefore find your best avenue of expression in study, writing or speaking.

You may find it difficult to concentrate for any length of time upon one subject, and are best suited for mental occupations that do not require continuity, like editing and reporting on newspapers where one must be on the alert for news and roam hither and thither for the purpose of gathering it.

Relatives and social contacts play an important part in the life — and it is necessary for your happiness that you mingle with others — discussing or exchanging ideas both personally and through correspondence.

You will be fond of journeying, and are likely to take many short trips. much of your personality finding expression in the Department of life described under your 'Local travel and social activities'.

🏠 fourth

The position of your *Moon* indicates that the true expression of your personality is found in all home affairs.

There is generally a close link with the mother, who exerts a strong influence, or in some other way makes it necessary to devote your time to domestic affairs, particularly in the early life. You will be happiest when you have your own home, and can devote your talents in this direction.

There are likely to be many changes of environment towards the latter part of life, therefore, don't plan for a permanent abode later.

A psychic awakening is more than possible in your closing years.

You could be successful in business matters including real estate, land, houses, property, mining or agriculture, much of your personality finding expression in the Department of life described under your 'Home and domestic affairs'.

🏠 seventh

The position of your *Moon* brings you in touch with the public in many ways and you will be happiest when linked with others whether in business, partnership or marriage and although you may not always find others dependable, for the *Moon* is fickle in nature and delights in change, you will always be popular in your own sphere, and will be best suited in a position of prominence or where the masses are concerned.

Your life is sure to be bound up with others but in most cases don't expect permanency.

You may find that your ambitions concerning companionships lead to an early marriage, as you can sometimes be a bit unsure of yourself.

Much of your personality will find expression in the Department of life described under your 'Marriage'.

🏠 eighth

The position of your *Moon* brings experiences through the deeper side of life, and makes you interested in the secrets of nature, which can range from birth and creation of life to the occult or passing of life. Coupled with this are the benefits derived through deaths, wills, legacies, etc., and the accumulation of material assets.

Your health in infancy may have caused some concern and you could be deeply affected by the passing of a female whether young or old.'

You will feel that security is of the utmost importance and therefore this emphasises an instinct to save for the future.

The mother or female relatives promise gain and a partner or co-workers will play an important part in your material benefits, further details of which are described under your 'Financial benefits through others'.

🏠 eleventh

The position of your *Moon* denotes many acquaintances and you will be happiest when mingling with your friends, for you have the ability to attract others to you easily. However, you may not always find your friends constant, and some will either travel away or prove unreliable.

You will be successful with groups, associations or societies, and will delight in the social activity that these will offer.

You are a deep student of human nature with humanitarian ideals, and are likely to be associated with some movement for the benefit of mankind, such as political, educational or scientific.

Friends are very important to you as you subconsciously draw strength and security from their presence.

Much of your personality will find expression in the Department of life described under your 'Friendships'.

🏠 twelfth

The position of your *Moon* indicates that your best expression will be along avenues that are away from the public gaze, in fact circumstances or your desires may limit or obstruct your personality coming too much to the fore, as you may be connected with nursing, hospitals, research laboratories, or where you are doing 'behind the scene work', i.e. historical research, study or writing.

There will be a great interest in psychic or mystical affairs, and you are likely to travel at some period of your life.

This position is likely to incur treachery or enmity at times, therefore look well into all your affairs.

Between the age of 27 and 29 some of the above conditions are likely to come to the fore.

To get the best out of your personality expression, study the write-up of 'Your personality' itself.

31

Mental qualifications

♈ arie

Mercury in this Sign endows you with a quick, alert, and aspiring mentality, with inventiveness and originality.

There is a tendency to be impulsive and fiery, rather argumentative, fond of disputes, quick at repartee, and apt to enlarge or exaggerate unconsciously.

The mind is studious, fond of reading, writing or lecturing, although there is a liability to be changeable, lacking in concentration and continuity of ideas. If this can be overcome, as well as moderation in expression, much progress can be attained.

♉ taur

Mercury in this Sign endows you with a practical and determined mentality, with patience and perseverance.

You are rather slow to make up your mind, but having done so are very fixed and firm, but see that this is based on reliable judgement, otherwise it is likely to be mere obstinancy.

You have strong likes and dislikes being greatly affected by feeling.

The disposition is sociable, being attracted to the opposite sex, pleasures, recreation, music, singing, art and light literature.

♌ leo

Mercury in this Sign endows you with a persevering, determined, ambitious and confident mentality with imagination, high ideals and a good deal of sympathy, although there is a tendency to be a little outspoken, and quick tempered at times.

The mind is balanced with feeling and finds a congenial outlet in all matters to do with pleasures, music, singing, sports, drama, fine arts, with a fondness for children, pets, etc.

You have positive assurance with governing, controlling or organising ability, and when you have once formed your plans you are not liable to change.

♍ virg

Mercury in this Sign endows you with a practical, versatile, discriminative, scientific and eloquent mentality, with the ability for reading, writing, studying, books, secretarial work and languages, although there is a tendency to be somewhat critical and sceptical at times, desiring proof before being convinced.

There is a taste for chemistry, dietetics, and mathematics, for you have wonderful ingenuity and dexterity.

The mentality is very tactful and adaptable, but needs co-operation to reach success.

♐ sagi

Mercury in this Sign endows you with an active, straightforward, generous and noble mentality, with religious, legal, scientific or philosophical inclinations, and a desire for freedom of thought and speech.

There is the ability to study more than one subject at a time, and the mind finds a congenial outlet in travel, and change of scenery, thus satisfying a certain restlessness and desire for knowledge.

Too much rashness, independence or rebelliousness will hold you back in life unless modified.

♑ capr

Mercury in this Sign endows you with a cautious, diplomatic, penetrating and subtle mentality, with keen ambitions which could find a congenial expression in architecture, surveying, agriculture, government and administrative positions.

The mind is really clever, and through method, persistency and tact, honour and recognition will be attained.

There is sometimes a certain amount of criticism, suspiciousness and restlessness, tendencies which need to be modified to attain success.

found from **merc** ☿ in **Sign**

(**As an example of Mercury in say Aries, it would read on the Chart like this -**
'MERC 24 ARIE 32' or ' ☿ 24 ♈ 32')

Ⅱ gemi

Mercury in this Sign endows you with a clever, active, ingenious and resourceful mentality, rather dualistic and variable, thus unbiased and very seldom prejudiced.

There is fondness for reading, literature, science, and the acquisition of knowledge, although the mind seems to absorb more through change and travel, there being a difficulty to concentrate too long upon one subject.

Anything new and novel appeals to Geminis and having versatility, shrewdness, a ready wit, the power of clear thinking, with facility of expression, you could have much success as speaker, orator, salesman, entertainer or lawyer.

♋ canc

Mercury in this Sign endows you with an active, discreet, tactful, although somewhat changeable mentality, with the ability to adapt yourself to conditions and surroundings.

The mind is impressionable and sensitive, with keen intuition and with an interest in all psychic and occult activities.

There is ingenuity and broadness of outlook with the power to argue and reason.

You are easily influenced by kindness and encouragement, and there is also a fondness for expression in movement, such as swimming, dancing, etc.

♎ libr

Mercury in this Sign endows you with a refined and well balanced mentality, with uncommon ability of expression which finds a congenial outlet in art, music, poetry, singing or public speaking, reading, writing and study.

The tendencies are not towards deep study, but judgement and comparison are good, and better results will be obtained when studying with another.

You have splendid natural abilities and aptitude for delicate mathematical work, and with suitable training could become proficient in oratory or literature.

♏ scor

Mercury in this Sign endows you with a keen, shrewd, forceful and somewhat obstinate mentality, with the desire of gaining knowledge and developing mental ability which could find a congenial outlet in scientific, mystical and metaphysical subjects, you also have manual dexterity for dentistry and surgery.

When not living up to your highest possibilities, the mind can be somewhat critical, suspicious and mistrustful, with a love for secrecy.

There is a ready wit and often a sharp and sarcastic tongue, tendencies which need to be modified to attain success.

♒ aqua

Mercury in this Sign endows you with a refined, original, strong, comprehensive and independent mentality, with keen judgement, good reasoning and concentrative powers which could find a congenial expression in science, mathematics, occult and Astrological activities.

The aspirations and ideals are high with strong intuitions.

Anyone original or intellectual appeals as friends, of which there are many, and there is the ability to entertain, bringing social success and popularity.

The opinions are rather fixed and sometimes unconventional, tendencies which need to be modified to attain success.

♓ pisc

Mercury in this Sign endows you with a receptive, imaginative, and psychic mentality, with strong intuitive perception, which senses things in an unexplainable manner.

The mind is diplomatic, ingenious, cautious, and versatile, tendencies which find a congenial expression in speaking, singing or writing.

There is also strong analytical ability which could bring success in chemistry and dietetics.

Mental indifference, worry, over-receptivity, and any tendency towards melancholy, will need to be modified to attain success.

33

Your financial capacity
found from **planets,** if any, in
the **second** 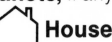 House

☉ sun

The Sun having influence over your earning capacity is good for finance, and helps you to secure a superior position.

You either work for yourself or hold an important post, under the Government or for some leading firm. At some period of life you could gain by speculation or through careful investment.

Much of 'Your individual nature' will find expression in the earning capacity. You love to lead or exercise authority over others, however, you are very fair and honest in all your dealings.

The Sun is always generous and tends to squander money unless care is taken.

As your financial conditions will be linked with the nature of your work or profession, refer also to 'Your vocational ability' for further insight into your financial capacity.

☽ moon

The Moon having influence over your earning capacity indicates that you are likely to experience many fluctuations in financial affairs.

Investments in public companies, especially those that deal in public commodities or associations catering for the general public in some form or other, should prove most successful.

At the age 27 to 29 financial matters will be very active.

Sometimes money is derived from the mother or her side of the family, or from occupations dealing with the feminine sex generally.

Much of 'Your personality' will find expression in the earning capacity, and you would do well to concentrate on business where there is a quick turnover and which deals directly with the public.

☿ merc

Mercury having influence over your earning capacity indicates that journalism, or work connected with printing, publishing, writing or literary matters in which the mind is more employed than the body, would furnish the most remunerative mode of income for you.

Much of 'Your mental qualifications' will find expression in the earning capacity, and you may have more success by working with, or for someone else, rather than in business on your own account.

Always use the utmost caution when signing financial documents for there is a liability of fraud and theft in this connection.

You will probably have the greatest success in any occupation connected with the information industry such as radio, recording, television and advertising and therefore these activities would be your best avenue of gain.

♀ venu

Venus having rule over your earning capacity is very favourable for finance, and a great deal of success in all money matters is indicated.

Business connected with artistic pursuits, interior decorating, music, jewellery, the fine arts, also all forms of entertainment, which give pleasure and happiness to others, should prove most successful.

You will always be fortunate in your financial transactions, and gain is promised either through business, your marriage partner, or by wills and legacies.

As Venus delights in spending, be careful that you do not develop wasteful habits, especially on pleasure, dress, or luxuries.

♂ mars

Mars having rule over your earning capacity denotes gain by your own energy, activity and strength. You should prosper on the whole as you have the ability to make money quickly, and should derive much happiness in earning it.

You can be practical where money is concerned, except where your feelings sway you, and should therefore, avoid over-generosity or carelessness and should never lend money without security for you will surely lose it.

There is a tendency to let money run quickly through your fingers, and unless you are very careful will have loss, either through your own or another's extravagance.

With this position of Mars there is often gain through partners or legacy.

♃ jup

Jupiter having rule over your earning capacity promises good fortune in matters connected with finance. You should never be poor and there is every prospect of accumulating wealth.

Jupiter has much to do with responsible business affairs, and tends to bring gain through Government, law, science, education, travel, or to do with those things that are necessary for the comfort of others.

It is a lucky planet and is often responsible for bringing gain through gifts, lotteries, shares, speculation, legacies or wealthy persons.

However, sometimes Jupiter brings an element of over-expansion when you may, due to your desire to increase finances, become too over-optimistic and hereby suffer some loss.

No matter which way your fortunes may turn you will always bounce back, ready for another fling.

♄ sat

Saturn having rule over your earning capacity shows that success will be achieved through steady perseverance and hard work.

Delay and hindrance are often met with in early life, but progress and financial advancement may be expected by slow plodding, thrift and economy, also by careful investment in land or property, and all things that are solid and concrete.

Architecture, surveying, contracting and mining, come under the rulership of Saturn, also municipal or state official positions.

After an uphill struggle success is assured, through your prudent financial ability.

♅ uran

Uranus having rule over your earning capacity indicates some very great and sudden changes in your fortunes, also peculiar and remarkable experiences in your financial affairs.

Gain and success is indicated in 'out of the ordinary' occupations — such as composing, inventing, creating new professions or adopting unique plans of work. Radio and aviation also come under Uranus, as well as antique furniture, curios, old books, occultism, astrology, etc.

This position tends to sudden gains and sudden losses. You should, therefore, be very careful in matters of a speculative or uncertain nature.

♆ nept

Neptune having rule over your earning capacity indicates that you will come into money by the most odd and eccentric means, or else by following some occupation of an uncommon nature.

This planet rules schemes, and has much to do with 'get rich quick' methods, the stock exchange, speculations, gambling, etc. It also rules the sea and its various industries, hospitals, public institutions, film work, photography, mystical and secret societies, detective work, etc.

Always be careful in your dealings with others, as this influence of Neptune gives a liability for your financial affairs to become tangled and you could easily lose through fraud or misrepresentation, as you are not sufficiently alert to others imposing upon you.

♇ plut

Pluto having rule over your earning capacity emphasises the urge to maintain security, with a desire to use any of your creative powers for monetary gain. Following the orders of an employer is difficult, as co-operation does not come to you easily. The one desire will be to own, or be at the head of a business, however small, but owing to an intense inner drive care must be taken against expanding too widely.

This position of Pluto gives a natural sense of public taste and demand, which could be used effectively in your earning capacity.

All businesses affiliated with large groups or franchise organisations would be your best avenue for gain.

Financial benefits through others

found from **planets** if any, in

the **eighth** House

☉ sun

Your material assets can be improved either through marriage or by linking yourself with others, such as partners or co-workers, for you will do better in sharing undertakings with another than by taking the sole responsibility upon yourself.

There are also indications of financial benefits through a legacy, gift or insurance, most likely from the male side of the family, or one who holds an influential position, either a relative or business partner.

The middle portion of life seems the most prosperous for the accumulation of money and material assets, especially those derived through sources other than your own earning capacity.

☽ moon

Your material assets can be improved either through marriage or by linking yourself with another in some way, such as a partner or co-worker, or by one who may be concerned with you in public undertakings.

There is a slight possibility of gaining through legacies, gifts or insurance, very probably from the female side of the family, or even from someone who is not directly related to you.

The period between your 27 and 29 birthday will be rather important in connection with above affairs, also money that could come to you through sources other than your own earning capacity.

☿ merc

Your material assets can be improved by linking with a partner or co-worker in business affairs, although there is bound to be a good deal of mental activity in this direction. Your prospects of gain through wills, legacies or insurance are rather fluctuating, for there shows a certain amount of worry in connection with papers, documents, etc.

You may be called upon to settle financial matters through legal or Government channels, and should never rely too much on the security of money that may be promised to you through others.

Your luck lies in pursuits where you can use your mental powers to advantage, particularly in partnership with another.

♀ venu

Your material assets can be improved either through marriage, or linking yourself with another in some way, such as a partner or co-worker, for there is a lucky influence surrounding you when connected with others in monetary affairs.

At some period of life you are likely to gain through money left by will or the goods of the dead, insurance, etc., and may benefit through gifts or lotteries. The middle portion of life seems the most prosperous for the accumulation of money and material assets, especially those derived through sources other than your own earning capacity.

♂ mars

Your material assets are likely to deteriorate if you link yourself with a partner or co-worker, for they could be extravagant or waste money foolishly.

There could be some financial gain through a will, legacy or insurance, but also some disputes or difficulties in connection with these.

Always see that you have your assets insured, for there is a tendency to lose things through fire, robbery, or accident, and don't overlook covering for war damage or natural disaster.

You could benefit at some time through Government or war compensation.

♃ jup

Your material assets are likely to be improved through marriage, or linking yourself with another in some way, such as a partner or co-worker, for there is good fortune surrounding you when connected with others in monetary affairs.

At some period of life you are likely to gain through money left by will or the goods of the dead, insurance, etc., and may also benefit through gifts or lotteries.

The middle portion of life seems the most prosperous for the accumulation of money and material assets, especially those derived through sources other than your own earning capacity.

♄ sat

Your material assets are not likely to be improved greatly through marriage, partnerships or co-workers, and it will be best for you to concentrate upon your own earning capacity for financial gain.

There is some likelihood of gaining through wills or legacies at some period of life, but it is more likely to be towards the latter years, or there could be much delay or some disappointment in your expectations concerning the amount of money due to you through others.

You could however, benefit through some land or property, or through insurance or securities that have accumulated during your life.

♅ uran

Nothing very definite or fixed can be defined regarding financial gains, for the sudden and unexpected surrounds material assets derived through sources other than your own earning capacity.

You could gain suddenly by legacy or lotteries, or through marriage, partnerships or co-workers. Yet, at other times in life you could have loss through a partner's income being suddenly depleted, or investments unexpectedly collapsing.

Do not count on a fixed income from outside sources, but enjoy the unexpected as it comes along.

♆ nept

Your material assets are not likely to be improved greatly through marriage, although there are indications of some peculiar gains through sources other than your own earning capacity.

At some period of life you are likely to gain through money left by a will or the goods of the dead, insurance, etc., or could benefit through unusual investments, shares, lotteries, art unions.

Look well into all partnerships, for there is the liability of financial affairs becoming involved, and you could easily lose through fraud and deception, or not get that to which you are entitled.

♇ plut

Your material assets could take a turn for the better by gain through a legacy from a distant or little known relative or even from some source that has been kept secret.

You could also suddenly lose your savings, through your faulty judgement, the extravagance of a partner, or victimisation from a misrepresented promise of a legacy or through a contested will.

As this position of Pluto indicates regeneration; assets lost could be replaced by their equivalent in some extraordinary way.

Your vocational ability

♈ arie March 21 to April 20

Due to your pioneering and ambitious nature, success could be achieved as a leader or explorer. You are intellectual, self reliant, active and energetic, though more idealistic than practical.

You will acquire some position of authority or responsibility in your particular sphere of life, as you feel capable of leading others, and assume such a position naturally. Even at a young age you tend to gravitate to the head of your department, and eventually to the head of the firm, if not in your own business.

Suitable occupations include: free-lance journalism, novelist, agencies of all kinds, company promoter, acting, designing, cutter, surveying, architecture, inspector, broker, hairdresser, milliner, wigmaker, optometrist, guide, lecturer and salesman. In the more martial occupations — success is shown as soldier, surgeon, dentist or electrician.

♉ taur April 21 to May 21

Due to your reliable, determined, fixed and practical nature, success could be achieved in all pursuits where you manufacture or build, for you have the ability to handle, mould and erect the material that others have created.

A suitable choice would be Government appointments or responsible positions with old established firms, and you could succeed as a banker, financial expert, accountant, builder, contractor, stockbroker or manufacturer.

As there is generally an inherent love of the land, farming, fruit growing and agricultural pursuits can be undertaken with success, and if so desired, you could become an excellent cook.

In the professional field — you could make a good doctor, nurse or masseur and with your artistic sense, excel in dressmaking, florist, painting or singing.

♌ leo July 24 to Aug 23

Due to your sociable and ambitious nature coupled with the ability to exercise authority over others, success could be achieved as an organiser, leader or manager, such as company promoter, stockbroker, chairman, politician, as well as president of societies or master of ceremonies.

You are however, better suited for a professional life than a business career, and could excel as an artist, actor and musician, or in occupations that minister to the joy, pleasure, entertainment or education of others, as a theatrical entrepreneur or tour promoter.

Your organising ability could find a suitable mental expression in social welfare work, kindergarten teaching, school master or instructor, or as a military officer, but where a more emotional expression is desired, musical or artistic activities are the most suitable, including television acting or directing.

♍ virg Aug 24 to Sept 23

Due to your methodical, industrious and discriminative nature, success could be achieved in commercial and mercantile pursuits generally. In fact, it is in your work that you show to your best advantage.

You are sensitive and reserved, yet analytical, tactful, ingenious and alert, qualities which suit you for an occupation such as — secretary, agent, buyer, seller, dealer, chemist, dietitian, nurse, or as an editor, literary critic, mathematician, statistician, efficiency expert, book-keeper, accountant, multi-copying, watchmaker, dental mechanic, jewellery designer.

There is also an artistic side to your nature, and loving detail, you should be good at drawing, painting, photography and designing.

As you have a highly strung nervous system, over-strain and worry will soon deplete you, therefore rest as much as possible.

♐ sagi Nov 23 to Dec 22

Due to your independent, enterprising and aspiring nature, success could be achieved in all philosophical or educational pursuits.

Suitable occupations include: journalism, college professor, clergyman, lawyer, politician, scientist, explorer, etc., or in advertising, publishing, the book trade or newspapers. The desire for change and exploring often finds expression in pursuits to do with travelling, shipping, modes of transit and foreign affairs, such as in travel agencies or the export-import business. It is more than probable that you will change your occupation during life, or follow two pursuits at the same time.

Success could also be achieved as civil engineer, advertising agent, commercial traveller or in a military career.

A fondness for animals sometimes brings work connected with horses, racing establishments or riding schools.

♑ capr Dec 23 to Jan 20

Due to your ambitious, practical and persevering nature with sometimes a desire for power and fame, success could be achieved in all enterprises of a public nature, where you can manage and organise.

Suitable occupations include: banker, financier, manager, director, builder and contractor, broker, estate agent, wholesale trader, economist, archivist, librarian or charity worker. You have wonderful capacity for work, combined with stability, tenacity, endurance and perseverance and have every opportunity of obtaining your goal in life.

Farming and agricultural pursuits sometimes appeal, in which case you would make a good builder or land worker.

With the power of debate added to your other characteristics, you could succeed as a politician, scientist or lawyer.

(If born on the first or last day of a Sign, the adjacent Sign should also be read due to its overlapping influence)

♊ gemi May 22 to June 21

Due to your adaptability, versatility and inclination towards intellectual pursuits, success could be achieved in all pursuits where you teach, speak or write. Your brain prefers mental work, which combines change and movement, rather than activities that are slow and laborious.

Suitable occupations include: lecturer, teacher, reporter, journalist, traveller, salesman, public speaker, auctioneer, artist, as well as all clerical and secretarial positions, receptionist, telephone operator, announcer, interpreter, postal employee, bus driver, pilot, or work connected with books and publishing such as linotypist, compositor, proof reader, etc.

Sometimes you can have two interests running at the same time, but to succeed, must check the tendency towards change and lack of concentration; you prefer reading short articles to long and tedious books, and in your own work are happiest when it can be quickly completed.

♋ canc June 22 to July 23

Due to your receptive, imaginative and romantic nature, success could be achieved in all pursuits where there is change, novelty, variety and sensation. Public concerns, where there is a good deal of change or a rapid turnover, would probably appeal to you most.

Suitable occupations include: selling, catering, managing, furnishing, manufacturing, and all activities that have to do with houses, land or property, such as estate agent, hotel-keeper, housekeeper, or as a dealer in antiques and curios, or renovations for reselling.

Your love of change and novelty could attract you to the sea, or your powers of mimicry and imitation suit you for acting, if you have the desire and opportunity of adopting it as a profession.

You may have to guard against the desire for too much change, and must not allow yourself to be affected by the vibrations of your fellow workers, otherwise you could become fretful and moody.

♎ libr Sept 24 to Oct 23

Due to your sociable and artistic nature, success could be achieved in all pursuits of a refined and intellectual nature.

Suitable occupations include: artist, designer, dressmaker, musician, singer, interior decorator, sculptor, librarian, secretary, social reporter, antique and art dealer, or to do with perfumery, jewellery, fabrics, fancy stationery, window dressing, beauty shop operator, manicurist, dressmaking or designing.

Being a lover of justice, and having the power to balance, reason and compare, you would make a good barrister, lawyer, accountant, personnel director, public relations officer, counsellor, or editor, but if responding to the more pleasurable side of your character, you would find happiness in the musical or theatrical world, and could have success in the direction or management of the artistic side of public amusements, set and stage design, ballet, teaching and choreography.

♏ scor Oct 24 to Nov 22

Due to your energy, force and self confidence, success could be achieved as a doctor, surgeon or nurse, also in any martial occupation where sharp instruments are used, such as mechanical engineer, soldier, electrician, or in sport as a fencing master.

Having a natural aptitude for delving into secrets of all kinds, you would make a good psychologist, magnetic healer, chemist, research worker, inventor, or detective, also Government official, policeman or fire investigator.

If attracted to the sea you would succeed in a naval career, diver, marine surveyor.

Sometimes there is an inclination towards occult or psychic work and success could be achieved along these lines.

Other occupations you could be attracted to are refrigeration, the meat trade, or connected with underground work, mining, oil field employee or funeral parlour, or in the science field, research to do with radiation, nuclear physics, astro-physics, or pollution monitoring.

♒ aqua Jan 21 to Feb 19

Due to your inventive, idealistic and refined nature, success could be achieved in literary, scientific or artistic pursuits.

Suitable occupations include: musician, librarian, artist, writer, secretary, advertising expert, radio-TV announcer or technician, electrical work in all its branches, engineering or surveying, also anything to do with aviation or car businesses.

You may have a desire to invent or be deeply interested in reforms, in which case associations, groups, popular movements, educational or political affairs would draw you, including occupations in social work, hospital benefits, co-op and human rights organisations.

Due to your interest in human behaviour patterns you could be drawn to sociology, psychology or psychoanalysis, leading to hypnology or Astrology and occult investigation.

You could also feel at home in occupations connected with the latest inventions, electronics, lasers, computers, jets and space probes.

♓ pisc Feb 20 to March 20

Due to your versatile nature and aptitude to combine the practical with the theoretical you have the ability for a variety of subjects.

Suitable occupations include: organising secretaries and agents of all kinds, literary workers, book-keepers, librarians and travellers. In the more artistic field, success is shown in music, acting or dancing, also film work and photography, or work in which fine detail is required.

As the sea generally has a strong fascination for you, a naval career often attracts, also the medical and nursing profession, ambulance officer, lifeguard, care of helpless animals, and chemical research or medical diagnoses.

It is quite possible that you will have more than one occupation running at the same time, or will change your position more than once during your life for you like change and novelty in your career.

You will be best fitted to hold some post under others, for you are liable to worry and apprehension, if you have too much responsibility placed upon you.

Your ambitions and career
found from **planets,** if any, in

the **tenth** House

☉ sun

The position of your Sun is very favourable for obtaining positions of authority, honour, or responsibility, and usually gives good hereditary conditions.

In a general sense there is power to lead, and this influence also denotes that you will most likely obtain the favour of persons of power and position.

Fortune and prosperity are generally experienced towards the middle of life.

Your career will be coloured a good deal by characteristics as described under 'Your vocational ability'.

For a non-career woman, these indications generally refer to the head of the house, the father, or if married, the husband.

☽ moon

The position of your Moon indicates that you will most likely experience a fluctuating and changeable career.

This influence favours all employment of a common or public and universal character, also in such work as performed in hospitals and institutions, or in professions which have to do with catering for the public and those in which a popular or well-known demand is made.

Avoid any profession or trade which has permanency as its base, for success is more likely where change and fluctuation is in evidence.

At the age 27 to 29 career matters will be very active. Your career will be coloured a good deal by characteristics as described under 'Your personality'.

These indications, for a non-career woman, generally refer to the head of the house, the father, or if married, the husband.

☿ merc

The position of your Mercury favours secretarial work and all pursuits where the mind is exercised, and shows that you usually adopt either a commercial career, or one connected with writing, teaching, lecturing, advertising or salesmanship.

This influence is not altogether favourable for permanency in professions, therefore you are likely to experience many changes throughout life.

A light employment is best suited for you, and where travel or movement is required, you will be in your element.

Your career will be coloured a good deal by characteristics as described under 'Your mental qualifications'.

For a non-career woman, these indications generally refer to the head of the house, the father, or if married, the husband.

♀ venu

The position of your Venus promises success in all matters that are concerned with the pleasure of others.

All those professions that are light and refined will be best suited to you, and if the artistic element is strong, a musical or artistic career is indicated.

This influence denotes that you will have many good friends who will help you, also that your employment should have some connection with the female sex and all their requirements, for in some way or other, your career will be greatly influenced by women and the pleasurable and social side of life generally.

For a non-career woman, these indications generally refer to the head of the house, the father, or if married, the husband.

♂ mars

The position of your Mars signifies that you are very ambitious and possess an enthusiastic nature with an inexhaustible fund of energy, so that no matter what obstacles are placed in your way, you usually surmount them.

This influence favours all forms of occupations where fire, iron or sharp instruments are used, in a skilled manner, therefore, you will most likely succeed as an engineer, soldier, surgeon or in a career where drive is a key factor.

Avoid hasty or rash decisions in career matters, for lack of discrimination may incur the enmity of persons who could accomplish your downfall and bring you into disrepute unless care is exercised.

These indications, for a non-career woman, generally refer to the head of the house, the father, or if married, the husband.

♄ sat

The position of your Saturn denotes power and authority in some way, but brings most fortune and success through industry and perseverance.

You may feel at times that you are under fate, but in spite of great odds your persistancy will help you achieve the success you have set out to gain.

If you use tact, foresight and systematic application to business you may become a top person in your field or hold other high positions involving great responsibility.

However, there is a tendency to misjudge the limit to which you can expand and you could easily lose that which you have gained, unless care is exercised, or this loss could be reflected through the affairs of a partner, or in early life, through the father.

Ψ nept

The position of your Neptune shows that you have high aspirations and inspirations, and that you are artistically inclined. There is also a love for mystery, hence success may be associated with some mystical society or through scientific research.

You would do best by following pursuits that are rare, unique or uncommon, for this influence favours literary genius, film acting, television, music, art, and also business connected with the sea and its products.

Guard against deception at all times, for Neptune is elusive in nature, which makes it difficult to judge between the false and the true.

These indications, for a non-career woman, generally refer to the head of the house, the father, or if married, the husband.

♃ jup

The position of your Jupiter will help you, both socially and financially.

There is also help from relatives or those in an influential position.

This influence favours professions such as law, religion, politics, metaphysics, also foreign affairs, shipping, commercial travelling and businesses that clothe and supply the general public with provisions.

Your employment is likely to be of a lucrative nature or you gain prestige through your marriage partner's career.

This position is one of the best indications of success, providing you do not over-expand or over-estimate in your aspirations when common sense should prevail.

♅ uran

The position of your Uranus denotes that you are endowed with an original and eccentric character, with a dislike for the usual conventions, hence you will most likely be attracted towards pursuits connected with exploring, pioneering or the development of new inventions, and all modes of transport.

This influence favours aviation, electronics, radio, television, computers, lasers, and all the latest inventions; in other fields, Astrology, curios and antiques.

Many sudden changes may be experienced in connection with business, and unless you are prepared to pay some attention to what other people say or think, disappointments trouble and reversals could easily occur.

For a non-career woman, these indications generally refer to the head of the house, the father, or if married, the husband.

♇ plut

The position of your Pluto denotes that you desire power and recognition and would like to be known as an authority.

You may get the urge to challenge the superficialities of your culture and society, and seek to reorganise humanity with your beliefs, but care should be taken that you do not endanger or undermine your position and reputation through too ruthless a manner.

You could at sometime be compelled or conscripted to undertake certain work in order to comply with the needs of a group.

This influence favours work connected with the latest discoveries and inventions; it also makes a good politician or official in an international organisation.

For a non-career woman, these indications generally refer to the head of the house, the father, or if married, the husband.

Romance and matters close to your heart

found from **planets,** if any, in

the **fifth** 🏠 **House**

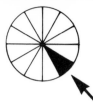

☉ sun

Romance and adventure are strongly marked in your life, with emphasis on love-affairs, pleasure seeking, speculations and all forms of enterprise, with a good deal of artistic creative capacity.

You will have scope for much individual effort and initiative, and will express much of your character as outlined under 'Your individual nature' in all matters of a creative nature.

You have speculative instinct and should be able to invest money to your advantage. The bigger the concern, the more success you will have.

You will be popular with the opposite sex, and will have honourable and successful attachments, also gain through social activity and entertainments. However, never let pride cause trouble in your heart affairs, or spoil your prospects.

There is fondness for children, through whom you should gain at some period of life, although a large family is not indicated.

As you are very enterprising and have creative ability, the above tendencies could be expressed through your work or profession, according to 'Your vocational ability'.

☽ moon

Romance and adventure are strongly marked in your life, for you love change, novelty, social pleasures and entertainment.

You also have strong creative capacity, which can find congenial expression according to the tendencies as outlined under 'Your personality'

In matters of enterprise and speculation, you will have much fluctuation, for you are inclined to favour those matters that have an element of uncertainty, with little or no permanency attached to them. However, you could have success in enterprise or investments that deal with the general public or places of amusement and entertainment.

In heart affairs you are inclined to be changeable, yet at some period of life could become deeply absorbed in someone who least deserves it.

Children are sure to play an important part in your life, one of whom could achieve popularity or fame.

At the age 27 to 29 these matters will become very active.

☿ merc

Adventure and enterprise are strongly marked in your life, particularly where you have scope to use your intellectual ability as outlined under 'Your mental qualifications'.

Your feelings and emotions are refined and your pleasures are likely to be more mental than physical. You could achieve success in enterprise connected with education, publishing, writing, public amusements, the theatre, or children's affairs.

Speculative interests are inclined to fluctuate, but favour those concerns that have a quick and rapid turnover. Be careful in signing or accepting any papers or documents with which you are not thoroughly acquainted, and avoid any urge to gamble.

Romance may come your way through correspondence, short journeys, education, business affairs or mental acitivity, but you must guard against anxiety in connection with matters close to your heart.

Children's affairs are likely to absorb your interest, nevertheless avoid undue worry concerning them.

♀ venu

Romance and adventure are strongly marked in your life, and there is every indication of successful love attachments, with much happiness through social pleasures and entertainments.

There is promise of success in all monetary affairs connected with investments and speculations, especially with stocks and similar securities. You could also gain through theatres, concerts, singing, music or some artistic creative capacity.

In heart affairs you are affectionate, and may have several love affairs before deciding on a permanent partner, details of which are outlined under 'Courtships'.

Much happiness from children and their affairs is shown, one of whom could be endowed with artistic or musical ability.

♂ mars

Romance and adventure are strongly marked in your life, for you have an ardent nature, and delight in pleasures, entertainments, and games of chance.

You are endowed with much energy and an enterprising spirit and if you avoid impulse, you may apply your energy to advantage in speculative matters, but you should carefully avoid gambling or any risky enterprises where you have to rely upon the honesty of others.

Your heart affairs may not always run smoothly, for you are rather impulsive. There is a tendency to involve yourself with the opposite sex if you are not cautious in dealing with them.

Try at all times to be moderate in your pleasures, amusements and love affairs.

A child will probably take up much of your time and attention at some period of life, but don't let it absorb too much of your energy.

♃ jup

Romance and adventure are strongly marked in your life, for you have a sociable and pleasure loving disposition.

Good fortune and success are promised through speculation, investments and enterprise, apart from any actual labour to acquire wealth, and by judicious investment you may, eventually, amass money in various ways.

You will be popular with the opposite sex and will have success in your heart affairs. There being one in particular, who will bring you happiness, being of a philosophical or social nature.

Children's affairs will play an important part in your life, one of whom will bring you gain, happiness and comfort.

Any activities that have to do with amusements, theatres, socials, schools, education, or publishing would benefit you.

♄ sat

Where investments and enterprise are concerned you will need to use extra care. However, if you invest in old established concerns, rather than risky and fluctuating speculations, you could have success. Well secured investments such as houses, land, mines, buildings or heavy industry will be most suitable.

In matters of the heart there may be some delay or disappointment in the earlier years, or else your affections will be centred upon someone older than yourself, in fact you will find the serious minded much more helpful to you than the more pleasure loving type.

You are likely to take your pleasures seriously, and may be more interested in enterprises of an educational nature or where you are creating in some way.

Children's affairs are not likely to bring you a great deal of happiness, in fact great respon⸺ ⸺surrounds anything to do with these matters.

♅ uran

Romance and adventure are strongly marked in your life, and you will be attracted to all new and strange things in your pursuit of pleasure.

You are very magnetic to the opposite sex, and in love matters will incline to original thought, with many strange, romantic, inconstant, or impulsive love affairs, some of which could be abruptly terminated.

In all enterprise and speculative matters sudden and unexpected events are indicated, and you would probably be safest in concerns dealing with inventions, electricity or original undertakings. You may have ability to entertain over the radio, or create in some other uncommon field.

Children's affairs are likely to affect your life in an unusual way, by you possibly adopting a child or even being separated from a child.

♆

Rom⸺ ⸺trongly marked in your life, and you may
exp⸺ ⸺ngs in your pursuit of pleasure.

In⸺ ⸺o careful, for there is a tendency to
⸺ ⸺entation and fraud of various kinds.

⸺ing emotional expression is in some
⸺ttachment with one of an advanced type.
⸺ative capacity to advantage in musical or

⸺ment is concerned, you will have to be
⸺s some possibility of gain through the stock
⸺.c.

⸺n could be described as intangible, as the
⸺ed more on the artistic and mental planes,
⸺alities.

♇ plut

This influence gives a need for creative expression, conquest and emotional drama.

Love is important to you and could be expressed in secret or unconventional ways, but be discreet and take great care of hygiene.

You are keen on recreation and could be a devoted theatre-goer, or there could be a strong interest in sports and athletics, with a tendency to do or die.

The desire for adventurous episodes could lead to gambling or other risks.

One of your children could be off-beat, but see that it is not due to too many of your rules.

If children are delayed, you may decide to adopt one, and it could even be of a different nationality.

Courtships

♈ arie

Venus the planet of love makes you impulsive in the expression of your affections. You will incline to be somewhat fickle, and therefore may have several courtships or love attachments.

Your feelings are sympathetic and quickly respond to appeals for worthy assistance, denoting generosity in gifts and expenditure.

Mistakes are likely regarding courtships, either through hasty decisions, such as falling in love at first sight or becoming entangled with another to such a degree that you may be forced into marriage, unless care is exercised in this direction.

Your position of Venus gives an idealistic love nature, generally making you anxious to obtain a mental affinity rather than a purely physical relationship.

♉ taur

Venus the planet of love indicates a very strong love nature, with a tendency to allow your feelings to influence decisions, as the emotions are much stronger than the mind.

You will have very set opinions concerning correct form and decorum in connection with pleasure, sociability and friendship, and once you have formed an opinion you will hold to it tenaciously.

You are likely to have only one real love throughout the course of your life, as you are inclined to be more fixed than fickle, and possess a very decided attachment to those whom you love, and for this reason care should be taken upon whom you bestow your affections.

Some misunderstandings could occur in connection with your love affairs, nevertheless you should gain financially and also socially through marriage.

♌ leo

Venus the planet of love favours marriage, and quickens the emotional nature to such an extent that your feelings are easily appealed to, producing attachments at the first opportunity.

You need love and to be loved; you have the magnetism, warmth and generosity to attract the opposite sex, though they may not always have the same amount to give.

It promises a successful courtship, for this influence lessens the liability of making errors in all matters of the heart, as your perceptions are very keen and active in this direction.

You will be very loyal in your affections and a considerable amount of happiness will come to you through your marriage partner.

You may be elevated to a higher position in life than that held at birth and should gain through social advantages, which will help considerably towards your happiness and welfare.

♍ virg

Venus the planet of love tends towards delay and disappointment in love, chiefly through the inability to gain the affections of those superior to yourself by birth, that is, so far as social status is concerned, or owing to the desire to make the love universal rather than particular.

There is a tendency for platonic attachments, secret or clandestine unions, and unless you can meet your ideal mate, you would probably prefer a life of freedom than legal union with another.

You will be attracted to those younger than yourself, or to those who need help or are in a lower social scale than your own, as weakness in others will call forth the sympathetic side of your love nature.

This position sometimes brings more than one marriage.

♐ sagi

Venus the planet of love shows that you are endowed with a sympathetic, kind and generous heart, and somewhat philosophically inclined.

Some peculiar episodes may take place in connection with your love affairs, and you could be involved in a love affair with a relative, or attracted to someone of a different nationality or religion.

You will probably marry more than once, and may meet your partner while travelling or during a visit to foreign parts. Your partner may also have been married before or have done much travelling.

You will have many experiences affecting your heart during the course of your life; but marriage should be good for you, promising success and advancement.

♑ capr

Venus the planet of love shows that you have great control over the feelings or they may be difficult to awaken to the fullest extent. However, when your affections are awakened you will become remarkably attached.

There is sometimes delay or hindrance in connection with marriage, and sometimes attachments to persons older than yourself.

Your love nature is ambitious, diplomatic and careful of honour, and marriage is usually for convenience or for social purposes. It conduces to social and business popularity, friends of high standing with gain and advancement through them.

Care may be necessary at times to avoid disappointment in love, also strange attachments, whereby your honour could be affected.

found from **venu** ♀ in **Sign**

(As an example of Venus in say Aries, it would read on the Chart like this -
'VENU 24 ARIE 32' or ' ♀ 24 ♈ 32')

♊ gemi

Venus the planet of love endows you with an artistic atmosphere where love affairs are concerned and tends to refine the feelings and intellect.

As a teenager you may go through a string of admirers and even when older, this position of Venus usually brings two love affairs into your life, or the likelihood of two attachments running at the same time, with perhaps difficulty in making a choice. Some troubles are indicated in this connection if care is not taken.

You will be extremely popular with the opposite sex, although danger of jealousy, also trouble through correspondence concerning matrimonial affairs may have to be watched.

In some way relatives could affect your love affairs and also exercise a decided influence over your marriage.

♋ canc

Venus the planet of love gives you a very fruitful imagination, and indicates there is a tendency to be rather fickle in your affections, and until you really become attached are liable to have many love affairs.

You will most likely meet your future partner through a journey or while travelling and will be attracted towards those with considerable difference in age, or become very much attached to one who is not of the same social standing as yourself.

Marriage may be a little delayed, owing to obstacles, either on account of parents, money or occupation; unforeseen difficulties, etc.

You are more receptive to the feelings of others than you suspect, and easily influenced through them.

The desire nature is ever seeking ideal love.

♎ libr

Venus the planet of love favours marriage, friendships, sociability, and popularity. It promises some gain through marriage and partnership. However, there may be a period during courtship when you will have a rival, who could cause some enmity or opposition to arise, but on the whole you should prosper in love affairs.

You will have very strong emotions, with kindness and sympathy, and tend to see good in everyone, yet through your sensitiveness can be easily hurt.

Affection is everything to you and you feel lost without a partner.

You will most likely be attracted towards those holding favourable positions in life and this influence could bring you elevation or spur you on to greater attainments in the material world.

♏ scor

Venus the planet of love increases the emotions and gives a love of sensation, luxury and pleasure.

With drive and persistency you don't easily let go of your mate.

You cannot be too discreet in connection with love affairs as there is a tendency to be attracted to, and by, persons with strong desires, who are inclined to form secret attachments. You have much self control, but will not always use it.

Avoid jealousy, and hasty unions or anything that could hurt your reputation, for there is a tendency towards risky attachments, which could cause you sorrow or disappointment.

There is the possibility of financial gain through marriage, as well as gifts, insurance or legacy.

♒ aqua

Venus the planet of love indicates a rather idealistic love nature with a desire to find your true soul mate.

You may expect some remarkable or strange, sudden and unexpected experiences of events in your love affairs and as you refuse to be bound by the usual restrictive rules of society and prefer to follow your heart's inclination, there is a tendency to form secret attachments or platonic friendships.

There is usually some faithful attachment and sometimes a long courtship, and you may fall in love with one formerly a friend.

This position sometimes delays marriage, or brings your true mate towards middle life.

Your temperament, loving personal freedom, can often finish a love affair at a moment's notice.

♓ pisc

Venus the planet of love indicates that you will most likely meet your future partner under rather peculiar circumstances.

You have a powerful emotional nature, and success is promised in love affairs if you guard against having more than one attachment going on at the same time, as there is danger of difficulties arising from rivals, unless care is exercised. It is, however, just possible that you may marry more than once, and should you survive your first partner, this will most certainly be the case.

Your attachments may have their origin in matters connected with sickness, or in a large place that deals with the public in some way, institutions, hospitals, etc.

Avoid secret alliances or attachments to inferiors, as you have a tendency to lack discrimination.

Marriage and partnership
found from **planets,** if any, in

the **seventh** 🏠 **House**

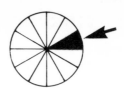

☉ sun

Your House of marriage indicates an honourable and ambitious partner, whose influence will be beneficial in your life, and although there is a tendency for marriage to be delayed, owing to pride or some condition surrounding position — you would eventually gain financially as well as socially.

During the early period of marriage there may not be complete harmony with your partner. Refer to 'Your individual nature' and see if you are unconsciously contributing to this. However, as time passes, happiness will come because of success in life and the fact that every opportunity will be presented for affection to increase.

A partner could also influence you in your work or profession or you could even take on a partner in business as you would be good in joint ventures, particularly those that harmonise with 'Your vocational ability'.

☽ moon

Your House of marriage indicates several opportunities to marry, but you will be inclined to waver or be undecided.

Your partner will be rather magnetic, sensitive and inclined to moods, will delight in change or travel and may deal with the public in some way.

Even though your marriage may not be considered a social success, you will probably be very happy, and for this reason should guard against outside influences, which may affect your marriage prospects.

Should inharmony occur, refer to your 'Personality' and see if you are unconsciously contributing to this.

Between the age of 27 and 29 will be a notable period in connection with this department of life.

☿ merc

Your House of marriage indicates an active, quick-witted and progressive partner. One who may have literary leanings, and although very intelligent and fluent in speech, may at times be irritable, critical and highly strung. Refer to 'Your mental qualifications' and see if you are unconsciously contributing to this.

Never allow worry, anxiety or difficulty to arise out of misunderstandings either through speech, travelling, relatives or correspondence.

Your partner will probably come strongly under the planet Mercury, could be a little younger than yourself, or not look their age.

Intellectual interests will contribute greatly to a happy marriage.

♀ venu

Your House of marriage indicates a partner whose influences upon your life will be beneficial, and according to other influences outlined under 'Courtships' should bring gain both socially and financially.

Your partner will be considerate and affectionate with probably an artistic temperament. Should marriage be delayed at all, you need not fear that it will not bring happiness and good fortune eventually, for it is shown as one of your most harmonious departments of life.

There is a love of offspring and a peaceful termination to any misunderstandings that may arise. Your partner is likely to be popular and attract many friends who will contribute to your social pleasures.

♂ mars

Your House of marriage tends towards an early union; as you are liable to fall in love at first sight, sometimes mistaking passion for love, you would do well to avoid a hasty marriage.

Your partner will be rather dominant, wishing to rule and be at the head of things, but at the same time capable, industrious, and untiring in the promotion of the welfare of the family.

You will probably be attracted by the qualities of boldness, fearlessness and courage in your partner who, although inclined to aggressiveness, will be ardent in feeling and emotions.

There is a liability for you to marry more than once as this position of Mars brings a tendency to short-lived partnerships.

♃ jup

Your House of marriage signifies happiness and success from your choice of a partner, whose nature will incline to be generous, optimistic and helpful. Your marriage should bring social and financial benefits, with a partner in a professional career, or of independent means, in which you share. Sometimes the partner has been married before, or is older and more philosophically inclined.

Marriage should turn your life into pleasant paths and favourable conditions with the opportunity to travel, which will bring both pleasure and profit as well as expansion to the mind.

Should anything occur to bring about the loss of your partner, you will most certainly marry again.

♄ sat

Your House of marriage indicates a tendency towards delay or hindrance in your early life. However, when marriage does take place you may be assured that your partner will be faithful and sincere. Probably a few years older than yourself and of a serious, industrious, persevering and thrifty nature.

There shows a great sense of duty and responsibility, with a tendency to loving deeds in preference to affections of the demonstrative and emotional order.

Care, therefore, should be taken not to allow coldness to come between you at any time. Your partner, although a great worker, may not necessarily rise to any position of social distinction, and may fall short of your aspirations.

There is every indication that you will outlive your marriage partner.

♅ uran

Your House of marriage denotes a rather original partner, one who is inventive or has ingenious methods of ministering to the domestic comforts.

You may meet your marriage partner under romantic conditions, but should avoid hasty or impulsive engagement. There may be an element of uncertainty about your marriage, and the unexpected is sure to occur. In fact you may end by marrying the last person you thought you would marry.

Your partner is bound to be magnetic and romantic, but unusual and original in many ways.

At some time in life, sudden and unexpected separations could occur in your partnership affairs, which may be beyond your control.

♆ nept

Your House of marriage is rather unusual, showing that although long expected happiness could meet with disappointment at the last moment due to deception on the part of another. When you do marry it will be quite unique and out of the common.

Your marriage partner could be connected with the sea in some way; or be of an original nature, interested in art, music, the occult, astrology or some kindred subject.

Don't be misled by 'personal magnetism', see that your intended partner is of an advanced spiritual type, for there is a tendency to attract shams, or those who pose as having superior qualities, or their weakness could be drugs or drink.

♇ plut

Your House of marriage attracts you to a dominant partner and due to the binding force of Pluto, tends to hold the partnership, either through the other's strength of will or by some other subtle methods.

You may feel that you are linked to your mate by fate, however, there may come a time when there is a clash of wills as your partner is likely to have intense desires and be somewhat unyielding.

If you wish the marriage to survive you will need to give your partner a certain amount of free rein.

Jealousy, separation, or death of a partner are the adverse features of this Pluto position.

Friendships
found from **planets,** if any, in
the **eleventh** 🏠 **House**

☉ sun

Your planetary influences show that you will contact firm, honourable and influential friends at some period of life, through whose help you will gain both in business as well as through the affections.

Some of your chief experiences are likely to come through your friends, and that part of your character as described under 'Your individual nature' will be broadened through your many contacts. It also promises the realisation of many of your hopes and wishes, through your strength of will or good luck to carry them out.

Friends coming under the sign of Leo as well as those of power and good position will benefit you.

This position is lucky and shows general good will to all. Read also other indications pertaining to love and friendships, for each will have a bearing upon your life.

Your work or profession could be furthered by the help of friendships, sometimes associated with committees, groups or companies, according to 'Your vocational ability'.

☽ moon

Your planetary influences tend to attract you to a large number of friends and acquaintances, especially among women, both in business and social circles.

You will be very popular where friendship is concerned as you have the ability to fraternise and mix easily with other people. Some of your main experiences will most likely come through your friendships, which play an important part in your life.

Those born under the sign Cancer will be congenial to you.

Owing to the fickle nature of the Moon there may be times when you will have to guard against insincerity, losses and disappointments among your friends.

Read also other indications pertaining to love and friendships, for each will have a bearing upon your life.

Between the age of 27 and 29 you will find yourself actively involved in friendship affairs and group activity.

☿ merc

Your planetary influences tend to attract you to many friends and acquaintances, although, owing to the changeable nature of Mercury there may be times when you will have unreliable friends, and incur loss through wrong advice or carelessness in their handling of facts.

Your most helpful friends will be found amongst those connected with literature or science, who will bring knowledge, inspiration and mental development.

Persons younger than yourself will be attracted to you, and those born under the signs Virgo and Gemini, probably the most congenial.

Never rely too much upon your acquaintances for assistance or go security for them.

Read also other indications pertaining to love and friendships, for each will have a bearing upon your life.

♀ venu

Your planetary influences incline you to a merry set of friends among the artistic and musically inclined, who in some way should do much to help you in the fulfilment of your hopes, wishes and aspirations.

Social success and popularity, as well as financial gain is indicated by this position and you will probably find those born under the signs Taurus and Libra the most helpful and congenial.

However, as Venus is rather carefree in nature, keep a watchful eye on all so-called friends who wish to impose on you.

Read also other indications pertaining to love and friendships, for each will have a bearing upon your life.

♂ mars

Your planetary influences indicate that you will make friends among ambitious, enthusiastic, enterprising, medical, military, or athletic persons, but tends to disagreement with acquaintances unless care is taken.

Be guarded in your choice of acquaintances, for Mars tends towards impulse or some form of extravagance.

Much energy and enthusiasm will be expended in the realisation of your hopes, wishes and aspirations, and you will always be a leader in your own particular social set.

Do not become surety for anyone, or lend your friends money, etc., or you will lose both friends and money.

Read also other indications pertaining to love and friendships, for each will have a bearing upon your life.

♃ jup

Your planetary influences tend to give friends and acquaintances among philosophical, social, wealthy and influential people, who may be relied upon to help the attainment of many of your hopes, wishes and desires.

It is an indication that there will never be a want of friends throughout life, and that you will be lucky in attracting just that type of friend who can benefit you. Those born under the sign Sagittarius, will probably be very congenial to you, also those who have travelled, and are broadened in outlook.

Any difficulties that may arise through Jupiter friendships are usually connected with religion, law or social activities.

Read also other indications pertaining to love and friendships, for each will have a bearing upon your life.

♄ sat

Your planetary influences tend to attract you to faithful and reliable friends, who are older, or more seriously minded than yourself.

Always choose those of a profound or scientific nature, for Saturn is not the most fortunate planet where gaiety or lightness is concerned, and does not show many real friends of this nature, in fact they would more likely disappoint or desert you when their help was most required.

It would seem that you have to learn some wisdom through friends of a Saturn nature, probably born under the signs Aquarius or Capricorn.

Read also other indications pertaining to love and friendships, for each will have a bearing upon your life.

♅ uran

Your planetary influences tend to attract you to people of an original, creative, or inventive turn of mind, also those who are interested in the mystical or occult, who will help you at some time of life.

This influence indicates rare and exceptional friendships with some strange and fascinating experiences. You may expect sudden and unusual attachments as well as sudden and unexpected estrangements.

Uranus is very original in nature, and will draw you to those who think more than the average individual, therefore, you can expect some interesting times where your friends are concerned.

Read also other indications pertaining to love and friendships, for each will have a bearing upon your life.

♆ nept

Your planetary influences tend to attract you to unique and strange acquaintances, some of whom will be interested in the artistic, romantic, musical, psychic or spiritual side of life.

Some remarkable experiences will most likely occur through your friends, and the fulfilment of your hopes and wishes will be brought about in quite a different manner to your expectations.

As Neptune is elusive and sometimes deceptive in nature, avoid any tendency to strange and unaccountable attractions, hypnotists, mesmerists, or those who drink heavily, or pose as mediums, etc.

Read also other indications pertaining to love and friendships, for each will have a bearing upon your life.

♇ plut

Your planetary influences tend to draw you to friends of a dominant nature, also to those intent upon reform movements or social improvements.

Any intrigue or secrecy with the opposite sex would cause the love life to get out of balance.

An awakening through one particular friend could affect your life at some period.

You can be quite intense over a friendship but keep in mind that this position of Pluto can attract you to the unscrupulous.

Any difficulties you may have with step-children could be the result of a hidden grudge they hold.

Read also the other indications pertaining to love and friendships, for each will have a bearing upon your life.

Your general health tendencies
found from **planets,** if any, in

the **sixth**  House

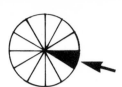

☉ sun

Your health prospects are fairly good, although care will have to be taken lest you weaken the constitution at some time in life, through some strenuous work, strain, or shock. Be careful also of contagious diseases and epidemics.

So much of the Sun's life force is bestowed upon your constitution, that you do not think sufficiently of conserving your energy.

However, you will obtain good attention when ill, and would find sun baths most beneficial as well as plenty of fresh air. The vitality is soon restored with a little rest, but don't indulge in too much medicine, nature's cures are the best for you.

You are likely to devote too much time to your working life or service to a cause, which could affect your health, therefore keep this in mind when choosing your work or profession, outlined under 'Your vocational ability'.

☽ moon

Your health prospects denote weakness during early life, and although this will improve, the constitution is not over-strong, consequently care must be taken at all times.

You are subject to functional more than organic complaints, therefore care should be exercised with regard to proper diet, otherwise you will suffer from indigestion and stomach complaints.

It would be advisable to avoid too much fluid or starchy foods, and stimulants should be taken in moderation.

Try to be quiet while eating and avoid uncongenial company, for the magnetism of others can have a marked effect upon your nerves and digestion.

Between the age of 27 to 29 health matters may need attention and you would be wise to have a check up at this time.

☿ merc

Your health prospects are not over-strong, due mainly to a highly strung nervous system, also a very active and ambitious mentality, which could easily over-tax the health unless care is taken.

Try to avoid worry, irritability, too much study or mental activity, otherwise the nerve centres will weaken, and the digestive system suffer. Headaches, neuralgia or insomnia are also common complaints although most of these tendencies can be overcome by avoiding worry, over-study and over-work.

Vitamin B Complex may help in this respect as a nerve fortifier.

Refer also to 'Your mental qualifications' as your mental qualities will have a lot to do with the state of your health.

♀ venu

Your health prospects are fairly good providing temperance is observed, especially with regard to diet and habits of living.

The nutritive system is easily affected, and should you indulge in the pleasures or luxuries of life to any extent, you may trace your indisposition to this fact.

The kidneys, tonsils, throat and generative system are subject to weakness, and there is a tendency to cysts through poor circulation of venous blood.

Vitamin C is recommended as it helps to ward off infections that might invade the blood stream.

However, most of these tendencies can be avoided by observing a proper diet most suitable to your constitution, also through the application of temperance in all things.

♂ mars

Your health prospects give a robust condition with an abundance of vitality. However, don't let your enthusiasm carry you too far for you are subject to overstrain, which could result in muscular weaknesses, operations, as well as accidents, scalds, burns, and cuts occurring in the course of your employment, unless care is taken.

Your sicknesses will tend to be sharp and sudden, with a likelihood of fever and inflammatory complaints, and although severe at the time, will not be lasting.

However, by exercising caution at all times, and by avoiding all excess of enthusiasm, over-work or over-indulgence in diet, much of the foregoing will be overcome.

Should any tendency towards impotency be noticed at any time, Vitamin E could have a wonderful toning effect.

♃ jup

Your health prospects are good, with little danger of sickness throughout life, except such as arise through excess or over-indulgence, in which case there would be a tendency to blood disorders and liver complaints, and in rare cases gout.

However, should you become ill, you will always be well looked after, and recover quickly, for the general tendency is towards good health, providing the blood is kept pure and indiscretions in diet are avoided.

The influence of Jupiter in this position can be responsible for the accumulation of too much sugar glycogen in the liver and arterial circulation, which could easily result in diabetes, tumours, boils and fatty degeneration. To cleanse the blood stream the mineral Calc. sulph. can be very beneficial.

♄ sat

Your health prospects can be difficult unless care is taken, for there is a tendency to colds, congestion, rheumatism or bronchial complaints, catarrh, etc., also poor circulation.

Your sicknesses could be the result of want or neglect, in which case the resistance would be lowered. Therefore, always see that you have nourishing food and warm clothing, etc.

There may be the tendency towards early teeth decay, so that regular check-ups would be advisable. However, much of the foregoing can be overcome by avoiding fear, depression or pessimism, as these tend to poison the blood stream and affect the liver. Cheerfulness and optimism will be the best weapons in defence of your health.

For the prevention of Saturn complaints, colds, influenza, bronchitis, sinus and phlegm, Vitamins A and C can be very beneficial.

♅ uran

Your health prospects are fairly good, although the nervous system is highly strung, and it would be advisable to avoid undue strain from over-work or mental fatigue at all times.

Most of your sicknesses will be due to a mental and nervous condition, and unless care is taken could weaken the nerve centres or bring on a breakdown.

Never eat when tired, nervous, excited or angry, for this would interfere with your digestion. Always try to have as much rest and sleep as possible, and in the case of any stubborn complaint, electrical treatment may prove beneficial.

For nerve complaints attributable to this Uranus position, Vitamin B Complex tablets are beneficial for feeding the nerves and the mineral Mag. phos. also has a very relaxing effect on the muscles and nervous system.

♆ nept

Your health prospects are fairly good, if you can avoid becoming too receptive to the people and conditions around you.

You seem to attract the conditions of those around you, particularly those who are not well, and may find it difficult to decide just why you are indisposed.

When you find yourself out of tune, an approach through psychology and psychiatric treatment would probably do more good than physical treatment.

Guard against the use of narcotics and never turn to drugs of a soothing nature. Excessive smoking or drinking will be detrimental to your health, and you should only eat the purest and freshest of food.

A vegetarian diet would suit your constitution better than animal matter.

♇ plut

Your health prospects can be affected through too much intensity and single-minded purpose in accepting responsibility to obtain desired results for large organisations or groups.

Your sicknesses can result from neglect of deep seated or hidden complaints and early medical attention should be obtained at the first sign of any physical blemish.

Some diseases result from self-poisoning, due to the absorption of toxins from the system and therefore much stress should be placed on proper elimination.

When gardening or bushwalking take great care to protect yourself against poisonous bites from insects or snakes.

You may be deeply interested in investigating the psyche, but danger lurks for you if you experiment with LSD, etc.

If females notice unusual symptoms of ill health, Pluto in this position could point to the contraceptive pill as the cause.

Points to watch regarding your health

♈ arie

Physically your constitution is strong, with good recuperative powers, but you are highly strung and apt to go to extremes, it being very difficult to 'keep cool' physically or mentally.

Your mind is particularly active, which makes it necessary to have a proper amount of natural sleep, bodily and mental rest, as well as peaceful and harmonious surroundings. There is nothing like worry, anxiety and overstrain of the brain to upset the general health, while excitement of all kinds is especially adverse.

Try not to overdo things either mentally or physically and observe regular hours for work and rest; otherwise you will tend to headaches, neuralgia, insomnia, eye strain, sinus, as well as feverish, infectious and inflammatory complaints, occasionally reacting upon the stomach and kidneys.

In matters of diet, brain food should be especially chosen and an avoidance of stimulants. Fresh air and daily walking exercise are most desirable.

♉ taur

Your constitution is strong and robust, and you tend to suffer from too much life, rather than too little, therefore, laziness is fatal to your health, while work is your best medicine.

Being fond of the good things of the earth, enjoying food, pleasures and ease, you may tend to become indolent, and unless discretion is used in both habits and diet, the blood becomes disordered and gives rise to complaints affecting the heart, throat, blood stream and generative system.

Every care should be taken in diet, and all food of a fattening and heating nature avoided, with temperance in drink essential.

Excitement and hurry should always be avoided and when run down or depressed, pleasures and company will act as a stimulant, music having an especially harmonious influence on the system.

♌ leo

Your constitution is strong, with an abundance of vitality, which enables you to resist the onslaught of disease, and also to quickly recuperate after any indisposition.

The heart and blood stream seem to be your weakest spots, and it may be necessary to guard the throat, back and generative system as life advances.

Temperate living is essential, because once your life gets into an inharmonious groove, or goes to extremes, disorders are likely to arise. Diet should be carefully attended to, and all heating and stimulating food or drink should be avoided, for nutritious blood-strengthening food is absolutely necessary.

Rest in solitude and peace is a wonderful curative agent with you.

♍ virg

Your constitution is fairly strong, although the condition of the mind has much to do with your general health: worry, anxiety and overwork soon deplete your system.

The general condition of business and financial matters greatly affects your health, and if your material affairs are upset, or going wrong, it will be found that your health and nervous system will suffer.

Diet is most important in your case, while regular habits should be observed in all things, especially meals, otherwise you will tend towards digestive and bowel disorders, and dyspeptic action arising from debility, and poorness of blood.

Every effort should be made to live naturally and quietly, as peace of mind means everything to you 'A healthy mind makes a healthy body'.

♐ sagi

You have a sound and wiry constitution with good vitality, but when your health is disturbed, the cause generally can be traced to over-activity and excessive worry.

Moderation is essential, as you do things with a rush and put too much exertion into actions, which in time tends to weaken the system. Everything should be done quietly and over-exertion avoided, otherwise you will be subject to nervous breakdowns, sciatica, rheumatism, varicose veins, too heated blood, fevers, etc. The condition of the blood will often need attention, guard also the hips and thighs, particularly if riding or engaged in sport.

When the health runs down, exercise, physical recreation, riding, cycling, or if possible a sea voyage will do more than medicine.

♑ capr

Your constitution may not be over strong during early life, but improves considerably as life advances. You seem to lack animal heat, your problem being to generate enough energy to keep warm.

Colds and chills should be guarded against, as your blood circulation is rather poor, and you are subject to rheumatism, catarrh, constipation, stomach and liver disorders. Be careful also of accidents to the knees.

There is sometimes a tendency to despond, therefore seek cheerful company and congenial surroundings whenever possible. A fair amount of physical exercise will prove beneficial as well as a heating and stimulating diet.

Should you at any time suffer from skin eruptions or complaints, you will be able to trace it to a sluggish condition of the kidneys and liver, which may need toning up from time to time.

found from the ASCENDANT SIGN
(i.e. The Sign in the middle of the left-hand side of
the circular Chart, the start of House number 1)
(The Ascendant point is sometimes marked in
Charts as ASC or A)

To find your Ascendant Sign without a Chart turn to page **83**

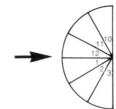

♊ gemi

Your mind and nervous system has chief influence over your health and although you have a fairly strong body, with quick recuperative powers, there is a danger of nervous disorders if you worry or become too mentally excited.

Try to avoid worry, irritability or too much restlessness, otherwise the nerve centres will weaken, and the digestive system suffer. It is essential that you have plenty of rest and a congenial atmosphere, for you easily get run down, giving rise to nervous complaints and disorders that affect the lungs and respiratory organs, such as bronchitis, asthma, catarrhal troubles, sciatica, and neuralgia.

You will find walking and gymnastic exercise helpful, and breathing exercises most beneficial for good health.

Warm clothing is important for lung protection and particular care is required in diet, mental and nerve foods being essential.

♋ canc

Your physical conditions are affected mainly through an over-receptive and sensitive nature, and all anxiety or overtaxing of the mind will disturb the digestive organs.

You should not worry over your health unnecessarily. as any indisposition can usually be traced to mental and emotional disturbances.

Colds and chills should be guarded against, as your blood circulation is rather poor, and you are subject to anaemia, catarrh, rheumatism and constipation; your problem being to generate enough energy to keep warm.

Any excessive emotion will give rise to gastric troubles and digestive derangements, and during these times extra care will be necessary with regard to diet. Pure, well cooked food is desirable, taking nothing that causes fermentation.

It would be advisable to avoid too much fluid, fatty or starchy foods, and stimulants should be taken in moderation. Drugs of all kinds should be particularly avoided.

♎ libr

Your constitution is fairly strong, although the blood is liable to get out of order quickly, particularly if you overdo your pleasures and are not careful in diet.

The kidneys, bladder and lumbar regions seem to be your weakest parts, and any pains across the lower part of the back should be given immediate attention, as this is a warning that your blood stream needs purifying, and if neglected could give rise to head and stomach disorders.

Excessive worry or impatience will soon deplete your health, so try to keep a balance in all things.

A congenial environment, plenty of fresh air, and mild physical exercises are necessary to keep your system in good order.

Beautiful and peaceful surroundings are your best medicine.

♏ scor

You have plenty of vitality, with good powers of resistance, but you should avoid all excess of enthusiasm, over-work, or over-indulgence in diet.

The excretory and generative organs are sensitive parts, as well as the heart, throat, and blood stream. You are also subject to infectious and inflammatory complaints, piles, ruptures, catarrh, sinus, kidney and bladder disorders.

All heating and stimulating foods should be avoided, very little meat taken, while intoxicants of all kinds should never be touched, unless medicinally. However, by exercising caution at all times, and avoiding overstrain, you will minimise any sickness. Having a strong intuitive sense, you will often find your own treatment your best medicine.

♒ aqua

You have a wiry and healthy constitution, but are liable to suffer from imperfect circulation of blood, therefore plenty of fresh air and exercise are necessary to keep the system in good order.

You also have a good deal of mental vitality, and it is quite essential that your mind is kept free from excessive worry and anxiety, otherwise your system could become depleted, giving rise to nervous disorders, corruption of blood, anaemia, varicose veins, palpitation of the heart, and various disorders, that tend to poison the blood or thicken the arteries.

Your diet should be of a brain and blood-building nature, but not too stimulating or over-heating. Always guard your ankles if riding or engaged in sport, and don't neglect any weakness of the eyes.

When indisposed you quickly recuperate when alone with nature.

♓ pisc

Your physical conditions are mainly weakened through over-anxiety, restlessness and worry, while you are apt to be careless of personal comforts and necessities.

There is also a tendency towards digestive disturbances, therefore temperance in both eating and drinking is absolutely necessary, in fact too much liquid is not good for you, particularly with meals.

Chills and colds are apt to cause catarrhal complaints, rheumatism, etc., and as you are subject to infectious and contagious disorders, care will be needed to always keep the blood and system in good order.

You may have a little trouble with the feet, such as corns, swellings, etc., and should always be careful of catching cold through damp feet.

A plain or vegetarian diet will suit you best, while intoxicants should be avoided.

Local travel and social activity
found from **planets,** if any, in

the **third**  House

⊙ sun

Your horoscope shows much activity both mentally and socially, for your mind is bright and observing and finds much pleasure in intellectual activities, or where you can express your characteristics as outlined under 'Your individual nature', for you aim at achievement and success and are suited for a good education.

Short journeys, reading and correspondence will widen your social activity and enable you to contact people who are ambitious and successful.

Most of your journeys will have some important mission or business activity connected with them, and you will always be well received on these occasions.

Your neighbours, relatives and social circles will benefit you in many ways, and will play an important part in your life.

As you are a good communicator in talking, interviewing or writing, these tendencies could be used to good effect when choosing your work or profession, according to 'Your vocational ability'.

☽ moon

Your horoscope shows an enquiring mind, ever alert for new information and possessing a fund of knowledge regarding public affairs and all that is going on.

You are very fond of travel and moving about, for you desire new material and surroundings for thought and action. In fact most of your mental experiences will come through change and social activity.

Although you are fond of mental pursuits, you may lack continuity and stability, and are therefore suited for short studies in preference to long and tedious training, for this would only result in unfinished education or accomplishments.

You are likely to come in contact with many people, some of whom may be in the public eye, and you will find your greatest enjoyment in social activity and personal expression as described under 'Your personality'.

Between the age of 27 and 29 will be a very active period for you in connection with the above affairs.

☿ merc

Your horoscope shows a fondness for change and travel, with a strong urge to investigate new places and people, and it is quite probable that you will be engaged in some pursuit that necessitates much moving about.

Your mentality is quick and perceptive, with an inclination towards study, research work, speaking, reading, lectures and writing, and according to your characteristics as described under 'Your mental qualifications', you should derive much pleasure through these activities.

Socially, you are a good mixer, being witty, good humoured and adaptable, and you will find that the more you converse with others the more your mental powers will increase

You may find it difficult to concentrate on one thing very long, and should never allow yourself to become over-active mentally, for any strain, anxiety or worry soon reacts on your nervous system, and depletes the health.

Brothers or sisters, relatives and neighbours, all tend to play an important part in your life.

♀ venu

Your horoscope shows much pleasure and happiness through journeys, travel and change, also benefit socially through your contact with others.

You have an optimistic and cheerful outlook, with the ability for expressing yourself in a happy and appropriate manner, both in speech or writing, which will add to your popularity.

You are very artistic, and should have ability for either art, music, singing, dancing, or designing, for you love the beautiful, especially in nature.

Much pleasure and social gaiety is likely to come your way, particularly through your contact with those who are travelled or artistically inclined, while neighbours, relatives, brothers or sisters should be well disposed, and capable of benefiting you in many ways.

♂ mars

Your horoscope shows a keen mind with plenty of energy, force and initiative, but as others may not always show your quickness in grasping points, it would be to your advantage to develop a little more patience and tact, for you could easily become combative and over-critical.

You are likely to have a good deal of change and travel throughout your life, but should never decide to move on impulse, or without sufficient thought, for there is a tendency towards mishaps and adverse conditions through hastiness.

Your inventive and executive ability could be used to advantage in some literary or educational activities, for you should be fond of writing, debating, and lecturing. However, never over-do your mental faculties, there being a tendency towards fevers, breakdowns, etc.

Neighbours, relatives, brothers or sisters could prove troublesome at some period of life, but always remember — a little tact can do wonders.

♃ jup

Your horoscope shows many benefits through journeys, travel and change, also your ability to take advantage of the education you will receive.

You should be very popular in your social circle, for you know how to be kind, courteous and sympathetic when the occasion arises. You are naturally optimistic and bright, and during the course of your life, will draw many interesting people to you.

Success is indicated in all mental pursuits, and you may benefit directly or indirectly through writings and publishings, or through books, correspondence and exchange of thought.

Brothers or sisters, neighbours and relatives will all be well disposed towards you, and you may expect some very interesting travel in connection with relatives or your social affairs.

♄ sat

Your horoscope shows a certain amount of delay in connection with any anticipated travel during your life, and you will probably find greater success if you devote your mind to mental pursuits, for you are capable of serious concentration and the study of deep or profound subjects.

You possess tact, diplomacy, justice and honesty and will attract people with these characteristics, and your social life will be more on the serious and intellectual side than the frivolous.

People older than yourself will be attracted to you, or those who hold responsible positions in society, although the earlier part of your life inclines to a little too much cautiousness or reserve.

Never allow worry, restlessness and anxiety to spoil your prospects, for a bright and optimistic mind must attract happiness and success.

♅ uran

Your horoscope shows many interesting experiences through sudden and unexpected journeys, travel and adventure.

Your mind is quite original and in no way conventional, and will possess qualities out of the ordinary, with the ability to study mystical, metaphysical and abstract subjects.

There is a touch of the eccentric, or a flash of genius especially if you are interested in music, writing or oratory. You are very intuitive and could study astrology with success or develop some psychic faculty.

You will never stay too long in one spot, for your restlessness will ever seek new schemes, projects, and discoveries, being always interested in social or mental reforms.

Social life will move at a high tempo, for you will delight in meeting new people and discussing interesting problems.

♆ nept

Your horoscope shows many interesting experiences through journeys and travel, many of which will be by water, or to holiday near the sea.

You have imaginative and fanciful mental tendencies, with a fondness for music, art, or matters pertaining to the occult and mystical. You could have poetic fancies or write a little, and for social reasons may change your name, have a nickname, 'nom de plume' or alias.

Some of your social contacts may be strange characters, interested in the unusual, and a relative, brother or sister may be difficult to understand, or could play an important part in your life.

Your intuitions are very strong, and you should always follow your first impressions, for among your social contacts you could easily contact schemers or those who would defraud you.

♇ plut

Your horoscope shows that you challenge superficial and obsolete modes of thinking, ever striving after new intellectual concepts. This may be a little shattering to those you live with, particularly if they conform to old established customs.

You are likely to change your environment or take many short journeys, also to read a good deal, for you love research.

Your educational activities are sure to include subjects dealing with psychology and delving into mental processes.

You would make a good investigator, detective or analyst.

Take care that your writings and communications do not reflect any biased opinions that you may have.

Travel and study - expansion of mind

found from **planets,** if any, in

the **ninth** 🏠 **House**

⊙ sun

You will achieve expansion of mind through higher educational pursuits, for you are creative, ambitious, and keen to investigate science, philosophy and truths worthy of benefiting others.

You can take very broad views of life generally as you are not bound too much by conventionality, and may interest yourself in the fine arts, music, science, philosophy, law, religion, or other profound subjects.

You are likely to travel overseas both for pleasure and profit, and may even take up residence abroad, or have an interest in the sea, shipping or foreign concerns.

The above tendencies could be expressed through your work or profession, therefore keep this in mind when reading 'Your vocational ability'.

☽ moon

You will achieve expansion of mind through philosophy, reading, change and travel, for you have an extremely fertile imagination, with a desire to investigate higher thought subjects.

You may take an interest in educational pursuits, writing, publishing, editing, or study science, philosophy, law, mysticism, etc., and could come into the limelight of publicity at some period of your life.

You are likely to travel a good deal, and may take up residence abroad, as you find your greatest happiness in moving about and exchanging ideas, the desire being to develop and enrich the mind.

Refer to 'Your personality' for added information regarding your expression in these fields.

Between the age of 27 and 29 will be a very active period for travel and mental stimulation.

☿ merc

You will achieve expansion of mind through travel, study and research work, for you are very intuitive and quick to learn and capable of delving into profound problems of life.

You may take an interest in reading, science, law, literary pursuits, writing, publishing, teaching, oratory, or take up metaphysical subjects, for you have the ability to become a philosopher, if you develop concentration and continuity.

You will undertake some long voyages or travel in foreign countries, or may take up residence abroad at some period of life, through which your mind will become broadened, flexible and adaptable.

Refer to 'Your mental qualifications' for added information regarding your expression in these fields.

♀ venu

You will achieve expansion of mind through travel and study of cultural activities, such as music, art or drama, also classical literature, and the exchange of ideas with artistic or literary persons.

You have a philosophical spirit with an appreciation for every form of mental improvement, and are likely to derive much pleasure from travel abroad.

You may have romantic experiences or become attached to one from another country, and could gain much happiness and expansion of mind through their spiritual, scientific or artistic disposition. Their relatives' influence could also be beneficial to you.

Refer to 'Courtships' for added information regarding these experiences.

♂ mars

You will achieve mental expansion through higher educational pursuits and will incline to much enthusiasm, force and independence regarding philosophical, scientific, educational or Government affairs.

You may take an interest in politics or law, being active in defence of rights, and you will combat or argue against any system of thought that does not meet with your approval. However, you will be wise not to become too expressive, or outspoken in your ideas, for you could arouse much strife and perhaps litigation.

You are fond of change, and are likely to travel abroad, but should avoid any rash impulses or decisions when travelling, for there is a tendency towards mishaps and accidents.

♃ jup

You will achieve mental expansion through travel, philosophy, or religion, and it is quite possible that you will develop some prophetic tendencies.

You will not be so scientific, as philosophical and artistic, for you are very intuitive, and incline more to accept the broad outlines than the limited and precise details of observation.

During your life you will undertake some long journeys, or travel in foreign lands, and will probably take up residence abroad, for gain is shown in some way through overseas affairs.

Legal or Government affairs may also affect you directly or indirectly and you could take up writing or literary activities at some period of life.

♄ sat

You will achieve mental expansion through the study of physics, science, philosophy and metaphysical or occult subjects, for you have a serious and thoughtful mind, capable of stability and concentration.

You are likely to be concerned with legal, travel, or foreign affairs at some period of your life, but must expect some obstacles, delay or hindrance in connection with these affairs. However, when these have cleared away, you should be able to expand your interests on a more stable footing.

Your mind is capable of bringing abstract thought down to practical demonstration, but you must avoid any tendency towards over-criticism or prejudice.

♅ uran

You will achieve mental expansion through the study of all advanced thought, such as Astrology, occultism, and kindred subjects, or by pioneer work of some kind, for you have an original, creative and inventive turn of mind.

You have a prophetic, intuitive faculty, desirous of travelling and exploring the region of the unknown, and all those subjects that are considered 'far fetched', and 'superstitious', but no matter how much critics may look upon you as a crank, your thought is of the advanced and progressive type.

During your life you will undertake some long journeys, or travel in foreign lands, possibly by air, and will probably gain more knowledge through your exploits in travelling about, than through any other source.

♆ nept

You will achieve mental expansion through psychic studies, philosophy, or perhaps spiritualistic phenomena and other kindred subjects, for you have an inspirational nature, capable of feeling the higher spiritual influences.

You could develop a gift for writing or prophecy, and will have some remarkable dreams and mental experiences. However, examine well all psychic impressions before putting them to practical use.

The sea could have a fascination for you, and you will probably undertake some long sea voyages, or take up residence abroad. Many fascinating and uncommon experiences will colour your life through travel.

♇ plut

You will achieve mental expansion through metaphysical subjects, as you desire to probe the depths of the unknown.

You refuse to conform to organised religion, but work to understand the laws of human existence.

These principles are best expressed through philosophy, writing, teaching or preaching.

Foreign travel may involve some secret mission or come about through a desire to pioneer a new idea.

Government, legal or war conditions could cause personal suffering at some time.

Your philosophies may lead to the desire to fight for the rights of others, but it may be wise to develop a love for the ideals rather than mere 'action'.

Home and domestic affairs
found from **planets,** if any, in

the **fourth**  **House**

☉ sun

Your environment and home conditions promise much success and realised ambitions during the close of life, either through your contact with helpful people or through conditions that you yourself have set in motion.

You could gain through houses, land or property, or occupations connected with these things, also benefit by means of parentage, inheritance, etc.

You may find the earlier years of life an uphill struggle or be unable to take full advantage of your abilities until later. However, according to your characteristics as outlined under 'Your individual nature', so will you be enabled to reap the fruit of what you have sown in your earlier years.

☽ moon

Your environment and home conditions tend to fluctuate as life advances and you may expect many changes of residence and moving about.

This could occur either through activity of parents or through your own restlessness and desire for expression as outlined under 'Your personality'.

A certain amount of domestic responsibility will colour your life, or you will have strong home ties, but should not bank on a settled abode in your latter years, for it would seem that change will be the best medium for the growth of your personality.

Possessions, prosperity, gain and benefits are all indicated from the home sphere, either through houses, land, property or the parents.

☿ merc

Your environment and home conditions indicate many changes as life advances. This could occur through your own restlessness or on the other hand through matters connected with business, and in the latter case would show success in pursuits as outlined under 'Your mental qualifications'.

Always be careful in dealing with sharp witted or clever persons, and use discrimination in regard to any papers you may have to sign, especially in connection with houses, land, property, or relatives' affairs, for the tendency is towards anxiety in connection with these matters.

In preference to a roaming life, you would be wise to engage in some occupation that keeps you physically stationary but mentally active.

♀ venu

Your environment and home conditions promise to be much happier and more harmonious during the latter half of life than the earlier years, for you will find yourself in better circumstances, and surrounded by those who can benefit you.

Your financial conditions will improve, and you should be able to add to your assets, either by acquiring land, a house or other securities for your old age.

You will have more pleasures and social activity, and will delight in decorating and furnishing your home, as well as buying attractive things to wear.

There is every possibility of gain through inheritance, parents, houses, property and investments.

♂ mars

Your environment and home conditions are subject to some disputes and difficulties as life moves on, possibly through the parents or those who have some authority or control in your life.

You would do well not to remain in one place too long, a change of residence being generally beneficial, as happiness lies for you in creating your own home.

You are subject to losses in connection with domestic affairs, and should therefore avoid speculations to do with property, lands and mines, also be careful of thefts or fire.

You are likely to lose a parent, but a legacy from them is almost assured, and although you may have obstacles to contend with, you will always have plenty of energy and aggressiveness to 'feather your nest' for a rainy day.

♃ jup

Your environment and home conditions promise to be peaceful and happy, in fact, the latter part of your life is the best, and a good termination to your existence is very plainly marked.

You will have successful family surroundings, gain and favour through parents, as well as benefits in all transactions that have to do with social or home affairs, and domestic life generally.

It would be much better for you to remain in, or near your native land and home, than to reside in a foreign country, or to travel from your home for success.

Gain through inheritance or the acquisition of assets in land or property is almost assured.

Every year of your life should be more and more prosperous, and comfort secure at the end.

♄ sat

Your environment and home conditions will not always run smoothly, but as life advances you could have success from investments and administration of anything to do with houses, land and property.

You will be anxious to save money for your closing years, but should guard against over-carefulness and too much work or responsibility, for this would tend to tie you down and make you too reserved and secluded.

You will have every opportunity to save money and accumulate assets so have no fear on this account, although you are likely to be more fortunate if you move away from your place of birth.

You may lose a parent in early life, or circumstances may necessitate you making your own way. However, success will grow as life advances.

♅ uran

Your environment and home conditions tend to be rather unsettled as life moves on, in fact towards the latter part, there is a likelihood of many changes, sudden surprises and unexpected events.

Changes may occur through restlessness, an inability to fit into your environment, or some inharmony with relatives or parents, and eventually you will find greater success by moving from your native place.

You are likely to take up studies or interests towards the close of life of which in the earlier part you had little, if any, idea and these are sure to be out-of-the-ordinary, for you will develop an advanced outlook, probably taking up astrology or occult sciences, or invent something unusual.

♆ nept

Your environment and home conditions tend to be unusual and unique, particularly towards the latter half of life, for there are sure to be some muddled, hampered or peculiar problems, either in your parents or your own domestic life.

You will have several changes of residence, and will either travel over water several times or live constantly near the sea.

There is some possibility of gaining through legacies, houses, land or property, but you must ever be alert for fraud, deception or schemes in connection with these.

Some psychic awakening is more than probable in your closing years, and you will either take a great interest in mysterious things, or have some secrecy or seclusion in your home surroundings.

♇ plut

Your environment and home conditions could have been insecure during your earlier life or there could have been broken family ties.

Houses, land or property could cause you some concern, but you will always desire to be king of your castle and when renting or purchasing a property, take care to check the basic structures and the surroundings for hidden snags.

Also, ensure that your property is adequately protected, as at some time you might be subject to robbery, arson or other unseen loss.

During the latter part of your life there may come to light a family secret or skeleton in the closet.

You could also take an interest in historic homes, or in genealogy.

Your children

found from **planets,** if any, in

the **Leo** ♌ **Sign**

(NOTE — The Sign Leo can be found anywhere around the Chart, part falling in one House and part in the next House, therefore a Planet in this Leo Sign can be in either House, but remember it must be in the LEO SIGN.)

(As an example of say, Jupiter in Leo, it would read on the Chart like this — 'JUP 24 LEO 32' or ' ♃ 24 ♌ 32')

Note — Not everybody has a Planet in the LEO Sign, so for other indications on Children's Affairs, check for any Planet in the 5th House and read under 'Romance and matters close to the heart'

☉ sun

The Leo position of the Sun denotes your children, or one in particular, who is important in your life and as the Sun is considered a male indicator, it favours boys rather than girls, although it rarely indicates more than one or two children.

Their nature as well as being warm-hearted, sociable and generous will also be proud and attract an air of authority.

As the Sun is a natural leader, it tends to lead a child into some more or less responsible or prominent position as organiser in Government affairs or high office.

A Sun child also has the ability to dramatise and is therefore at home in the entertainment world, where success could come, in occupations connected with the stage and television acting, theatre management, etc.

As a parent, you will need to use discipline with a certain amount of affection, as if you are too possessive or dominant, your offspring will become resentful or arrogant.

☾ moon

The Leo position of the Moon denotes your children, or one in particular, who is important in your life and as the Moon is considered a female indicator, it tends to bring more girls than boys.

This lunar position brings your children success in matters concerning the public, as they have a natural understanding of public needs and conditions and at some time in life a child is sure to achieve popularity or recognition.

Moon children are not necessarily of a scholastic nature and express best through their emotions, and therefore they should be encouraged to take an interest in acting, music or painting.

If these children at times appear to be fickle, it can be traced to their sensitivity to people and places, but when something does take their fancy they can be very tenacious and clinging.

☿ merc

The Leo position of Mercury denotes your children, or one in particular, who is important in your life. As Mercury is a mental planet, your creative interests may be more along these lines and therefore you may not be interested in a large family.

This planet indicates children who are intellectual and clever, with creative ability along the lines of art, drama, writing, editing or teaching, with an aptitude for mimicry or acting.

Detail work is never too much for this type of child, although care should be taken not to let them over-study as their nature is rather highly strung.

Mercury children easily change their mind 'on the double' and therefore need training early in life to stand on their own feet and make firm decisions.

As this planet is the 'message carrier', occupations connected with communications will suit them.

♀ venu

The Leo position of Venus denotes your children, or one in particular, who is important in your life and as this is a fruitful planet, it denotes gain and happiness through your children.

As well as being good looking, their nature will be easy to get on with, being loving and affectionate, with an appreciation for all forms of beauty.

Venus leans towards a full social life and luck should surround many of your children's ventures, particularly financially, socially and in matters of the heart, for they will attract friends and popularity.

Their success is indicated in some artistic or musical career and due to their love of life and people, occupations connected with the theatre, pleasure and amusements will draw them.

They have the ability for painting, acting or singing and could also excel at modelling, interior decorating, fashion designing or beautician work.

♂ mars

The Leo position of Mars denotes your children, or one in particular, who is important in your life and as this planet stands for self-reliance, courage and ambition, you are likely to recognise these characteristics in a child, possibly a male.

Due to the war-like influence of Mars, there could, at some time, be disputes over a child, or even estrangement for a period.

The force of Mars can both build and destroy and it is therefore essential to use wise direction in steering this Mars child into some constructive channel, such as pioneering, debating, or a profession that needs organisation and leadership, otherwise they could become destructive, aggressive and difficult to control.

Their motto is generally 'act now, think later', but as a pioneer type they are sure to leave their mark. Occupations best suited for them are those of a martial nature and sometimes they excel as athletes or in physical sports.

♃ jup

The Leo position of Jupiter denotes your children, or one in particular, who is important in your life and as this planet rules expansion, children could bring much happiness into your life, as their nature will have a natural optimism.

As well as being popular they attract luck, socially and financially, particularly in investments and speculation.

They could become active in travel, sports, and exercise in the outdoors and success comes their way by attracting people of influence and so expand the whole domestic scene.

However, their natural optimism and generosity may need curbing at times so that they do not become over-expansive.

Occupations connected with education, publishing, overseas or diplomatic affairs are bound to capture their interest and they are likely to achieve positions of social and professional prominence.

♄ sat

The Leo position of Saturn denotes your children, or one in particular, who is important in your life and as this planet causes delay and hindrance in children's affairs, there may be a delay in your having a child or a certain amount of responsibility in connection with children.

Saturn indicates a child who is likely to have a disposition that is serious and reserved, with a natural inclination to prudence and cautiousness.

They may not be very demonstrative and will therefore need more loving care than given to other children. In the early years they should be encouraged and given authority, with lots of praise for all their efforts.

Although their progress at first may be a little slow, there shows credit and gain as their life advances and when choosing a profession for them, you will find they respond best to positions of trust and responsibility. Gain could also accrue through careful investment in land and property on their behalf.

♅ uran

The Leo position of Uranus denotes your children, or one in particular, who is important in your life and as Uranus brings the extraordinary and unusual, you are sure to encounter these tendencies concerning their affairs.

One in particular is likely to be 'different and way out' and may at times be difficult to understand, but do not let this cause you anxiety, for although their character may be detached, your offspring will be quite inventive and original, and these qualities could mark an outstanding career.

A certain amount of latitude for self-expression will be necessary with this type of child, although they should be taught how to organise their thoughts so that they do not go overboard with their ideas.

Electronics, lasers, computers, jets and the latest inventions are accepted by them as part of the natural environment and occupations in these fields are just a 'piece of cake' for them.

♆ nept

The Leo position of Neptune denotes your children, or one in particular, who is important in your life, and as this planet rules the emotions, imagination and intuition, it will be found that these intangible qualities describe the nature of these children.

Neptune children are dreamers, looking for moonbeams with a tendency to wrap their fantasies in rainbow colours. However, if they cannot find a practical expression for these dreams in their daily life, they may try to capture the fleeting ecstasy of Neptune in other sensational ways, which could lead, if not careful, to drink, drugs or moral lapses.

A suitable avenue of expression for these sensitive children would be music, art, or theatre, or on a more physical level, dancing or swimming.

Occupations connected with sea travel, film work and photography, or work of fine detail could attract them.

♇ plut

The Leo position of Pluto denotes your children, or one in particular, who is important in your life and as this planet gives plenty of energy and strong willpower, you will recognise the hidden strength and force of these qualities in the child as life goes on.

Due to the regenerative nature of Pluto there is likely to be in one of your children a pull towards group activities involved with social reform, and once knowing what they want, they can plug away with quiet strength and patience to break down all opposition and obstacles.

The force of Pluto if used constructively, can move mountains, but if used destructively, tends towards subversive activities.

If this type of child shows a desire to join the local gang, a better expression would be in sports where their group consciousness can express in a team.

With this planetary position a child could go out of your life at some time, only to reappear at a later date.

3

HOW TO FIND
THE 'FUTURE'

**READINGS FOR ANY HOROSCOPE CHART
FUTURE PROSPECTS
THE PROGRESSED MOON
ADDITIONAL FUTURE PROSPECTS
THE TRANSITS**

How to find future prospects

As the Horoscope Chart is a clock face of life, the Progressed Moon can be likened to the hand of this clock and its position can be plotted for any year ahead to read 'Future prospects'.

As the Progressed Moon moves through each Sign and House, it brings a change of outlook and therefore a change of activity.

In the John Doe example Chart progressed to say his 21st birthday, you can see how this Moon has progressed in the 21 years from its birth position in AQUA around the Chart to the SCOR Sign and 9th HOUSE.

The 'Future Prospects' read-up for SCOR indicates benefits through a Will while the 9th HOUSE read-up promises long journeys, therefore it can be concluded that this young man would inherit a legacy and travel overseas during these cycles. Likewise, the 'Future' story for any Chart can be foretold.

example horoscope chart - progressed moon

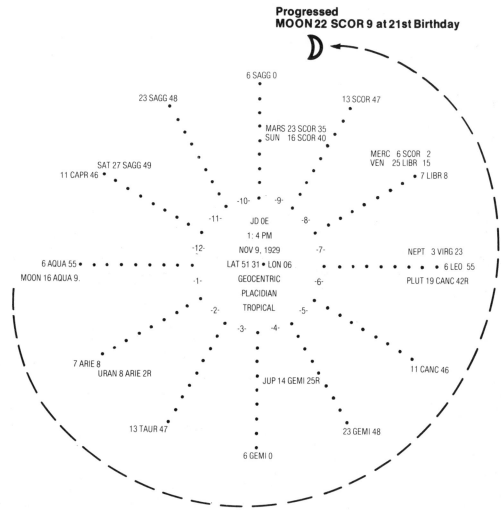

The Progressed Moon's position can be quickly worked out from instructions on the next page; or can be ordered from the Computer Services as 'Progressions'.
For 'Additional Future Prospects', by Transits, which reveal the highlights and timing of current events, see further on in this Section.

future prospects

These are found by ascertaining the position of the Progressed Moon, which is the progression of the birth Moon through the Signs to the present or desired year ahead.

A quick way to find the Sign (and House) position of the Progressed Moon without the necessity of doing astronomical calculations, is given as follows.

Consult the *table* on page **65** and opposite the year of age will be seen an amount made up of signs and degrees. When the amount appropriate to the age selected is added to the original position of the Moon in the Birth Chart, it gives the position of the progressed Moon on that birthday.

To help count in Signs, their running order is:

ARIE ♈ TAUR ♉ GEMI ♊ CANC ♋ LEO ♌ VIRG ♍ LIBR ♎ SCOR ♏
SAGI ♐ CAPR ♑ AQUA ♒ PISC ♓ ARIE ♈ TAUR ♉ GEMI ♊ CANC ♋
LEO ♌ VIRG ♍ LIBR ♎ SCOR ♏ SAGI ♐ CAPR ♑ AQUA ♒ PISC ♓

In the case of the John Doe example (if the 'Future prospects' were desired for the age of 21) it would be noted from the *table* the amount the Progressed Moon had travelled in the twenty-one years, namely 9 Signs and 6 degrees. When this is added to the original position of the Moon on the Birth Chart, we would have the following sum -

Moon at Birth	=	AQUA	Sign	16 degrees	9 minutes
Add for 21st birthday	=	9	Signs	6 degrees	0 minutes
As 9 Signs further on from AQUA is SCOR, we get	=	SCOR	Sign	22 degrees	9 minutes

(If the 'degrees' column adds to more than 30 degrees, take 30 as an extra Sign.)

Having now established that his Progressed Moon is in the Sign *SCOR,* we read *that* Interpretation for his 'Future prospects' surrounding his 21st birthday, November 1950 (i.e. birth in November 1929 plus 21 years).

However, another cycle applying at the same time is the House position of the Progressed Moon and to find this we would see, by glancing at his Chart, that the Progressed Moon, (which moves in a counter-clockwise direction), being at 22 degrees SCOR, has progressed beyond the SCOR 13 degrees on the dividing line and falls in the *9th House.* Therefore, we also read *this House* position Interpretation and as both Sign and House cycles apply at the same time, they can be read together to give the 'Future' story, such as briefly outlined previously.

For reference the Horoscope Reader would be filled in as follows -

FUTURE PROSPECTS Age 21 (NOV 50) Year PROGRESSED MOON IN SCOR SIGN

FUTURE PROSPECTS Age 21 (NOV 50) Year PROGRESSED MOON IN 9th HOUSE

table to find the position of the progressed moon

ADD to the position of the Moon in the Birth Chart the following number of - 'signs and degrees' (*Note:*- Signs contain 30 degrees each)

Age	Age	Age	Signs	Degrees	Minutes
1	28	55	0	13	0
2	29	56	0	26	0
3	30	57	1	9	0
4	31	58	1	23	0
5	32	59	2	6	0
6	33	60	2	19	0
7	34	61	3	2	0
8	35	62	3	15	0
9	36	63	3	28	0
10	37	64	4	12	0
11	38	65	4	25	0
12	39	66	5	8	0
13	40	67	5	21	0
14	41	68	6	4	0
15	42	69	6	17	0
16	43	70	7	1	0
17	44	71	7	14	0
18	45	72	7	27	0
19	46	73	8	10	0
20	47	74	8	23	0
21	48	75	9	6	0
22	49	76	9	20	0
23	50	77	10	3	0
24	51	78	10	16	0
25	52	79	10	29	0
26	53	80	11	12	0
27	54	81	11	25	0

It will be noted that after the 27th birthday, the Progressed Moon has gone right around the Birth Chart and reached its original position again — so for the 28th birthday start again at the top of the column for the amount to add to the original Birth Moon position, likewise for the 55th birthday.

'Progressions', ordered with a Computer Chart show the Progressed Moon's position and the exact date it enters a new Sign or House cycle, by an entry like this, 'Moon LIBR to SCOR' or 'Moon enters SCOR'; 'Moon 8 to 9' or 'Moon enters House No. 9'.

Future prospects

Found by the Progressed Moon, brings two cycles of experience at the same time, one by SIGN position, the other by HOUSE position. Each cycle lasting two and a half years but overlapping each other

arie   🏠 first

The influence in force during this period will tend to awaken that part of your character as described under 'Your physical temperament'. This will cause you to gain new and special experiences, which will not only increase the energetic side of your nature, but will advance your interests and bring you more prominently to the front. A splendid year for personal effort and initiative.

You will probably feel restless and unsettled and will desire change. You can therefore expect either travel, removals or some change in your surroundings and environment. It will be well for you to note carefully the kind of change you desire, so that you do not make mistakes, for this cycle tends to break up existing conditions.

With this general change of environment and outlook, there is sometimes a corresponding change in the health, and it would be advisable to refer to that part of your horoscope which describes 'Points to watch regarding your health'.

It is a year when many new opportunities will open, you should therefore make the most of your personality and appearance.

☿ taur   🏠 second

Financial affairs are now to the fore; and you will find that during this cycle money will be the cause of more concern than before, and you will find yourself having more to do with finance, either by your income fluctuating or by your mind being more than usually taken up with monetary and business affairs.

The influence now in operation should help you to increase your income, either through judicious investment or by getting busy with new ideas whereby you can improve your material assets, for the present cycle is that of your personal earning capacity.

New resources are bound to open and you will be wise to grasp every opportunity to increase your financial prospects either through improving your job or business, turning a hobby into a source of income, selling or purchasing to your advantage or opening a new banking account, all according to the general indications of your horoscope outlining financial capacity and 'Your vocational ability'.

♌ leo   🏠 fifth

The influence in force during this period will awaken all matters that are close to your heart, and will exert a strong influence on the social, pleasure loving and affectional side of your nature.

You will be more than usually anxious to have pleasures and will either invest or speculate or desire to increase your income. You will be drawn towards social gatherings and favour entertainments, therefore accept and enjoy all pleasures while the stars are in your favour.

This cycle also rules children and the artistic creative capacity, therefore you will find it a splendid time in which to establish any creative plans, or get busy with some new enterprise.

Romantic attachments are sure to play an important part in your life either directly or indirectly, while new adventure should add an extra zest to life.

♍ virg   🏠 sixth

During this cycle you will probably have more work thrust upon you, or conditions may necessitate you taking up some new type of work or even changing your position.

However, do not let energy and enthusiasm overtire you for you could easily get run down. Take particular care with your diet and try to get sufficient rest, otherwise health tendencies as outlined in your horoscope are liable to come to the fore.

This cycle is just as powerful for benefiting the health as for impairing it, providing you guard against over-work, worry or unsuitable diet, for it is related to the regulation or adjustment of the physical system generally.

You may also be more concerned with servants, or those in your employ, and should be extra careful in all dealing with inferiors.

It is a year to press for business advantages, also to be energetic and industrious.

sagi   ninth

A splendid period in which to enrich and develop your mind, either through writings, study, travel or through contact with artistic and intellectual people.

Your mental vision will widen and your outlook become more philosophical than usual. This will make you more active and alert and anxious to study deeper subjects than formerly.

You will either take a long journey or travel during this cycle and will come in contact with some very deep thinkers, or have your mind stimulated through contact with travelled, and interesting people.

You may also have activity to do with Government, legal, or educational affairs, or some activity with writings or publications, but only if your horoscope shows tendencies in this direction.

It is an excellent year in which to expand your intellectual and social life and plan for the future.

♑ capr   tenth

You are now in your destiny cycle, which has chief rule over your ambitions and career, and during this period are likely to come more to the front than formerly, obtaining either publicity, advancement or recognition from your efforts.

You should seek to make all the progress that you can; for you will be able to command authority, and have far greater opportunities to advance in life, and make your activities more useful than hitherto.

You are likely to have more responsibility during this period, also some activity to do with a parent or the rearrangement of domestic affairs.

The whole of your horoscope is strengthened by this cycle, with a field of new opportunity opening for you. However, much will depend upon your abilities as outlined in your horoscope under Vocation, Ambitions and Career, as to how this cycle will benefit you.

**These Moon cycles are applying at the birthday of the Progressed year.
A check for the next birthday will show whether the Moon's Sign or House
Reading continues, or has changed.
Each of the twelve read-ups can be read either as a Sign or a House,
whichever applies**

gemi   third

The present cycle will give greater activity in all matters connected with the mind, stimulating to greater thought, and also tending to bring changes. A feeling of restlessness will prevail and you may incline to brood over your conditions, desiring to alter in some way the environment in which you are placed. It will also bring you in contact with relatives, or some persons who have a claim upon you. However, don't let them interfere with your peace of mind.

Short journeys or travel are sure to engage your attention, also writings, correspondence, and all activity as outlined under your 'Mental qualifications'. Social contacts could inspire many new ideas, you should therefore take advantage of every opportunity to visit and entertain, discuss or debate, for your mind will have an extra zest, and will be more eager for knowledge than usual.

This cycle sometimes makes it difficult to concentrate, but if you can see things through to a conclusion, much progress can be made. It is your year for the quest of knowledge, and if you take advantage of all opportunities to expand your intellectual life, so will it lead you to new mental horizons.

canc   fourth

Your interests will now be centred upon home and domestic affairs, and during this period you may expect some changes, either removals, alterations or variable conditions which will tend, in a certain manner to upset your plans.

You will in all probability have fresh occupants in your residence or abode, or have persons in the same house as yourself who will in some manner affect you.

You may decide to remove or take a holiday, or if your horoscope indicates, take an interest in houses, land or property, by building or purchasing.

If these tendencies are not previously outlined in your horoscope, then conditions will arise that will make it necessary for you to concentrate upon your environment, parents or the etablishing of a new home.

This cycle will precipitate many things that have been held in suspension, and you will find it a particularly active time in which to attend to all affairs that need rearranging in the home sphere.

 libr  seventh

Your interest will now be centred upon marriage, partnerships or association with others, and during this cycle you are likely to make new ties and attachments. Some other life will run parallel with your own, either through marriage or through entering upon some partnership, either of a business or personal nature.

Marriage sometimes takes place in the family or some binding attachment is entered upon. Refer to tendencies outlining love and marriage for details in this direction.

Conditions will arise that will bring you more before the public than usual, and you will take a more prominent position than hitherto.

This cycle also rules law, litigation and the public, therefore avoid all legal disputes should they arise. However, this could only occur if your horoscope shows tendencies in this direction.

The above cycle promises to be an important one in your life, and you should grasp all opportunities to extend your social circle and cement close ties.

scor   eighth

You are now in a cycle that has much to do with matters surrounding finance and your material assets, not so much through your individual earning capacity, as through the help or co-operation of partners or co-workers.

You could benefit financially through wills, legacies, insurance, lotteries or deaths, or a marriage, business partner or co-worker could either benefit you or have some change in their financial conditions which could indirectly affect you.

This cycle generally brings experiences through the deeper side of life, and you could take an interest in the secrets of nature, occultism, etc. or be affected in some way through the loss of a friend or relative, or hear of births or deaths.

Grasp all opportunities this year to increase your financial security and add to your material assets, for a busy time is foreshadowed.

 aqua  eleventh

During this cycle you will find friendships playing a very active part in your life. You will make many new acquaintances and have opportunities to form some permanent friends, some of whom will assist and benefit you.

Your hopes and wishes will become more active and you will find personal relationships most important, whether in connection with associations or groups of people, or with one of a more personal nature.

You may revive an old friendship and will find yourself more than usually drawn toward the study of human nature and character, and will, during this cycle, find your greatest pleasure in mingling with others.

You could now use your mind to advantage in all artistic matters and will find your desires more likely to be fulfilled, as this cycle favours all wishes.

Make the most of all opportunities, for friends should prove particularly entertaining and inspiring during this cycle.

pisc   twelfth

The present cycle exerts a strong influence in all matters of a hidden nature and you may find yourself more than usually restricted or hampered, or have some unfortunate episodes more or less thrust upon you, including sickness.

Don't take unnecessary risks or force any important issue just yet and be on the alert for deceit or treachery from the hidden enmity of others.

These temporary setbacks are sometimes necessary to stir into activity the deeper emotions and bring out some special feature of your character.

It will probably cause you to meditate and think more deeply, or give you the desire to investigate psychic or mystical affairs.

It is a splendid cycle in which to do 'behind the scenes work' such as research or study, should your horoscope indicate this tendency, but is not altogether a favourable cycle for worldly prosperity.

additional future prospects

These are found by 'Transits', which are the current passage of planets in the heavens over a planet in the Birth Chart.

The full effect of a 'Transit' will be felt when it is in conjunction with a Birth Planet (in the same Sign and at the same degree) or is in conjunction with the Ascendant Sign degree or the MC Sign degree. When the 'Transit' opposes these degrees from the opposite Sign across the Chart, the effect will also be felt, but the read-up for the House it is passing through is still read.

The slower the transiting planet moves the stronger and longer will its influence be felt. Therefore, we concern ourselves only with the six slow moving planets,

MARS ♂ JUP ♃ SAT ♄ URAN ♅ NEPT ♆ PLUT ♇

The transits of the other faster moving planets are of such short duration as to be almost negligible in effect.

To find 'Transits' first consult the following Transit Ephemeris (compiled by the author in simple form for the next four years), and opposite each Sign will be seen the degree of the 'Transit' at the middle of each month, intervening degrees falling between.

Next, check if any 'Transit' is in conjunction with, any Birth Planet, the Ascendant, the MC point, or is opposing them, remembering that the 'Transit' must pass over the same degree in the same Sign or in the same degree in the opposite Sign.

Having found such a conjunction or opposition, note this 'Transit's' HOUSE position and turn to the 'Additional future prospects' interpretations for the appropriate read-up.

As you will need to consult your Birth Chart a number of times to check if a Transit is applying, it might be useful if you first write down a list of the Sign and degree that holds your Birth Planets, including the Ascendant and MC from your circular Birth Chart, not forgetting their opposite Sign degrees. As there are 10 Birth Planets plus the Ascendant and MC, and their opposites, you will always have 24 birth Sign degrees to check Transits against.

As a handy reference the following are the Signs opposite each other across the Chart: (Arie-Libr) (Taur-Scor) (Gemi-Sagi) (Canc-Capr) (Leo-Aqua) (Virg-Pisc).

In the case of the John Doe example, if we wanted the prospects for early 1981, in consulting the Transit Ephemeris, we would see that in LIBR, the Transiting Planet JUP had reached 8 degrees in March.

Next, looking at his circular Birth Chart, (or at the list suggested above) we see that this Transit at 8 degrees LIBR, would make an exact opposition to his birth URAN in ARIE (the opposite Sign to LIBR) and as the Transit was itself going through the 8th House we would read the Interpretation - JUP in the 8th House.

For reference the Horoscope Reader would be filled in as follows:

for *MARCH* Month *1981* Year   Transit *Jup.* in *8th* House

Likewise you would work through the year's Ephemeris to find other Transits contacting Birth planets in the Chart, remembering that like billiards the Transit has actually got to hit a Birth planet or be exactly opposite it across the Chart.

Transit Ephemeris

1980	JAN.	FEB.	MAR.	APR	MAY	JUNE	JULY	AUG.	SEPT.	OCT.	NOV.	DEC.
MARS	14 VIRG	Rx 14 VIRG	Rx 4 VIRG	Rx 26 LEO	29 LEO	10 VIRG	25 VIRG	12 LIBR	2 SCOR	22 SCOR	14 SAGI	7 CAPR
JUPITER	10 VIRG	Rx 8 VIRG	Rx 5 VIRG	Rx 1 VIRG	0 VIRG	2 VIRG	6 VIRG	12 VIRG	18 VIRG	25 VIRG	1 LIBR	6 LIBR
SATURN	27 VIRG	Rx 26 VIRG	Rx 25 VIRG	Rx 22 VIRG	Rx 21 VIRG	20 VIRG	21 VIRG	24 VIRG	27 VIRG	1 LIBR	5 LIBR	8 LIBR
URANUS	24 SCOR	25 SCOR	Rx 26 SCOR	Rx 25 SCOR	Rx 24 SCOR	Rx 23 SCOR	Rx 22 SCOR	21 SCOR	22 SCOR	23 SCOR	25 SCOR	27 SCOR
NEPTUNE	21 SAGI	22 SAGI	23 SAGI	Rx 23 SAGI	Rx 22 SAGI	Rx 22 SAGI	Rx 21 SAGI	Rx 20 SAGI	20 SAGI	20 SAGI	21 SAGI	22 SAGI
PLUTO	22 LIBR	Rx 22 LIBR	Rx 21 LIBR	Rx 21 LIBR	Rx 20 LIBR	Rx 19 LIBR	19 LIBR	19 LIBR	20 LIBR	21 LIBR	22 LIBR	23 LIBR

1981	JAN.	FEB.	MAR.	APR	MAY	JUNE	JULY	AUG.	SEPT.	OCT.	NOV.	DEC.
MARS	1 AQUA	26 AQUA	17 PISC	11 ARIE	4 TAUR	27 TAUR	18 GEMI	9 CANC	29 CANC	18 LEO	6 VIRG	22 VIRG
JUPITER	9 LIBR	Rx 10 LIBR	Rx 8 LIBR	Rx 4 LIBR	Rx 1 LIBR	0 LIBR	2 LIBR	6 LIBR	11 LIBR	18 LIBR	24 LIBR	0 SCOR
SATURN	9 LIBR	Rx 10 LIBR	Rx 8 LIBR	Rx 5 LIBR	Rx 3 LIBR	Rx 3 LIBR	3 LIBR	5 LIBR	8 LIBR	12 LIBR	16 LIBR	19 LIBR
URANUS	28 SCOR	29 SCOR	0 SAGI	Rx 29 SCOR	Rx 28 SCOR	Rx 27 SCOR	Rx 26 SCOR	Rx 26 SCOR	Rx 26 SCOR	27 SCOR	29 SCOR	0 SAGI
NEPTUNE	23 SAGI	24 SAGI	24 SAGI	24 SAGI	24 SAGI	Rx 23 SAGI	Rx 23 SAGI	Rx 22 SAGI	22 SAGI	22 SAGI	23 SAGI	24 SAGI
PLUTO	24 LIBR	Rx 24 LIBR	Rx 24 LIBR	Rx 23 LIBR	Rx 22 LIBR	Rx 21 LIBR	21 LIBR	21 LIBR	23 LIBR	23 LIBR	24 LIBR	25 LIBR

1982	JAN.	FEB.	MAR.	APR	MAY	JUNE	JULY	AUG.	SEPT.	OCT.	NOV.	DEC.
MARS	7 LIBR	17 LIBR	Rx 18 LIBR	Rx 9 LIBR	Rx 0 LIBR	2 LIBR	13 LIBR	29 LIBR	17 SCOR	7 SAGI	1 CAPR	23 CAPR
JUPITER	6 SCOR	9 SCOR	Rx 10 SCOR	Rx 8 SCOR	Rx 4 SCOR	Rx 1 SCOR	0 SCOR	2 SCOR	6 SCOR	11 SCOR	18 SCOR	25 SCOR
SATURN	21 LIBR	22 LIBR	Rx 21 LIBR	Rx 19 LIBR	Rx 17 LIBR	Rx 15 LIBR	15 LIBR	17 LIBR	19 LIBR	23 LIBR	26 LIBR	0 SCOR
URANUS	2 SAGI	4 SAGI	4 SAGI	4 SAGI	3 SAGI	2 SAGI	1 SAGI	0 SAGI	0 SAGI	1 SAGI	3 SAGI	5 SAGI
NEPTUNE	25 SAGI	26 SAGI	26 SAGI	Rx 27 SAGI	Rx 26 SAGI	Rx 26 SAGI	Rx 25 SAGI	Rx 24 SAGI	Rx 24 SAGI	Rx 24 SAGI	25 SAGI	26 SAGI
PLUTO	26 LIBR	Rx 26 LIBR	Rx 26 LIBR	Rx 25 LIBR	Rx 25 LIBR	Rx 24 LIBR	Rx 24 LIBR	24 LIBR	25 LIBR	26 LIBR	27 LIBR	28 LIBR

1983	JAN.	FEB.	MAR.	APR	MAY	JUNE	JULY	AUG.	SEPT.	OCT.	NOV.	DEC.
MARS	18 AQUA	11 PISC	3 ARIE	26 ARIE	19 TAUR	10 GEMI	2 CANC	22 CANC	12 LEO	0 VIRG	19 VIRG	7 LIBR
JUPITER	1 SAGI	6 SAGI	9 SAGI	10 SAGI	Rx 9 SAGI	Rx 5 SAGI	Rx 2 SAGI	1 SAGI	2 SAGI	6 SAGI	12 SAGI	19 SAGI
SATURN	3 SCOR	4 SCOR	Rx 4 SCOR	Rx 2 SCOR	Rx 0 SCOR	Rx 28 LIBR	27 LIBR	28 LIBR	0 SCOR	3 SCOR	7 SCOR	11 SCOR
URANUS	7 SAGI	8 SAGI	9 SAGI	8 SAGI	Rx 8 SAGI	Rx 6 SAGI	Rx 5 SAGI	Rx 5 SAGI	5 SAGI	6 SAGI	7 SAGI	9 SAGI
NEPTUNE	27 SAGI	28 SAGI	28 SAGI	29 SAGI	28 SAGI	Rx 28 SAGI	Rx 27 SAGI	Rx 26 SAGI	Rx 26 SAGI	Rx 26 SAGI	27 SAGI	28 SAGI
PLUTO	29 LIBR	Rx 29 LIBR	Rx 29 LIBR	Rx 28 LIBR	Rx 27 LIBR	Rx 27 LIBR	Rx 26 LIBR	26 LIBR	27 LIBR	28 LIBR	29 LIBR	0 SCOR

NOTE: THE ABOVE POSITIONS ARE FOR THE FIRST DAY OF EACH MONTH.
Rx = RETROGRADE — MEANS THE PLANET IS TRAVELLING BACKWARDS IN THE SIGN, RATHER THAN FORWARD. THE EFFECT IS TO SOMEWHAT REPRESS THE ENERGY OF THE ASPECT.

Additional future prospects

The Houses show the Department of life activated,
while the Transit shows how it will affect you.
For opposing Transits read as adverse

TRANSITING PLANETS →
IN HOUSES
↓

♂ mars

House	Description	Mars
1st HOUSE	When a Transiting Planet first enters this House it contacts the Degree of the Ascendant Sign, which has a very strong effect, accentuating conditions described in 'Your physical temperament' and 'Points to watch regarding your health'. Can also bring changes in the environment or reflect conditions of relatives; or when opposing from this House will involve your partner.	Gives extra energy, impulsiveness, feverish and dental complaints; also restlessness causing change.
2nd HOUSE	Will activate conditions as described in 'Your financial capacity', or when opposing from this House, will activate conditions as described under 'Financial benefits through others'.	Extra earning capacity but impulse to spend. Avoid over-generosity.
3rd HOUSE	Will activate conditions as described in your 'Local travel and social activity', or when opposing from this House, will activate conditions as described under 'Travel and study'.	Your mind active and restless, controversy in speech, writing or over journeys.
4th HOUSE	When a Transiting Planet first enters this House it opposes the exact Degree of the MC point, which will activate conditions described in 'Your ambitions and career'. Whilst moving through this 4th House, will activate conditions described in your 'Home and domestic affairs'.	Activity to do with home, parents, real estate. Avoid impulse.
5th HOUSE	Will activate conditions as described under 'Romance and matters close to your heart', or when opposing from this House, will activate conditions as described under 'Friendships'.	Fire to the emotions, good creative capacity, risky for games of chance.
6th HOUSE	Will activate conditions as described in 'Your general health tendencies', or when opposing from this House, will activate conditions to do with hospitals, institutions or behind-the-scenes work.	High tension through over-work, tendency to feverishness, cuts or burns.
7th HOUSE	When a Transiting Planet first enters this House it opposes the exact Degree of the Ascendant point, which will activate conditions described under 'Points to watch regarding your health'. Whilst moving through this 7th House, will activate conditions described under 'Partnerships and marriage'.	Quarrels, opposition or litigation in attachments or partnerships. Health troubles through hastiness, mishaps.
8th HOUSE	Will activate conditions as described under 'Financial benefits through others', or when opposing from this House, will activate conditions as described under 'Your financial capacity'.	Expended energy or aggressiveness over assets or money due. Loss of assets.
9th HOUSE	Will activate conditions described under 'Travel and study', or when opposing from this House, will activate conditions as described under 'Local travel and social activity'.	Stimulates interest in the higher sciences, tends to controversy over government or legal affairs
10th HOUSE	When a Transiting Planet first enters this House it contacts the Degree of the MC point, which will open up your destiny cycle, commanding fresh interest in your aspirations, more fully described in 'Your ambitions and career'. Can also reflect conditions pertaining to your boss or head of the house. When opposing from this House, will involve 'Home and domestic affairs'.	Renewed ambitions, rash ventures, loss of credit, ill health of parent.
11th HOUSE	Will activate conditions described under 'Friendships', or when opposing from this House, will activate conditions as described under 'Romance and matters close to your heart'.	Discord with old friends, but likelihood of meeting new friends of martial type.
12th HOUSE	Will activate conditions, which could be described as 'Your debts of destiny', or involve behind-the-scenes work, or when opposing from this House, will activate conditions as described under 'Your general health tendencies'.	Some activity in connection with hospitals, either directly or indirectly. Trouble through ill wishers.

These interpretations will take your future readings a stage further - found from Transiting Planets conjunction or opposing birth planets

♃ jup	♄ sat	♅ uran	♆ nept	♇ plut
Renews vitality, increases weight, attracts good luck and opportunity. Travel prospects, but curb over-adventure.	Brings over-work, responsibility, set-backs, colds and reduced weight. Any success comes through caution.	Breaks old habits and ties, brings high nervous tension and unexpected changes.	Promotes artistic capacity, attracts to the sea, tends towards confusion and intrigue.	Tends towards dangerous enterprise, neglected ill health, which could undermine constitution.
Increase in financial prospects and general good furtune. Avoid tendency to fritter it away.	Money comes the hard way, best enterprise property or solid concerns. A time to check over your budget and resources.	Sudden or unusual transactions, which may need care. Possibility of unexpected gain.	Look well into 'get-rich-quick' propositions. Chance for fringe benefits.	Hidden things come to the surface — either money owed or money due to you.
Lucky for interviews or correspondence, happy pleasure trips. Curb any boastfulness or you could miss out.	Deeper concentration, disappointment over letters, interviews or relatives.	Mind stimulated into new channels. Time for advertising, air travel and inventive ideas.	Mental anxieties, vague fears, sea journeys, psychic interests. May take up music interest.	Deeper interest in psychology, greater energy for study, writing or teaching.
Chance for removals, property investments or redecorating the home. Don't spend more than is practical.	Heavier responsibilities regarding parents and domestic conditions. Good for securing family benefits.	Alterations and surprises, complete removal from the home or certain amount of upheaval.	Confused home affairs, beware of deception, fire or robbery. Sea interests could involve you.	Treachery or jealousy, some defect in property deals. Guard your reputation.
Pleasures, romance, engagement, luck in lotteries or speculation. Don't be blind to gambler's risk.	Disappointments and delay over love or investments. Children's affairs could involve you.	Unusual attachments, unexpected happenings, speculation hunches. New hobby or social ideas.	Confusion or deception in love. Stimulation of artistic capacity. Friends could easily let you down.	Hidden love affairs, jealousy, risky for new enterprises, broken ties.
Added confidence, uplift in job, good health, journeys. Prospects could be spoilt through any over-indulgence.	Loss of vitality, tendency to catch colds, obstacles in employment. Any benefits result from a practical approach.	Unexpected change in employment, nerve energy stimulated. Avoid sudden quarrels. Trips imminent.	Unsatisfactory working conditions, health affected through germs or narcotics. Possible inoculation.	Treachery from employees or work mates, organic complaints. Time for a check-up.
Excellent for partnerships of all kinds, but don't expect everything to come easily. Avoid excess, watch weight.	Delay or misunderstandings in matrimonial affairs. Health suffers colds, rheumatism.	Sudden unions, broken bonds, unexpected lawsuits, physical complaints of nervous origin.	Anxiety about partners, contracts, deception or broken engagement. Nervous disorders.	Undermining influence in partnership or legal affairs. Medical treatment for stubborn complaints.
Some gift or added security, gain through partner or legacy, but these things could be lost through wastefulness.	Concern over diminishing assets, delay in transaction or monetary settlement. Loss of a dear one.	Unexpected situations regarding partner's income or financial affairs. Sudden loss of a friend.	Confusion or deceit over money due to you. News of a death. Watch waste of resources.	Double-crossing over lawsuits regarding legacies. Lost wills, hidden snags.
Best time for long journeys or foreign affairs, increased knowledge. But over-expansion could cause you confusion.	Steadies the mind, hinders progress in legal affairs, education or publications.	Stimulates the imagination and intuition, good for science or philosophy. Unexpected air travel.	Contact with higher planes of consciousness, but care needed to keep one foot on the ground.	Deeper subjects are studied reform or improvement of existing laws, a desire to command.
Good for promotion, reputation and starting new projects. Watch you don't throw discretion to the winds.	Delays and set-backs in your career, responsibility, trouble with superiors or parents.	Sudden changes in occupation, sometimes reversal of fortune, unexpected news regarding parents.	Unrealistic attitude over career, tendency to be deceived. Parents death.	Some undermining of reputation — difficult to trace. Revolutionary projects, a desire for power.
Gain from new friends or important persons. Over-generosity could deplete your resources.	Activity with older or more serious acquaintances, ill feeling or coolness from a friend.	Joining new group activities, or estrangement with some of your friends.	Greater attraction towards artistic people, treachery among one of your friends likely.	Some double-crossing, intrigue or secrecy from a so-called friend.
Satisfaction through institutional or behind-the-scenes activity. Avoid giving too much of yourself.	Strange realisations, the mind becomes more reflective. Loneliness or slow progress.	Unexpected happenings, both good and bad, whether deserved or otherwise.	An interest in mystical subjects. Medical treatment may be necessary. Secret enemies may try to harm.	Activity in behind-the-scene affairs, either research in science or medical treatment.

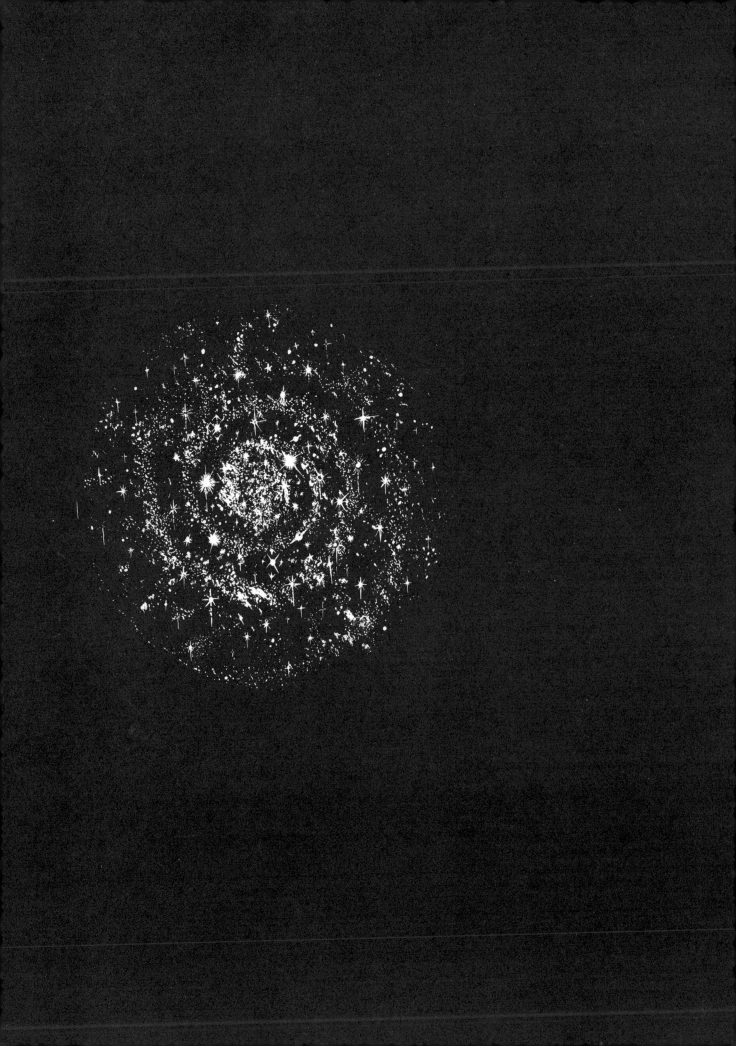

4

COMPATIBILITY BETWEEN THE SEXES

LOVE RELATIONSHIPS
OPPOSITE SIGN READINGS
COMPATIBILITY COMPARISON
USING CHARTS
HOW WILL MY PARTNER AFFECT MY LIFE?

Love relationships

This is a Zodiac guide to your character, to the way you feel about love. It tells you what you need in a soulmate to find lasting happiness. To find your ideal partner the questions you will want to know are - do you share common interests? Do you like the same pleasures? Will your partner have the natural characteristics that will supply the strength or balance that you feel you need?

Some Zodiac Signs are compatible, others will leave you cold or even irritate you. By comparing the nature of the Signs, the compatibility factors will be shown. You can compare either Sun Signs or Ascendant Signs. Ascendant Signs are given on page **83**. Certain groups of Signs have a common element, Fire, Earth, Air or Water. Some groups mix well, others not so well.

Gemini, Libra and Aquarius types have an airy nature, making them versatile and good mixers. Team two of these together and they will float around happily in an intellectual stratosphere. However, Airy types with Watery types are harder to mix, as Air with Water only makes bubbles that float away. Then again, these Airy types blend well with the Fiery types - Air fanning Fire into greater activity.

Aries, Leo and Sagittarius are fiery types, having an adventurous nature, are impetuous and make good lovers - and being of the same element of course mix well with each other. However, Fiery types are difficult to mix with Watery Signs - as Water tends to quench Fire and Fire sets Water on the boil.

The Watery types are Cancer, Scorpio and Pisces, being romantic and imaginative, like calm waters - run deep, but mix well with each other. Watery and Earth types blend harmoniously - as Water softens the hardness of Earth, while Earth moulds the other into a more solid expression.

The Earth types are Taurus, Virgo and Capricorn, which are down to earth, dependable and excel as home makers, mix well with each other.

However the combination of Earth types with Fire Signs can be heavy going as Earth tends to smother Fire, while the combination of Earth types with Air types, merely raises clouds of dust.

As a general guide we find that the Zodiacal Sun or Ascendant Signs are invariably attracted to their opposite Signs as they complement each other - what one partner lacks the other helps to supply.

For compatibility, study your own Sign on the following pages and compare it with your opposite Sign, which appears beside it.

Opposite sign readings

ARIES
March 21 to April 20

Adventurous! Ambitious!
You'll never be domestic like some Signs, but can hold your mate through your enthusiastic and affectionate nature. Liable to impulse and hasty decisions in love. Your choice of the right mate is important to your happiness.
Aries with capacity for leadership, may clash with a Sign that needs to dominate, such as another Aries. Your enthusiasm could be quenched by analytical Virgo or conservative Capricorn. You're bored by indecisive Pisces or clinging Cancer. However, Sagittarius and Leo whirl you into exciting and romantic ventures, while Libra gives you calm and peace you sometimes lack.

LIBRA
Sept. 24 to Oct. 23

Romantic! Artistic!
You flourish with companionship, wilt if left alone. Forever searching for an impossible ideal, your procrastination can often lose you quite a compatible mate.
Charm and tolerance with a flair for listening instead of chattering makes you popular with practically all Signs of the Zodiac. Gemini and Aquarius are a good match for your social activity, while Aries would be a marvellous tonic to liven your passivity into action. Although you may date many of the other Signs, you will spend a lot of time weighing them up.

TAURUS
April 21 to May 21

Dependable! Practical!
You need the good things of this Earth, invariably drawn to a partner of financial stability. You're more fixed than fickle, with a strong love nature.
You need a partner who appreciates your ability to provide good food and manage finance, also one who shares your artistic sense, either in the arts of music. Your sense of promptness and routine would be severely taxed by any unconventional type like Aquarius or the volatile Sagittarius and Gemini Signs. Best fall in love with cautious but loyal Virgo or Capricorn, or perhaps Scorpio who aims for the comfort and luxury you need.

SCORPIO
Oct. 24 to Nov. 22

Courageous! Magnetic!
Intense feelings and smouldering temperament hidden in a calm exterior, soon form a magnet for the opposite sex. With drive and persistency you don't easily let go of your chosen partner.
Bounding energy allows you to keep pace with any mate, but for long range compatibility you enjoy adaptable Cancer or Pisces, who can share your psychic interests. And Taurus can help you acquire the good things of life.
Don't waste time over Aquarius - they are too remote for you, or Leo - who likes to boss.

75

GEMINI
May 22 to June 21

Versatile! Restless!
With your on-the-move mentality choose a partner who allows you scope for your rapidly changing interests.
You can handle many things at one time, so you need hobbies or a career, as well as domesticity. As a teenager you may go through a string of admirers but you will be happiest with a mate who offers intellectual stimulation, such as Sagittarius. Libra and Aquarius are also bright and sociable and would enjoy your Gemini interests. Take it easy with Scorpio or Taurus, they could be a bit too possessive.

SAGITTARIUS
Nov. 23 to Dec. 22

Optimistic! Adventurous!
Your outlook is expansive - ever seeking new horizons through travel, reading and exploring.
You love freedom, and a reluctance to restrict yourself sometimes makes you hesitant about that wedding ring. But once married you make a very amiable marriage partner. You're happy-go-lucky, great fun and a marvellous entertainer. A partner who won't allow you personal freedom, like Scorpio or Taurus, soon find themselves out in the cold. Ambitious Aries or enterprising Leo are good bets for you, while Gemini offers a good mental bond.

CANCER
June 22 to July 23

Sensitive! Protective!
With plenty of charm. Romances change quite often with your moods, but when truly in love you are the real clinger.
You're a born homemaker, with a reluctance to say NO.
Don't let your sympathies decide your fate. You need a mate that spells security such as Scorpio or Taurus, whilst Capricorn could be a good anchor for you. For a stimulant to your imagination the Pisces mate could be a good tonic. Go easy with the fiery Signs, Aries, Sagittarius and Leo, as they could keep your watery sign too much on the boil.

CAPRICORN
Dec. 23 to Jan. 20

Conscientious! Tireless!
Your aim is high and by careful planning and hard work you eventually reach your goal. Being very selective in your love life you do not marry in haste. However, this gives you time to choose a mate who will equal your own desire for success. In fact a career in double harness would suit your temperament nicely.
Age is not as important to you as a mate who echoes your own values. Either methodical Virgo, practical Taurus or your own sign Capricorn could develop into a long and successful marriage. Cancer could offer the sentiment and imagination that your nature often needs.

LEO

July 24 to Aug. 23

Affectionate!   Enterprising!
Full of self-esteem. Never the back
seat for you, it bores and frustr-
ates.
You need love and to be loved, you
have the magnetism, warmth and
generosity to attract the opposite
sex, though they may not always
have the same amount to give.
Don't be hoodwinked by money
alone, practical Virgo, Capricorn
and Taurus are not exciting
enough for you. Best keep an eye
out for dynamic Sagittarius or ambitious Aries, not forgetting
Aquarius, who like yourself, has a
zest for life and social contacts.

AQUARIUS

Jan. 21 to Feb. 19

Self-contained! Unconventional!
You share more of your time with
friends and groups than any other
Signs.
Your temperament, loving personal freedom, can often finish a
love affair at a moment's notice.
Not terribly domesticated but
charming and gay you can make a
dovoted partner when mated to
the right person. Not interested in
growing roots. You can pick up
sticks at any time. Therefore you'll
find Gemini, Sagittarius or Libra
best suited to you. Leo can also be
compatible if you combine your
forces.

VIRGO

August 24 to Sept. 23

Methodical! Discriminative!
Being cool and detached you are
able to steer round the snares of
romance. However, this gives you
time to choose a partner who
echoes your own values.
Your mate, beyond all things, must
be intelligent, neat and orderly.
Security conscious Capricorn
would suit you. Although Pisces
can give you the warmth and romance that your nature often
needs. Your patience could soon
wear thin with restless Aries,
Gemini or Sagittarius, who have a
constant need for change.

PISCES

Feb. 20 to March 20

Sensitive! Versatile!
You are as unpredictable as the
weather - the mystery Sign of the
Zodiac. With your illusive and
affectionate nature you act as a
magnet to the opposite sex. Deep
as the sea, you often have secret
love affairs. You can be very indecisive in choosing a permanent
mate. Your head seldom rules
your heart, so it's important to
choose someone compatible with
your sensitive nature, such as
Cancer or Scorpio. Virgo could
also work out well by adding the
practical streak you sometimes
need.

Compatibility comparison using charts

Chart comparison is another fascinating way to check on compatibility. For this you need the individual Horoscope Charts of both persons.

The author has found that the Moon, Venus and Mars in their Zodiac Signs, indicate other factors that can attract and make for harmony, either in business, marriage or personal relationships.

In all cases of partnership, where we need to adjust our personality to another, the closer we are in accord or harmony the more successful the partnership will be, and it has been found that one of the strongest affinities is when the male's Moon (representing a female) is found to fall in the Sign of the female's Sun (representing a male) or when the female's Sun is in the same Sign as the male's Moon.

An example of this harmonious exchange of the luminaries is when the male's Moon is in Taurus and the female's Sun is in Taurus; or say when the female's Sun is in Libra and the male's Moon is in Libra.

Another very strong bond between the sexes is found when the Moon in the male's Chart falls in the Ascendant Sign of the female's Chart; or when the Sun in a female's Chart falls in the Ascendant Sign of the male's Chart.

A strong physical attraction between male and female (although not necessarily a permanent partnership) is indicated by the exchange of the planets Venus and Mars, an example being, one having their Venus in Cancer and the other having Mars in Cancer.

If there are any Planets in the 7th House, the general strength or weakness of a person's partnership can be read under 'Marriage'.

Summarised, compatibility between two Charts is shown when the following exchanges are found:

Male's Chart		Female's Chart	
His SUN Sign	to be the opposite	her SUN Sign	(or vice versa)
His ASCENDANT Sign	to be the opposite	her ASCENDANT Sign	(or vice versa)
His MOON Sign	to be the same as	her SUN Sign	(or vice versa)
His MOON Sign	to be the same as	her ASCENDANT Sign	
His ASCENDANT Sign	to be the same as	her SUN Sign	
His VENUS Sign	to be the same as	her MARS Sign	
His MARS Sign	to be the same as	her VENUS Sign	

How will my partner affect my life?

To answer this question you will need individual Horoscope Charts for both persons.

Next, it is necessary for you to transpose your partner's Planets, by their Sign and degree position, into your own Chart, (perhaps entering them in your Chart in pencil), then read the Interpretations in the usual way of these pencilled-in Planetary positions, bearing in mind as you read them that they are now referring to *your partner's effect on you and your life,* therefore read 'You' or 'Your' as 'Your partner -'. As there are only ten Planets, including the Sun and Moon, you cannot expect more than ten readings to examine in this light, and the readings to concern yourself with are those for the *House* divisions in which your partner's Planets fall.*

For quick reference the following list gives the Department headings to read for each House in which one or more of your partner's Planets may fall in your Chart, together with a brief indication here as to the main effect they will have.

1st House   *and in the same Ascendant Sign as your own,* read under 'Your special characteristics', as this indicates, *personal development or restriction through partner,* according to the nature of the read-up.

2nd House   read under 'Your financial capacity' as this indicates, *financial aid or expense because of partner,* according to the nature of the read-up.

3rd House   read under 'Local travel and social activity', as this indicates, *mental stimulation and activity through partner.*

4th House   read under 'Home and domestic affairs', as this indicates, *home life with partner.*

5th House   read under 'Romance and matters close to the heart', as this indicates, *affection or lack of it from partner and the desire for children,* according to the nature of the read-up.

6th House   read under 'Your general health tendencies', as this indicates, *health helped or hindered* according to the nature of the read-up.

7th House   read under 'Marriage and partnership', as this indicates, *complementary or opposing viewpoints.*

8th House   read under 'Financial benefits through others', as this indicates, *gain or loss through partner,* according to the nature of the read-up.

9th House   read under 'Travel and study - expansion of mind', as this indicates, *intellectual influence of partner* and could reflect in-laws' attitude.

10th House read under 'Your ambitions and career', as this indicates, *occupational or reputational influence of partner.*

11th House	read under 'Friendships', as this indicates, *friendships, mutual acquaintances stimulated by partner,* according to the type described in the read-up.
12th House	there are *no* individual readings as this is the *House of Destiny,* or a fated position showing that any of your partner's Planets falling here indicate, *links behind the scenes of everyday affairs.*

To try this method of transposing Planets, we will do an example using John Doe's Chart, found at the start of this book. Say, his wife had her *JUP* at 12 degrees in *ARIE.* Transposing this to John Doe's own Chart we would see that it falls into his *2nd House.* As readings for this House are covered by 'Your financial capacity', we would read under this heading the Interpretation for *JUP.* This reading promises 'good fortune in matters connected with finance', so it is easy to see that this is the effect John Doe's partner will have on him - bringing him gain financially. Likewise, his wife's other nine Planets could be transposed on to John Doe's Chart and read accordingly.

To help place your partner's Planets in their correct position in your own Chart, it should be remembered that besides the Sign in which the Planet is placed, the actual degree has to be taken into account, as this decides which House they fall in.

The *degree* of the *Sign* at the dividing line (the spoke) is the guide - Planets with a *less degree* are pencilled-in *before* the line and those with a *greater degree* are pencilled-in *after* the dividing line. The Sign degrees increase in a counter-clockwise direction, the same direction as the Houses are numbered.

If you cannot locate a *Sign* in a Computer Chart, it might be that it is not typed in, being an 'Intercepted Sign', which is entirely in one House, between its two consecutive neighbouring Signs. To check see the sequence of the Signs under 'The Horoscope Chart and its Symbols' on page **9** and first enter any missing Sign in the Chart. Any partner's Planet falling in such an 'Intercepted Sign' is entered in the appropriate House.

Remember, the resulting readings are *not* those of your partner, but are *how your partner will affect your life,* and they should be read in this light.

* 'Chart Comparison' ordered as an additional option with your Computer Chart, lists the House position of your partner's Planets in the terms of your Chart, which would save you listing them yourself. In this case it would be necessary to give the full birth data of your partner.

5
FINDING YOUR BIRTH TIME

FOR THOSE PERSONS UNABLE TO OBTAIN THEIR BIRTH TIME, THE FOLLOWING TABLES AND CHARTS ARE SPECIALLY DESIGNED BY THE AUTHOR TO ASSIST YOU IN DISCOVERING THIS VITAL DATA

How to find your time of birth

If the birth hour is not known it may be an idea to first try narrowing the time to day/night, morning/afternoon, etc., by enquiring from parents, relatives or hospital, even consulting the family Bible, (unless of course you were born in a country where the time is put on the Birth Certificate. Some hospitals, upon request, will search their records and advise you of Birth Time information by mail. Often, a fee is charged).

In the event of your being successful in ascertaining what part of the day or night birth took place, you can then refer to the 'Ascendant Sign Graph' to tentatively narrow down the choice to two or three possible Ascendant Signs, as the Ascendant Sign is a vital factor in finding the time of birth.

Of course if the time of birth cannot be narrowed down, the whole 12 Signs will have to be considered.*

The Ascendant Sign indicates the time of birth and is directly related to the Temperament and Appearance of the individual. In fact, by examining these two factors of Temperament and Appearance, the time of birth can be found.

The first step is to read on the following pages the Temperament descriptions and choose the Ascendant Sign that describes the temperament best, next thoroughly examine the Appearance descriptions and choose the Sign that also fits best.

When the two resultant chosen Signs are the same, it can be considered that this is the Ascendant Sign and therefore by consulting the Graph you can ascertain the time of birth.

Having found the hour of birth, you can use this to order a Computer Calculated Chart or can plot a Chart yourself from the instructions in Section 6.

* When the time of birth is totally unknown, the examination of Astrological Heredity can sometimes help to find a likely Ascendant Sign, this subject being fully covered in my book *Human Destiny*, where I explain how the Ascendant Sign is often shown to be inherited from the parents' Sun or Moon Sign. In fact where there is the necessity to choose the Ascendant by this method, the one to assume would be the Sign prominent in the family tree, or due to the laws of polarity it can be the opposite Sign, i.e. six Signs ahead. Another way to get a strong clue, when there is little or no idea of the birth time is to ask, 'what is the weakest part of the body, where ailments usually strike?' Then match the answer to one of the Signs' appearance descriptions.

Birth time - ascendant sign graph

The following graph can be used for two purposes - either to find the Time of Birth after examining the Temperament and Appearance Descriptions on the following pages - or to find the Ascendant Sign when you know the approximate Time of Birth.

If born at, or near, the uneven hour, between two Ascendant Signs, then check the Temperament and Appearance descriptions to decide which Sign on either side fits best.

This checking may also be necessary if Daylight Saving Time was in use on the birth date, as this could make the Ascendant Sign the one earlier.

These Signs are calculated for 45° north latitude, approximately correct for major Canadian cities.

	ARIES	TAURUS	GEMINI	CANCER	LEO	VIRGO	LIBRA	SCORPIO	SAGITTARIUS	CAPRICORN	AQUARIUS	PISCES
	Mar. 21 to Apr. 20	Apr. 21 to May 21	May 22 to June 21	June 22 to July 23	July 24 to Aug. 23	Aug. 24 to Sept. 23	Sept. 24 to Oct. 23	Oct. 24 to Nov. 22	Nov. 23 to Dec. 22	Dec. 23 to Jan. 20	Jan. 21 to Feb. 19	Feb. 20 to Mar. 20
1 am	CAPR	AQUA	PISC	TAUR	GEMI	CANC	LEO	VIRG	VIRG	LIBR	SCOR	SCOR
2	CAPR	PISC	ARIE	GEMI	CANC	LEO	LEO	VIRG	LIBR	SCOR	SCOR	SAGI
3	AQUA	PISC	TAUR	GEMI	CANC	LEO	VIRG	VIRG	LIBR	SCOR	SAGI	SAGI
4	AQUA	ARIE	GEMI	CANC	LEO	VIRG	VIRG	LIBR	SCOR	-SCOR	SAGI	CAPR
5	PISC	TAUR	GEMI	CANC	LEO	VIRG	VIRG	LIBR	SCOR	SAGI	SAGI	CAPR
6	ARIE	GEMI	CANC	LEO	LEO	VIRG	LIBR	SCOR	SCOR	SAGI	CAPR	AQUA
7	TAUR	GEMI	CANC	LEO	LEO	LIBR	LIBR	SCOR	SAGI	CAPR	CAPR	AQUA
8	GEMI	CANC	LEO	LEO	VIRG	LIBR	SCOR	SAGI	SAGI	CAPR	AQUA	PISC
9	GEMI	CANC	LEO	LEO	VIRG	LIBR	SCOR	SAGI	CAPR	AQUA	PISC	ARIE
10	CANC	LEO	LEO	VIRG	VIRG	SCOR	SCOR	SAGI	CAPR	AQUA	ARIE	TAUR
11	CANC	LEO	VIRG	VIRG	LIBR	SCOR	SAGI	CAPR	AQUA	PISC	TAUR	GEMI
12 noon	LEO	LEO	VIRG	LIBR	LIBR	SAGI	SAGI	CAPR	AQUA	ARIE	GEMI	GEMI
1 pm	LEO	VIRG	VIRG	LIBR	SCOR	SAGI	CAPR	AQUA	PISC	TAUR	GEMI	CANC
2	LEO	VIRG	LIBR	SCOR	SCOR	CAPR	CAPR	AQUA	ARIE	GEMI	CANC	CANC
3	VIRG	VIRG	LIBR	SCOR	SAGI	CAPR	AQUA	PISC	TAUR	GEMI	CANC	LEO
4	VIRG	LIBR	SCOR	SCOR	SAGI	AQUA	AQUA	ARIE	GEMI	CANC	LEO	LEO
5	VIRG	LIBR	SCOR	SAGI	CAPR	AQUA	PISC	TAUR	GEMI	CANC	LEO	LEO
6	LIBR	SCOR	SCOR	SAGI	CAPR	PISC	ARIE	GEMI	CANC	LEO	LEO	VIRG
7	LIBR	SCOR	SAGI	CAPR	AQUA	ARIE	TAUR	GEMI	CANC	LEO	VIRG	VIRG
8	SCOR	SCOR	SAGI	CAPR	AQUA	TAUR	GEMI	CANC	LEO	LEO	VIRG	LIBR
9	SCOR	SAGI	CAPR	AQUA	PISC	GEMI	GEMI	CANC	LEO	VIRG	VIRG	LIBR
10	SCOR	SAGI	CAPR	AQUA	ARIE	GEMI	CANC	LEO	LEO	VIRG	LIBR	SCOR
11	SAGI	CAPR	AQUA	PISC	TAUR	CANC	CANC	LEO	VIRG	VIRG	LIBR	SCOR
12 Midnight	SAGI	CAPR	AQUA	ARIE	GEMI	CANC	LEO	LEO	VIRG	LIBR	SCOR	SCOR

Interpretations of each Ascendant Sign are given in Section 2 under the heading, 'Your physical temperament'. The following pages also give descriptions of the Temperament and the Appearance ascribed to each Ascendant Sign.

83

Temperament descriptions

As each Ascendant Sign gives temperament characteristics, which are distinctly individual, they are easily recognised by asking the following questions applicable to each Sign.

When the answer is 'yes' to the majority of the twelve questions for any one Sign, then this Sign could be considered the Ascendant

♈ arie

1 Have you plenty of energy and self-confidence?
2 Do you like travelling and exploring?
3 Are you hasty in speech and sometimes a little too positive in manner?
4 Have you changed your occupation several times?
5 Do you feel fitted for some position of authority or responsibility?
6 Do you like to be your own boss - resent being driven or restricted?
7 Do you get impatient, irritable and restless at times?
8 Do you shine in an emergency?
9 Do you like to take the floor in conversation?
10 Does worry, overwork, anxiety, etc., soon deplete your health?
11 Do you resent being corrected?
12 Do you progress better when praised?

♉ taur

1 Are you reserved, practical, determined and plodding?
2 Do you like handling materials and building things?
3 Are you fond of the earth and the things it grows?
4 Are you interested in property, houses, real estate?
5 Do you desire security, assets, money and your own home?
6 Have you been in the one position for some time?
7 Are you fond of good food and worldly pleasures?
8 Do you dislike change?
9 Can you recognise obstinacy in your nature?
10 Does it take a lot of goading to excite you?
11 Can you get through plenty of work without tiring?
12 Are you musical or artistic?

♌ leo

1 Have you a fondness for pleasures and amusements?
2 Are you warm-hearted and generous - cheerful and sociable?
3 Do you love children?
4 Are you capable of long sustained effort in carrying out your schemes?
5 Are you interested in matters of an enterprising or speculative nature?
6 Perhaps there is a tendency to gamble or dabble in games of chance?
7 Do you feel happier when organising than when serving?
8 Have you dramatic ability — able to sing or entertain?
9 Are you easily appealed to, through the heart?
10 Do your friends influence you a good deal?
11 Do you aim high - set yourself a target?
12 Do you like frankness?

♍ virg

1 Are you analytical, tactful and discriminative?
2 Would you prefer to work quietly and unobserved?
3 Does untidiness get on your nerves?
4 Do you study the vitamin value of your food?
5 Are you clever in detail work, tabulation, etc.?
6 Do you feel that too much responsibility is a strain on you?
7 Do you like to maintain a cool and dignified attitude?
8 Would you consider yourself an alert business person?
9 Are you capable of seeing many angles to a problem, and thus hesitate to make a decision?
10 Would you rather improve upon another's idea than create yourself?
11 Do you vacillate and at times lack self-confidence?
12 Would you say that you are rather fastidious and retiring?

♐ sagi

1 Do you like exercise, walking, sport?
2 Are you inclined to be too outspoken?
3 Do you dislike restraint or control?
4 Do you like travelling - long voyages?
5 Are you naturally intuitive, have dreams - are you prophetic?
6 Have you the ability to write?
7 Do you find that an unfinished task worries you?
8 Have you a keen sense of justice?
9 Are you fond of animals - especially horses?
10 Are you inclined to expect too much of others?
11 Have you the ability to preach or teach?
12 Do you like reading - philosophy - travel - educational matters?

♑ capr

1 Are you economical, practical and cautious?
2 Do you admire people of intellect?
3 Are you particularly careful in money matters and business affairs?
4 Do you get on better with older than younger people?
5 Have you a deep sense of responsibility towards your family?
6 Do you set a great value upon the opinion of the world?
7 Do you like to mingle with those of good birth?
8 Do you dislike any especial demonstration of affection?
9 Are you a good worker, especially for yourself?
10 Do you get into fits of depression?
11 Do you hesitate in spending too much on clothes, etc.?
12 Do you feel that you can make money go farther than most people?

When first attempting to discover the Ascendant Sign, the characteristics of the Sun Sign may also be recognised, but should be disregarded; unless it is a case of the Ascendant and Sun Sign being the same, which happens if the birth is at sunrise, about 6.00 am.

Additional information in non-question form, describing the Temperament of the Twelve Ascendant Signs can be found in Section 2, under 'Your physical temperament'

♊ gemi

1 Do you talk, read and write a good deal?
2 Do you find it difficult to stick to one thing very long?
3 Have you had many changes of environment or short journeys?
4 Do you reason, analyse and criticise a good deal?
5 Are you clever with your hands?
6 Do you express more in action and thought than in feeling and emotion?
7 Do you find it difficult to make up your mind?
.8 Do you delight in hearing or telling a good story or pun?
9 Are you a bachelor or spinster?
10 Do you find it difficult to finish one thing before starting another?
11 Does a brother or sister play an important part in your life?
12 Do you admit that you have too many irons in the fire?

♋ canc

1 Are you shy and reserved, especially among many people?
2 Are you adaptable, cautious and economical?
3 Have you strong emotions and feelings?
4 Do you let others impose upon you?
5 Have you home responsibilities or parental ties?
6 Do you often have an inner nervousness?
7 Do you spoil your children?
8 Are you tenacious, able to see a thing through to a conclusion if important?
9 Are you moody at times?
10 Are you keen on ancient customs, antiques, curios?
11 Are you romantic, idealistic, imaginative?
12 Although shy, do you love to be noticed?

♎ libr

1 Have you a keen sense of justice?
2 Are you fond of pleasure and the good things of life?
3 Are you fond of comparing and criticising?
4 Are you a good listener?
5 Do you dislike hard and dirty work?
6 Do you feel it your duty to help people?
7 Would you say that association with others has moulded your life a good deal?
8 Are you careless with your belongings - sometimes losing things?
9 Are you a keen follower of fashion, beauty, dress, etc.?
10 Do you sometimes delay decisions until it is too late?
11 Are you impatient of method and necessary routine?
12 Have you strong feelings and emotions?

♏ scor

1 Have you strong likes and dislikes?
2 Are you determined, critical and secretive?
3 Have you strong powers of attraction and attachment?
4 Have you ever inherited money, or won money?
5 Can you keep a secret?
6 Is your mentality subtle and acute?
7 Have you a lot of physical energy?
8 Are you lucky in receiving gifts?
9 Are you sometimes jealous - angry - passionate?
10 Do you dread being ill?
11 Have you suffered from deception and misplaced confidence?
12 Are you skilful with your hands?

♒ aqua

1 Have you inventive ability or originality?
2 Are you unobtrusive, humane and kind?
3 Have you heard others say that you 'are difficult to understand'?
4 Are you reserved or retiring?
5 Do you like original or unusual people?
6 Do you trust most people and are sometimes let down?
7 Do you gather many friends and acquaintances?
8 Have you a desire to be quite alone at times?
9 Are you a lover of dumb animals?
10 Have you the tendency to forget advice after you have asked for it?
11 Do you like checks, dots or uncommon dressing?
12 Have you lost opportunities through indifference or laziness?

♓ pisc

1 Have you a tendency to become over-anxious and restless?
2 Are you careless of personal comforts and necessities?
3 Are you well informed on a great variety of subjects?
4 Are you inclined to show a better front than you can maintain?
5 Are you good at detail work - liking method and order?
6 Do you know how to use subtlety and persuasion to advantage?
7 Have you an inferiority complex at times?
8 Can you keep a secret?
9 Do you get despondent?
10 Would you rather suffer injury than fight for your rights?
11 Are you fond of dumb creatures and those who are helpless?
12 Are your feet a tender spot - standing or walking - dancing - fond of new shoes?

Appearance descriptions
of the twelve Ascendant Sign types

arie ♈

BODY - Lean and wiry, moderate stature.

FACE - Broad forehead, narrowing down to chin, sometimes prominent nose, converse profile.

EYES - Blue or grey, (often wears glasses).

HAIR - Coarse, sometimes ruddy tinge, tends to grey early in life and later balding at temples.

COMPLEXION - Ruddy.

MANNERISMS - Bossy, argumentative, 'I am' in speech.

AILMENTS AFFECT - Head, eyes, ears, (headaches).

taur ♉

BODY - Heavy and solid, short and thick neck.

FACE - Straight up and down square face, thick lips, often dimples.

EYES - Dark, big and prominent.

HAIR - Dark, grows low in peak on forehead.

COMPLEXION - Dark.

MANNERISMS - Rather undemonstrative expression, hard to rouse.

AILMENTS AFFECT - Neck, throat, larynx, tonsils.

leo ♌

BODY - Tall to average stature, big boned, wide chest, somewhat narrow hips, (women small breasted).

FACE - Big round face and head, chin sometimes receding, lips are full, the lower inclined to protrude, nose heavy and full at tip.

EYES - Blue or grey, or sometimes grey-brown, smouldering brightness.

HAIR - Fair, fine, curly and mane-like, (men often bald at temples).

COMPLEXION - Sanguine or florid.

MANNERISMS - Air of importance and confidence, vital and magnetic personality.

AILMENTS AFFECT - Heart, spine and back.

virg ♍

BODY - Small boned, good proportion, keeps age well, sometimes slightly pigeon-toed.

FACE - Oval, high forehead, nose sometimes sharp with prominent tip, good bone structure generally.

EYES - Usually hazel, although sometimes dark, rather detached gaze.

HAIR - Medium.

COMPLEXION - Medium.

MANNERISMS - Particularly neat, giving a refined appearance, reserved and thoughtful manner.

AILMENTS AFFECT - Bowels, digestive system.

sagi ♐

BODY - Above the average stature, wiry, loose limbed, long legs, large hands and feet, stooping shoulders.

FACE - Long, nose long, high forehead, ears stick out, peculiarity about the two upper front teeth, which are either widely spaced or uneven.

EYES - Expressive and open looking, colour varies from hazel-brown to purple-blue.

HAIR - Chestnut or light brown, very fine texture.

COMPLEXION - Sunburnt, ruddy to rosy.

MANNERISMS - Hail-fellow-well-met attitude, sometimes speaks out of turn, full of enthusiasm, keen on the outdoors and sports, good walker.

AILMENTS AFFECT - Liver, hips, thighs, (sciatica).

capr ♑

BODY - Average to short stature, bony structure evident, narrow chest, thin and bony knees, skin somewhat crinkled and dry looking.

FACE - Angular, with long chin and nose (nose inclined to turn down at tip to meet chin, which sometimes turns up), thin neck, bony face.

EYES - Brown and deep-set, with prominent brow area.

HAIR - Dark, thin and lank.

COMPLEXION - Leathery and sometimes lined.

MANNERISMS - Close with their money, economises on clothes, food and comfort. Grasps every opportunity for their own acquisition and progress.

AILMENTS AFFECT - Knees, bones in general, teeth, (rheumatism) skin blemishes.

☉ sun	☽ moon	☿ merc	♀ venu	♂ mars
Will intensify the above description, as the Sun being in the same Sign as the Ascendant, means that this is a 'double' Sign type.	Gives full round face, double chin, pale skin, and tends to fleshiness.	Slims the body, gives more elasticity, quickness of movement, small bones and hazel eyes.	Bestows greater physical beauty, adds flesh and places dimples in cheeks.	Makes the body thicker and more muscular, gives a ruddy tinge to the colouring, wavy or kinky hair and perhaps an accident scar.
Sun's Sign position is found from Month of Birth, i.e. March 21 to April 20 = ARIE. Note - The SUN is only in the Ascendant Sign if birth was at sunrise, about 6.00 am.	◄- To find if any of these Planets are in the *proposed* Ascendant Sign, you would need to consult an Astrological Ephemeris ── for the day, month and year of birth.			

To help find the correct Ascendant Sign, a pertinent clue can be obtained by asking, 'what is the weakest part of the body where ailments usually strike?'

gemi ♊

BODY - Tallish, slim, noticeable thin tipped fingers.

FACE - Longish, bumps at temples, small hump at bridge of nose. Teeth recede from view at each side.

EYES - Hazel (this being a noted feature of this Sign), although sometimes brown.

HAIR - Mousy to dark brown, thins with age.

COMPLEXION - Sanguine.

MANNERISMS - Talks a lot, quick and active in thought and movement, sometimes has impediment in speech, or bites finger-nails, or is left-handed.

AILMENTS AFFECT - Arms, shoulders, lungs, (bronchial troubles).

canc ♋

BODY - Average to small stature, sometimes fleshy, (women particularly full busted).

FACE - Moon-like, round and full, brow bulges, slightly double chin, nose generally snub or upturned with septum showing below nostrils.

EYES - Small, blue or grey.

HAIR - Fair to medium.

COMPLEXION - Very pale.

MANNERISMS - Shy and timid, home conscious, (men in some instances have high-pitched voices).

AILMENTS AFFECT - Breasts, stomach, indigestion, (ulcers).

libr ♎

BODY - Tall to average stature, well formed usually beautiful body, inclined to stoutness after youth.

FACE - Almond shaped, often dimples in cheeks, grecian short nose, with sometimes very little bridge, cupid-bow lips, small white even teeth.

EYES - Blue eyes, bright, large and very round in shape.

HAIR - Soft, silky blonde, with a low hair line.

COMPLEXION - Pink and white, soft skin.

MANNERISMS - Charm, good listener, elegant in dress, physically can be a bit lazy.

AILMENTS AFFECT - Kidneys, (blotchy skin).

scor ♏

BODY - Average stature, muscular and strong body, usually very hairy, legs particularly thick.

FACE - Square, strong facial bones, well developed over eyes, often bullet shaped top part of head. Nose large, sometimes ill-shapen or hooked. Mouth has corners that droop.

EYES - Magnetic, dark, piercing and compelling.

HAIR - Rather thick, dark, course and curling, low hair-line, pointed brows meeting over nose.

COMPLEXION - Dusky.

MANNERISMS - Positive but secretive in speech and expression.

AILMENTS AFFECT - Bladder, sex organs.

aqua ♒

BODY - Tall erect carriage, dignified, healthy robust appearance, (men rather good looking), weak ankles.

FACE - Square chiseled features. Prominent broad forehead is a noted feature of this Sign.

EYES - Deep blue or hazel-green magnetic eyes, eye corners tilt up, broad delta between widely spaced eyes.

HAIR - Good head of hair, sometimes wavy, fair or dark.

COMPLEXION - Good clear complexion with fine skin.

MANNERISMS - Sociable, may display unconventional trend through individual dress, converses with humanitarian ideals.

AILMENTS AFFECT - Lower leg, shins, ankles, circulation, (varicose veins).

pisc ♓

BODY - Average to short stature, fleshy or soft, shoulders droop, pot bellied, tender feet.

FACE - Sensitive face with liquid eyes. Nose joins brow with very little indentation, nostrils flare upwards, protruding upper lip.

EYES - Protrude with well defined upper lids, dreamy soulful expression, sometimes fishy-looking, blue-green in colour.

HAIR - Fine and soft, generally dark.

COMPLEXION - Particularly pale and soft skin.

MANNERISMS - Sympathetic, a 'feeler' rather than a 'doer', dreamy preoccupied expression. Puts on a bigger 'front' than can maintain.

AILMENTS AFFECT - Feet and toes, (cold feet).

♃ jup	♄ sat	♅ uran	♆ nept	♇ plut
Adds fullness and size and gives a jovial expression. Good luck in early life.	Darkens the hair, emphasises bony structure and gives a plain appearance. Struggle in early life.	Gives height, length of limb, steely expression to the eyes, independent manner.	Gives more delicate features, pales the skin and gives a noted blueness to the whites of the eyes.	Sometimes brings inherent physical or organic imperfection, such as birthmark or skin eruptions or boils.
	→	URAN'S Sign position - 1912-1919 AQUA 1919-1927 PISC 1927-1934/5 ARIE 1934/5-1941/2 TAUR 1941/2-1948/9 GEMI 1948/9-1955/6 CANC 1955/6-1961/2 LEO 1961/2-1968/9 VIRG	NEPT'S Sign position - 1915-1928/9 LEO 1928/9-1942/3 VIRG 1942/3-1956/7 LIBR 1956/7-1970 SCOR 1970-1984/5 SAGI	PLUT'S Sign position - 1913/4-1937/8 CANC 1938/8-1957/8 LEO 1957/8-1971/2 VIRG 1971/21983/4 LIBR

6

HOW TO PLOT
A HOROSCOPE CHART

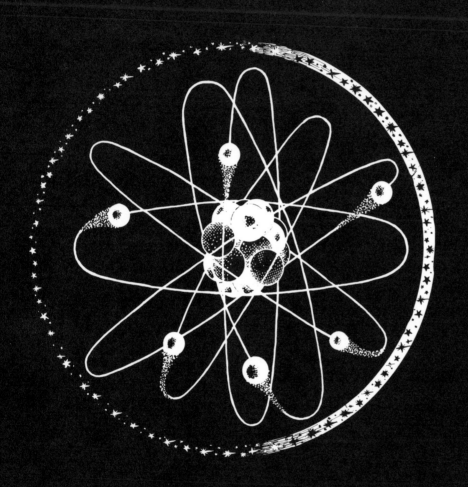

Plotting a horoscope chart

If not ordering a Computer Calculated Chart and intend to plot one yourself, you will need to obtain an Astrological **Ephemeris,** *for the year of birth.* Among several available are, *Raphael's Astronomical Ephemeris,* published in London each year, which is calculated for Noon Greenwich; the *Rosicrucian Fellowship Simplified* (USA) in yearly volumes, also calculated for Noon Greenwich. Another, *Die Deutsche Ephemeride* (Germany) in 10 year volumes is calculated from 1931 for Midnight at Greenwich (i.e. the start of the new day's date).

method 1: for unknown birth time or approximate hour of birth

Having assumed a Birth Time within a two hour period and chosen a corresponding Ascendant Sign from the instructions in Section 5, proceed as follows:

Place this Ascendant Sign on the Blank Chart at the start of House Number 1 and fill in the other 11 Signs counter-clockwise around the Chart in their consecutive order at the head of each dividing line.

Mark each Sign '15 degrees', which means that half of the Sign's thirty degrees falls in one House and half in the next.

The next step to complete a Chart is to place the planets in their appropriate Sign and House, according to their positions on the birth date shown in the Ephemeris and to do this turn to the next chapter, 'Entering the Planets in the Chart'.

This method will give accurate readings according to Sign, while the House readings will only be approximate.

method 2: for known birth time (if not using computer facilities)

This method enables the correct degree of the Ascendant Sign to be found, together with the individual Sign degrees, which will give greater accuracy in placing the planets in the Houses and therefore a truer reading of both the Birth Chart and 'Future Prospects'.

To proceed with this method, in addition to the Ephemeris for the birth year already mentioned, you will need to use a **Tables of Houses** for either north or south latitude, depending on whether the birth was in the northern or southern hemisphere. These Tables are needed to find the correct Sign degrees for the House dividing lines and are good for any year.

There are a number of Tables of Houses published, and, like the Ephemerides, are obtainable from astrological and occult bookshops in the capital cities.

In the back of *Raphael's Ephemeris* there are Tables of Houses for the northern latitudes of London, Liverpool and New York.

Tables of Houses for northern latitudes, covering the main cities of Canada, are included in the Appendix of this book. Tables for other latitudes in Canada can be found in most Astrological bookstores.

Method 2 is best shown by doing an example Chart. For simplicity a birth in London is used, as this city is right on the Standard Time longitude of 0 degrees Greenwich and therefore in London the birth time shown on the clock is exactly true to Greenwich Standard longitude.

However, if the birth had been in Liverpool, England, (which is 3 degrees west of the Greenwich longitude), the real time there based on its longitude position would be some 12 minutes earlier than the clocks show as the Standard Time all over England.

This local time factor has to be taken into account and can be found by referring to the chapter, 'Adjustment for Finding True Local Time of Birth'. Also included in that chapter is another adjustment for Daylight Saving Time if in practice on the birth date.

We will now proceed to do the example, using the same birth data as for the Computer Calculated Chart earlier in this book, for John Doe, born in London, on 9th November 1929 at 1.04 pm by the clock.

As the birth place, London, does not call for any local time adjustment by longitude, and Daylight Saving Time was not in operation on the birth date, we can proceed using the birth time of 1.04 pm without prior adjustment.

		Hrs	Min	Sec
From a 1929 *Raphael's Ephemeris*, opposite date of birth extract the Sidereal Time (which represents 12 Noon)	=	15	12	41
Add, as it is pm, the Clock Time of Birth (If it were am, subtract the interval before Noon)	=	1	4	0
Correct Sidereal Time to find Ascendant Sign degree is	=	16	16	41

(If the Sidereal Time given in the Ephemeris is too small to subtract from, add 24 hours, or if the total exceeds 24 hours, subtract 24 hours)

With the correct Sidereal Time found above, next refer to a *Northern Table of Houses* for the latitude of birthplace, in this case latitude 51 degrees 32 minutes north, which represents London. (as shown in part of the Table which follows) and find the nearest Sidereal Time to 16 16 41, which is 16 16 26. In line with this are found the Signs and their degrees for the dividing lines of the Chart, with an Ascendant Sign - Aquarius ♒ 6° 32'.

Note: in the Table of Houses, sometimes the Sign shown at the top of the column changes on the way down the column - therefore watch for it.

The blank Chart can now be filled in with the Signs and their degrees

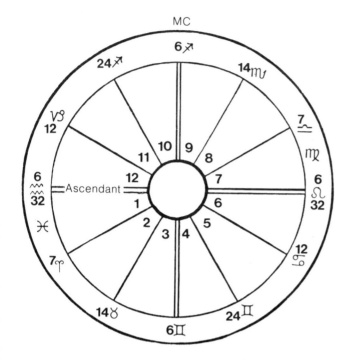

Part of Northern Table of Houses for London latitude

Sidereal Time.	10 ♐	11 ♐	12 ♑	Ascen ♑	2 ♓	3 ♉
Latitude 51° 32' N.						
H. M. S.	°	°	°	° '	°	°
15 51 15	0	18	6	27 15	26	6
15 55 25	1	19	7	28 42	28	7
15 59 36	2	20	8	0 ♒ 11	♈	9
16 3 48	3	21	9	1 42	2	10
16 8 0	4	22	10	3 16	3	11
16 12 13	5	23	11	4 53	5	12
16 16 26	6	24	12	6 32	7	14
16 20 40	7	25	13	8 13	9	15
16 24 55	8	26	14	9 57	11	16
16 29 10	9	27	16	11 44	12	17
16 33 26	10	28	17	13 34	14	18
16 37 42	11	29	18	15 26	16	20
16 41 59	12	♑	19	17 20	18	21
16 46 16	13	1	20	19 18	20	22
16 50 34	14	2	21	21 22	21	23
16 54 52	15	3	22	23 29	23	25
16 59 10	16	4	24	25 36	25	26
17 3 29	17	5	25	27 46	27	27
17 7 49	18	6	26	0 ♓ 0	28	28
17 12 9	19	7	27	2 19	♉	29

(Placidus House System)

starting at the MC point (start of House division 10) and continuing counter-clockwise around to House division 3, as shown in the example Chart.

It will be noticed that Sagittarius ♐ is repeated, at different degrees, at Houses 10 and 11, and also that the Table of Houses have skipped the Sign Pisces ♓ in the consecutive order and therefore this 'intercepted' Sign has to be entered in the middle of House division 1, between the Signs on each dividing line.

Repeated and 'intercepted' Signs appear according to the latitude of the birth place. Signs rise evenly at the equator but vary in northern and southern latitudes.

To complete the chart, fill in the opposite Signs on the start of House division 4 to 9 and use the same degrees as the opposite Signs.

Also insert the intercepted Sign, Virgo ♍ opposite Pisces ♓ . Placing the Signs around the example chart is now complete and it only remains to enter the planets in their correct Signs and House divisions.

For practical working all the steps mentioned in this Chapter such as, 'Daylight Saving Time', 'Adjustment for Finding True Local Time of Birth', 'Sidereal Time Calculation' and 'Ascertaining the Ascendant and Sign Degrees', are all set out on the Blank Working Chart at the end of this Section. There is one working sheet for use with a Noon Ephemeris (such as *Raphael's*) and one for use with a Midnight Ephemeris (such as *Die Deutsche*).

Entering the planets in the chart

An Ephemeris for the year of birth is now used to locate the Planets positions.

Using METHOD 1 it will be remembered that each Sign placed around the Chart has been marked as 15 degrees at the dividing line of each House division.

The Planets are entered into the Chart from the Ephemeris according to their Sign and degree, as shown in the longitude columns opposite the date of birth.

The Planets move in a counter-clockwise direction in the same order as the numbered Houses.

If a Planet is less than 15 degrees it is entered in the House before its Sign's dividing line and if more than 15 degrees it is entered in the House after the dividing line.

Using METHOD 2, which gives the individual Sign degrees, we continue with the example Chart of John Doe by entering the Planets into their correct House divisions, guided by the Sign degrees shown at the dividing lines.

In the 1929 *Raphael's Ephemeris,* opposite the date of birth, November 9, the Zodiacal position of the Planets appear under columns headed by their symbols and the word **Long**, which are as follows:

☉ Sun	16°	♏ 36′	♃ Jupiter	14°	♊	25′
☾ Moon	15°	♒ 37′	♂ Mars	23°	♏	33′
♆ Neptune	3°	♍ 23′	♀ Venus	25°	♎	12′
♅ Uranus	8°	♈ 2′	☿ Mercury	5°	♏	58′
♄ Saturn	27°	♐ 49′	♇ Pluto	19°	♋	40′

Note: The longitude position of Pluto is found in the back, or in supplementary Ephemerides.

The first Planet to enter is the Sun at 16° ♏ 36′ and being a greater degree than its Sign Scorpio at 14° on the dividing line, it is entered in the following 9th House division close to the dividing line as shown in the example Chart which follows.

All the Planets are entered into the Chart direct from the *Noon Ephemeris* with the exception of the Moon. The latter moves quickly at the average of ½ a degree per hour and therefore a correction is necessary for the number of hours the birth time was before or after noon, more fully explained in 'Moon Correction Details'.

From the *Ephemeris,* the Moon shown at 15° ♒ 37′ is corrected to 16° ♒ 9′, due to the birth time of 1.04 pm being one hour later than Noon Greenwich. This Moon is placed in the 1st House division as its degree is greater than that of the Aquarius Sign at the Ascendant.

The remaining Planets are extracted from the *Ephemeris* and according to their Sign and degree are entered into their correct House divisions as shown in the completed example Chart which follows.

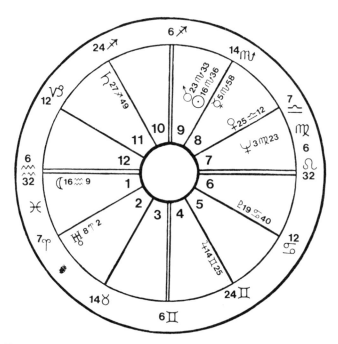

The above example Chart for John Doe is now ready to read - see Section 1.

Remember that the Planets are moving in a counter-clockwise direction and those with a less degree than their Sign degree at the dividing line are entered in the House before, while Planets with a greater degree have crossed over the dividing line and are therefore entered in the next House.

Note that the 7th House contains the intercepted Sign ♍ holding the Planet Neptune ♆ . Care should be taken to write-in the Planets close to their appropriate Sign and in their correct House division. Also count that you have entered ten Planets in all, as sometimes Pluto ♇ can be missed.

Here is John Doe's birth chart calculation done by a computer calculating service, which gives the same information as the completed example Chart above, although only in list form. By comparing them you can see how the computer information could be transferred to a circular Chart for reading.

	POSITION OF PLANETS				POSITION OF HOUSES		
SUN	16	DEGREES	SCORPIO	I	ASCENDANT	6 DEGREES	AQUARIUS
MOON	16	DEGREES	AQUARIUS	II		7 DEGREES	ARIES
NEPTUNE	3	DEGREES	VIRGO	III		14 DEGREES	TAURUS
URANUS	8	DEGREES	ARIES	IV	NADIR	6 DEGREES	GEMINI
SATURN	28	DEGREES	SAGITTARIUS	V		24 DEGREES	GEMINI
JUPITER	14	DEGREES	GEMINI	VI		12 DEGREES	CANCER
MARS	23	DEGREES	SCORPIO	VII	DESCENDANT	6 DEGREES	LEO
VENUS	25	DEGREES	LIBRA	VIII		7 DEGREES	LIBRA
MERCURY	6	DEGREES	SCORPIO	IX		14 DEGREES	SCORPIO
PLUTO	20	DEGREES	CANCER	X	MID-HEAVEN	6 DEGREES	SAGITTARIUS
				XI		24 DEGREES	SAGITTARIUS
				XII		12 DEGREES	CAPRICORN

moon correction details

The correction for the movement of the Moon between its position given in the *Ephemeris* at Noon Greenwich and its position at the time of birth is explained as follows.

These instructions also take in to consideration a birth place being in a Time Zone other than Greenwich.

First remember to check if Daylight Saving Time was in use on the birth date and subtract any such advance from the birth time before you start.

1 The Moon's position in *Raphael's Ephemeris* is calculated for Noon Greenwich, but when the birth place is in another time zone, east or west of Greenwich it is necessary to establish a new 'Noon Mark', equivalent to Noon Greenwich, and consider the *Ephemeris* as having been calculated for that time at the place of birth.

This is easily done by consulting the Standard Zone Time list and note where this Zone Time falls on the following 'time reckoner'. This point is the new 'Noon Mark'.

Midnight	am	Noon	pm	Midnight
(Start of Day)		Greenwich		
12 1 2 3 4 5 6 7 8 9 10 11		12 1 2 3 4 5 6 7 8 9 10 11 12		
11 10 9 8 7 6 5 4 3 2 1				
(Hours before Noon)				

2 Keeping the 'Noon Mark' in mind, next work out how much the birth time is before or after this point.

3 This difference is then converted to degrees and minutes by consulting the Correction for Moon chart, and is then subtracted or added accordingly, to the long. position of the Moon given in the *Ephemeris* for the date of birth.

EXAMPLE - for a birth in Toronto, Canada at 1:00 pm

1 As the Zone Time for Toronto is 5 hours behind Greenwich, the 'Noon Mark' would fall at 7:00 am

2 The Birth Time at 1:00 pm is therefore 6 hours after the 'Noon Mark'

3 This 6 hours is then converted to 3°12′ and is added to the Moon's long. position in the *Ephemeris*

EXAMPLE - for a birth in Vancouver, Canada at 1:00 pm

1 As the Zone Time for Vancouver is 8 hours behind Greenwich the 'Noon Mark' would fall at 4:00 am

2 The Birth Time at 1:00 pm is therefore 9 hours after the 'Noon Mark'.

3 This 9 hours is converted to 4°48′ and is added to the Moon's long. position in the *Ephemeris*

(By following the above examples on the 'time reckoner' you will soon understand how to do Moon corrections.)

If using a *Midnight Ephemeris*, it will be necessary in Step 1 to work from Midnight (start of the day) on the 'time reckoner' to establish the new 'Mark', which in this case will be equivalent to Midnight Greenwich and then proceed as previously described.

Note: for west longitude birth places this 'Midnight Mark' will fall into the day before the birth date so you will have to work from there in this case.

Correction for moon - average movement in 12 hours

Hours	°	′	Hours	°	′
½	0	16	6½	3	28
1	0	32	7	3	44
1½	0	48	7½	4	00
2	1	04	8	4	16
2½	1	20	8½	4	32
3	1	36	9	4	48
3½	1	52	9½	5	04
4	2	08	10	5	20
4½	2	24	10½	5	36
5	2	40	11	5	52
5½	2	56	11½	6	08
6	3	12	12	6	24

When adding or subtracting the Moon correction remember that each Sign has 30 degrees and each degree has 60 minutes. If the degrees of the Moon's position after adjustment come to a total of more than 30 degrees, it is in the next Sign, or if less than zero it falls into the previous Sign.

progressed moon

For the advanced student plotting his own Chart, there is another method of finding the position of the Progressed Moon for 'Future prospects'.

Due to the Moon's variation in its rate of travel, this method will be found to be a little more accurate than the 'average' method used in Section 3.

Using the traditional method of one day equals one year, count down the *Ephemeris* page from the birth date, at the rate of one day for every year of age, making the next day down the first year and so on, remembering that the progression falls due on the birth-day.

Having arrived at the desired progression date, note the longitude and Sign position of the Moon in the *Ephemeris,* which then has to be corrected as per instructions for Moon Correction. In fact if you have already corrected the Birth Moon use the same correction for the Progressed Moon.

A quick method to check correct plotting

Having completed a Horoscope Chart for any birthplace, the position of the Sun must appear in the correct position in the Chart of the heavens, corresponding to the hour of birth, shown around the Chart below, (first, less any artificial advance due to Daylight Saving Time)

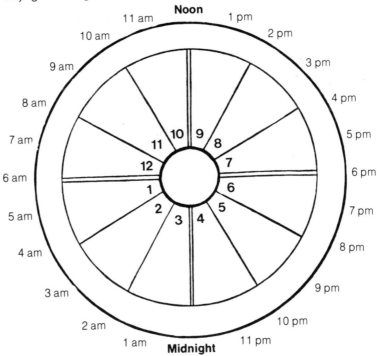

Example: For a birth at 1.04 pm (as in the John Doe example) the correct place for the Sun to fall would be in the 9th House division. If the completed Chart does not show the Sun in its correct position, then a mistake has been made, perhaps in the calculations, or check to see whether the *Ephemeris* used was set up for Noon or Midnight, or check if the correct *Tables of Houses* was used corresponding to north or south latitude of the birth place.

If the Chart has already been done, even by a Computer Calculating Service, it is wise to check its correct Sun position against the time of birth given, as sometimes a mix-up can occur in the coding of am or pm, especially when the birth time is just after 12.00 o'clock.

daylight saving time

An adjustment that may have to be considered is 'Daylight Saving Time', as if in vogue at the time and place of birth, the clock reading would have been advanced usually by one hour and in the UK for 'Double Summer Time', advanced by two hours, and therefore this advancement would have to be *first subtracted from the birth time*.

Daylight Saving Time details for various countries can be found in *New Waite's Compendium of Natal Astrology*, *Whitaker's Almanack* and two books by Doris Doane, *World Time Changes* and *Time Changes in Canada and Mexico*. Up-to-date information on Daylight Saving Times in major Canadian cities are given in the Appendix of this book.

Adjustment for finding true local time of birth

The time shown by the clock at the birth place is the Standard or Zone time adopted by a country for convenience, but is not necessarily the true Local Time as measured by longitude. (Standard Zone Times are given in the Appendix.)

The world is divided into twenty-four Standard Time Zones, each one being 15 degrees of longitude in width and the time used for each Zone is the longitude at its centre; birthplaces *east* of *centre,* need something *added* to clock time; birth places *west* of *centre* need something *subtracted* from clock time, and this rule applies for both east and west longitudes of the world, as clock time accelerates consistently towards the East.

To find the true Local Time, first divide the longitude of the birth place (found from an Atlas) by 15 to convert it to time in hours and minutes.

The difference between this time and the Standard Zone Time is the longitude difference in time, and this is added to, or subtracted from, the clock time of birth to give True Local Time of Birth.

This adjustment is shown by the following example for a birth in Toronto, Ontario at 1:04 pm by the clock.

	H	M	S
Divide longitude 79°W 22' of Toronto by 15	5	17	28
Zone Time of Toronto at 75° is 5 hours	5	00	00
Longitude Difference in Time		17	28

Being west of the Zone Time Centre, this difference must be subtracted from the Clock Time of Birth. Since the subtrahend is greater than the minuend, the Clock Time must be converted into minutes and seconds. (1:04 becomes 63' 60")

Clock Time	12	63	60
Difference		17	28
True Local Time of Birth	12	46	32

If this birth was in Montreal, divide the longitude of Montreal 73°35' by 15 = 4 hours, 54 minutes, 20 seconds. As this is east of the Zone Time Centre of 75° at 5 hours, the difference of 5'40" is added to the Clock Time of Birth.

Blank working charts

using a **noon** ephemeris

NAME .... Sex ....

Birth Place .... Longitude .... E / W Latitude .... N / S

Time .... am / pm Date........... Month .... Year ....

First remember to check if Daylight Saving Time was in use on the birth date and subtract any such advance from the birth time before you start.

Step 1 Adjustment for Finding True Local Time of Birth   Hrs Min Sec

Divide longitude ....of (Birth place) by 15   =

Zone Time of Birth Place   = _____

Longitude difference in Time   =

which, according to rule on previous page, is added to, or subtracted from,

The Clock Time of Birth (first, less any D.S. Time)   = _____

True Local Time of Birth   = _____

Step 2
From a *Noon* Ephemeris in line with the date of birth extract the Sidereal Time   =

For pm birth add the True Local Time of Birth   }
For am birth subtract the interval between the True Local Time and Noon   }   =
          _____

Corrected Sidereal Time of Birth   = _____

(If Sidereal Time is too small to subtract from, add 24 hrs, or if Total exceeds 24 hours, subtract 24 hours)

Step 3
From an appropriate Table of Houses (north or south latitude) use nearest Sidereal Time to the corrected Sidereal Time of Birth found above.

          o Sign '

10th.....................................

11th.....................................

12th.....................................

ASCEN............................

2nd.....................................

3rd.....................................

Step 4
Now enter the Planets in the Chart.

blank working chart
using a **midnight** ephemeris

NAME .... Sex ....

Birth Place .... Longitude .... $\begin{smallmatrix}E\\W\end{smallmatrix}$ Latitude,............. $\begin{smallmatrix}N\\S\end{smallmatrix}$

Time .... $\begin{smallmatrix}am\\pm\end{smallmatrix}$ Date........... Month .... Year ....

First remember to check if Daylight Saving Time was in use on the birth date
and subtract any such advance from the birth time before you start.

Step 1   Adjustment for Finding True Local Time of Birth   Hrs Min Sec

Divide longitude ....of (Birth place) by 15   =

Zone Time of Birth Place   = _____

Longitude difference in Time   =

which, according to rule on previous page, is added to, or
subtracted from,

The Clock Time of Birth (first, less any D.S. Time)   = _____

True Local Time of Birth   = _____
                                                                        ===============

Step 2
From a *Midnight* Ephemeris in line with the date of birth
extract the Sidereal Time   =

For pm birth add the True Local Time of Birth plus ⎫
12 hours from midnight to noon   ⎬   =
                                                   ⎪
For am birth add the True Local Time of Birth   ⎭   _____

Corrected Sidereal Time of Birth   = _____
                                                                        ===============

(If Total exceeds 24 hours, subtract 24 hours)

MC

Step 3
From an appropriate Table of Houses (north or south latitude)
use nearest Sidereal Time to the corrected Sidereal Time
of Birth found above.

     o Sign '

10th.......................................

11th.......................................

12th.......................................   Ascendant

ASCEN.....................................

2nd..

3rd..

Step 4
Now enter the Planets in the Chart.

99

7
APPENDIX

STANDARD TIME ZONES IN CANADA
DAYLIGHT SAVING TIMES
TABLES OF HOUSES
COMPUTER CALCULATING SERVICES

Standard time zones in Canada

Included for those doing their own calculations is a quick reference list of corrections to convert Zone Clock Time to True Local Time (TLT) for births in major cities.

Note: Time Zone boundaries have changed frequently in the past, sometimes for scientific reasons, sometimes as the result of popular referenda. In Saskatchewan, such votes are still common, with the result that the boundary between the Central and Mountain Standard Time Zones often shifts. The boundary between the Atlantic and the Eastern Standard Time Zones has also changed occasionally, while Labrador, once included in the Newfoundland Standard Time Zone, is now included in the Atlantic Standard Time Zone. Also, some communities near the Zone boundaries adopt whatever time suits them best, regardless of their location within a particular zone. All this is said as a caution to those born in communities near the boundaries — they should check with their municipal offices to determine the system in effect at the time of their births.

Newfoundland Standard Time is based on $52\frac{1}{2}°$ west longitude and is $3\frac{1}{2}$ hours behind Greenwich. It is used throughout Newfoundland.
For TLT in St. John's NFLD add 40′ to clock time

Atlantic Standard Time is based on 60° west longitude and is 4 hours behind Greenwich. It is used in Prince Edward Island, Nova Scotia, New Brunswick, Labrador, Quebec east of the 63° west longitude meridian, and the Northwest Territories east of the 68° west longitude meridian.

For TLT in		
	Charlottetown, PEI	subtract 12′28″ from clock time
	Halifax, NS	subtract 14′40″ from clock time
	Fredericton, NB	subtract 27′ from clock time

Eastern Standard Time is based on 75° west longitude and is 5 hours behind Greenwich. It is used throughout most of Ontario, in Quebec west of 63° west longitude, and in the Northwest Territories between the 68° and 85° west longitude meridians.

For TLT in		
	Quebec City, PQ	add 15′08″ to clock time
	Montreal, PQ	add 5′40″ to clock time
	Ottawa, ON	subtract 2′40″ from clock time
	Toronto, ON	subtract 17′28″ from clock time
	Windsor, ON	subtract 32′ from clock time
	Thunder Bay, ON	subtract 57′08″ from clock time

Central Standard Time is based on 90° west longitude and is 6 hours behind Greenwich. It is used in Ontario west of 90°, Manitoba, parts of south-eastern Saskatchewan, and in the Northwest Territories between the 80° and 102° west longitude meridians.

For TLT in		
	Winnipeg, MAN	add 1′28″ to clock time
	Regina, SASK	subtract 58′20″ from clock time

Mountain Standard Time is based on 105° west longitude and is 7 hours behind Greenwich. It is used in Alberta, parts of western Saskatchewan, parts of British Columbia, and in the Northwest Territories west of the 102° west longitude meridian.

For TLT in		
	Edmonton, ALTA	subtract 34′30″ from clock time
	Calgary, ALTA	subtract 36′ from clock time

Pacific Standard Time is based on 120° west longitude and is 8 hours behind Greenwich. It is used in the Yukon and most of British Columbia.

For TLT in		
	Vancouver, BC	subtract 12′ from clock time
	Victoria, BC	subtract 12′40″ from clock time

Yukon Standard Time, based on 135° west longitude and 9 hours behind Greenwich, was in effect in the Yukon for many years. On October 28, 1973 the Zone was abolished and the Yukon was incorporated into the Pacific Zone.

Time Zones of Canada

Newfoundland Standard Time 8:30 pm

Atlantic Standard Time 8 pm

Eastern Standard Time 7 pm

Central Standard Time 6 pm

Mountain Standard Time 5 pm

Pacific Standard Time 4 pm

QUEBEC

ONTARIO

MANITOBA

SASKATCHEWAN

ALBERTA

BRITISH COLUMBIA

NORTHWEST TERRITORIES

YUKON

N.S.

P.E.I.

N.B.

Daylight Saving Times

Daylight Saving Time (DST) in Canada is a nightmare for astrologers and others who have to use time calculations. Only recently has some small degree of consistency been obtained in its use, though twice, during the two World Wars, the entire country observed DST at the same times.

Before 1918, only St. John's, Halifax, Montreal, Hamilton, Winnipeg and Brandon had experimented with DST. Then from April 14 to October 31, 1918 all Canada observed fast time. During World War II, War Time (DST) came into effect on different dates in various parts of the country. Those communities in Ontario and Quebec that had been observing DST in the summer of 1940 were ordered to continue using it throughout the War. Other communities in those two provinces went on DST on September 29, 1940. In Alberta, British Columbia, Manitoba, New Brunswick, the Northwest Territories, Nova Scotia, Prince Edward Island, Saskatchewan and the Yukon, DST came into effect on February 9, 1942. Newfoundland and Labrador adopted DST on May 11, 1942. In all provinces and territories, War Time continued until September 30, 1945.

In the lists that follow, common dates for each province and dates for major cities are given. People born in other communities should write to their municipal offices to determine dates. Unless otherwise stated, changes took effect at 2:00 AM.

ALBERTA. Some communities observed DST after 1945, but its observance was outlawed in 1948. Beginning in 1973, the use of DST was standardized in the province.

1918 Apl 14 - Oct 31	1973 Apl 29 - Oct 28	1977 Apl 24 - Oct 30
1919 Apl 13 - May 27	1974 Apl 28 - Oct 27	1978 Apl 30 - Oct 29
1942 Feb 9 -	1975 Apl 27 - Oct 26	1979 Apl 29 - Oct 28
1945 - Sept 30	1976 Apl 25 - Oct 31	

Calgary
1946 May 15 - Oct 5	1947 Apl 27 - Sept 27

Edmonton
1920 Apl 25 - Oct 31	1922 Apl 30 - Sept 24	1947 Apl 27 - Sept 27
1921 Apl 24 - Sept 25	1923 Apl 29 - Sept 30	

BRITISH COLUMBIA. The observance of DST was standardized throughout the province in 1947.

1918 Apl 14 - Oct 31	1956 Apl 29 - Sept 30	1968 Apl 28 - Oct 27
1942 Feb 9 -	1957 Apl 28 - Sept 28	1969 Apl 27 - Oct 26
1945 - Sept 30	1958 Apl 27 - Sept 27	1970 Apl 26 - Oct 25
1947 Apl 27 - Sept 28	1959 Apl 26 - Sept 27	1971 Apl 25 - Oct 31
1948 Apl 25 - Sept 26	1960 Apl 24 - Sept 25	1972 Apl 30 - Oct 29
1949 Apl 24 - Sept 25	1961 Apl 30 - Sept 24	1973 Apl 29 - Oct 28
1950 Apl 30 - Sept 24	1962 Apl 29 - Oct 28	1974 Apl 28 - Oct 27
1951 Apl 29 - Sept 30	1963 Apl 28 - Oct 27	1975 Apl 27 - Oct 26
1952 Apl 27 - Sept 28	1964 Apl 26 - Oct 25	1976 Apl 25 - Oct 31
1953 Apl 26 - Sept 27	1965 Apl 25 - Oct 31	1977 Apl 24 - Oct 30
1954 Apl 25 - Sept 26	1966 Apl 24 - Oct 30	1978 Apl 30 - Oct 29
1955 Apl 24 - Sept 25	1967 Apl 30 - Oct 29	1979 Apl 29 - Oct 28

Vancouver
1946 Apl 28 - Oct 31

Victoria
1921 May 1 - Oct 1	1923 May 6 - Sept 9
1922 Apl 30 - Sept 5	1946 Apl 28 - Sept 29

MANITOBA. DST was not observed province-wide between the Wars, from 1946 to 1962, or in 1966. Its use was standardized in 1967.

1918 Apl 14	- Oct 31	1968 Apl 28	- Oct 27	1974 Apl 28	- Oct 27
1942 Feb 9	-	1969 Apl 27	- Oct 26	1975 Apl 27	- Oct 26
1945	- Sept 30	1970 Apl 26	- Oct 25	1976 Apl 25	- Oct 31
1964 Apl 26	- Sept 13	1971 Apl 25	- Oct 31	1977 Apl 24	- Oct 30
1965 Apl 25	- Sept 12	1972 Apl 30	- Oct 29	1978 Apl 30	- Oct 29
1967 Apl 30	- Oct 29	1973 Apl 29	- Oct 28	1979 Apl 29	- Oct 28

Winnipeg

1916 Apl 23	- Sept 17	1950 May 1	- Sept 30	1956 Apl 29	- Sept 30
1937 May 16	- Sept 26	1951 Apl 29	- Sept 30	1957 Apl 28	- Sept 29
1946 May 12	- Oct 13	1952 Apl 27	- Sept 29	1958 Apl 27	- Sept 27
1947 Apl 27	- Sept 28	1953 Apl 26	- Sept 28	1959 Apl 26	- Oct 25
1948 Apl 25	- Sept 26	1954 Apl 25	- Sept 26	1960 Apl 24	- Sept 25
1949 Apl 24	- Sept 25	1955 Apl 24	- Sept 25	1966 Apl 24	- Oct 30

Brandon

1916 Apl 17	- June 19	1963 June 1	- Sept 1
1946 Apl 28	- Sept 29	1966 Apl 30	- Oct 29

Note: Changes in 1916 in Winnipeg and Brandon took effect at 0 hour.

NEW BRUNSWICK. DST has been observed province-wide since 1966.

1918 Apl 14	- Oct 31	1969 Apl 27	- Oct 26	1975 Apl 27	- Oct 26
1942 Feb 9	-	1970 Apl 26	- Oct 25	1976 Apl 25	- Oct 31
1945	- Sept 30	1971 Apl 25	- Oct 31	1977 Apl 24	- Oct 30
1966 Apl 24	- Oct 30	1972 Apl 30	- Oct 29	1978 Apl 30	- Oct 29
1967 Apl 30	- Oct 29	1973 Apl 29	- Oct 28	1979 Apl 29	- Oct 28
1968 Apl 28	- Oct 27	1974 Apl 28	- Oct 27		

St. John

1924 May 19	- Sept 8	1937 May 23	- Sept 26	1954 Apl 25	- Sept 26
1925 May 4	- Sept 28	1938 May 22	- Sept 25	1955 Apl 24	- Sept 25
1926 May 3	- Sept 8	1939 May 21	- Sept 24	1956 Apl 29	- Sept 30
1927 May 2	- Sept 26	1940 May 26	- Sept 29	1957 Apl 28	- Oct 27
1928 May 21	- Sept 5	1941 May 25	- Sept 28	1958 Apl 27	- Oct 26
1929 May 13	- Sept 4	1946 Apl 28	- Sept 29	1959 Apl 26	- Oct 25
1930 June 2	- Sept 3	1947 Apl 27	- Sept 28	1960 Apl 24	- Oct 30
1931 May 18	- Sept 14	1948 Apl 25	- Sept 26	1961 Apl 30	- Oct 29
1932 May 29	- Sept 26	1949 Apl 24	- Sept 25	1962 Apl 29	- Oct 28
1933 May 28	- Oct 1	1950 Apl 30	- Sept 25	1963 Apl 28	- Oct 27
1934 May 27	- Sept 30	1951 Apl 29	- Sept 30	1964 Apl 26	- Oct 25
1935 May 26	- Sept 29	1952 Apl 27	- Sept 29	1965 Apl 25	- Oct 31
1936 May 24	- Sept 27	1953 Apl 26	- Sept 28		

Fredericton

1946 Apl 28	- Sept 29	1954 Apl 25	- Sept 26	1961 Apl 30	- Oct 29
1948 Apl 25	- Sept 26	1955 Apl 24	- Sept 25	1962 Apl 29	- Oct 28
1949 Apl 24	- Sept 25	1956 Apl 29	- Sept 30	1963 Apl 28	- Oct 27
1950 Apl 30	- Sept 25	1957 Apl 28	- Sept 29	1964 Apl 26	- Oct 25
1951 Apl 29	- Sept 30	1958 Apl 27	- Sept 27	1965 Apl 25	- Oct 31
1952 Apl 27	- Sept 29	1959 Apl 26	- Oct 25		
1953 Apl 26	- Sept 28	1960 Apl 24	- Oct 30		

Note: Changes in St. John from 1924 to 1941 took effect at 0 hour.

NEWFOUNDLAND. DST has been observed province-wide since 1951.

1918 Apl 14	- Oct 31	1959 Apl 26	- Sept 27	1970 Apl 26	- Oct 25
1942 May 11	-	1960 Apl 24	- Oct 29	1971 Apl 25	- Oct 31
1945	- Sept 30	1961 Apl 30	- Oct 28	1972 Apl 30	- Oct 29
1951 Apl 29	- Sept 30	1962 Apl 29	- Oct 28	1973 Apl 29	- Oct 28
1952 Apl 27	- Sept 29	1963 Apl 28	- Oct 27	1974 Apl 28	- Oct 27
1953 Apl 26	- Sept 28	1964 Apl 26	- Oct 25	1975 Apl 27	- Oct 26
1954 Apl 25	- Sept 26	1965 Apl 25	- Oct 31	1976 Apl 25	- Oct 31
1955 Apl 24	- Sept 25	1966 Apl 24	- Oct 30	1977 Apl 24	- Oct 30
1956 Apl 29	- Sept 30	1967 Apl 30	- Oct 29	1978 Apl 30	- Oct 29
1957 Apl 28	- Sept 29	1968 Apl 28	- Oct 27	1979 Apl 29	- Oct 28
1958 Apl 27	- Sept 28	1969 Apl 27	- Oct 26		

St. John's

1917 Apl 8	- Sept 17	1926 May 2	- Oct 31	1934 May 6	- Oct 28
1919 May 5	- Aug 12	1927 May 1	- Oct 30	1935 May 5	- Oct 27
1920 May 2	- Oct 31	1928 May 6	- Oct 28	1936 May 11	- Oct 5
1921 May 1	- Oct 30	1929 May 5	- Oct 27	1937 May 10	- Oct 4
1922 May 7	- Oct 29	1930 May 4	- Oct 26	1938 May 9	- Oct 3
1923 May 6	- Oct 28	1931 May 3	- Oct 25	1939 May 15	- Oct 2
1924 May 4	- Oct 26	1932 May 1	- Oct 30	1940 May 13	- Oct 17
1925 May 3	- Oct 25	1933 May 7	- Sept 29	1941 May 12	- Oct 6

Note: Changes in St. John's from 1919 to 1935 took effect at 11:00 PM. Changes from 1936 to 1941 took effect at 0 hour.

NOVA SCOTIA. Since 1968, almost all communities in Nova Scotia have observed DST on the same dates.

1918 Apl 14	- Oct 31	1970 Apl 26	- Oct 25	1975 Apl 27	- Oct 26
1942 Feb 9	-	1971 Apl 25	- Oct 24	1976 Apl 25	- Oct 31
1945	- Sept 30	1972 Apl 30	- Oct 29	1977 Apl 24	- Oct 30
1968 Apl 28	- Oct 27	1973 Apl 29	- Oct 28	1978 Apl 30	- Oct 29
1969 Apl 27	- Oct 26	1974 Apl 28	- Oct 27	1979 Apl 29	- Oct 28

Halifax

1916 Apl 30	- Oct 1	1932 May 1	- Sept 25	1951 Apl 24	- Sept 30
1920 May 9	- Aug 28	1933 Apl 30	- Sept 24	1952 Apl 27	- Sept 28
1921 May 6	- Sept 4	1934 Apl 29	- Sept 30	1953 Apl 26	- Sept 27
1922 Apl 30	- Sept 4	1935 May 4	- Sept 29	1954 Apl 25	- Sept 26
1923 May 6	- Sept 3	1936 May 3	- Sept 27	1956 Apl 29	- Sept 30
1924 May 4	- Sept 14	1937 May 2	- Sept 26	1957 Apl 28	- Oct 27
1925 May 3	- Sept 27	1938 May 1	- Sept 25	1958 Apl 27	- Oct 26
1926 May 16	- Sept 12	1939 May 26	- Sept 24	1962 Apl 29	- Oct 28
1927 May 1	- Sept 25	1940 May 5	- Sept 29	1963 Apl 28	- Oct 27
1928 May 13	- Sept 8	1941 May 4	- Sept 28	1964 Apl 26	- Oct 25
1929 May 12	- Sept 2	1946 Apl 28	- Sept 29	1965 Apl 25	- Oct 31
1930 May 11	- Sept 14	1947 Apl 27	- Sept 28	1966 Apl 24	- Oct 30
1931 Apl 29	- Sept 27	1948 Apl 25	- Sept 26	1967 Apl 30	- Oct 29

Note: Changes in Halifax in 1916 took effect at 0 hour. Changes from 1920 to 1941 took effect at 0 hour for the spring change, 2400 hours for the fall change.

ONTARIO. Although there have been many attempts to standardize DST in Ontario, no bill to that effect has ever made it through the legislature.

1918 Apl 14	- Oct 31	1940 Sept 29	-	1945	- Sept 30

Toronto

1919 Mar 30	- Oct 25	1938 Apl 24	- Sept 25	1962 Apl 29	- Oct 28
1920 May 2	- Sept 25	1939 Apl 30	- Sept 24	1963 Apl 28	- Oct 27
1921 May 15	- Sept 16	1940 Apl 28	-	1964 Apl 26	- Oct 25
1922 May 14	- Sept 17	1946 Apl 28	- Sept 29	1965 Apl 25	- Oct 31
1923 May 13	- Sept 9	1947 Apl 27	- Sept 28	1966 Apl 24	- Oct 30
1924 May 4	- Sept 21	1948 Apl 25	- Sept 26	1967 Apl 30	- Oct 29
1925 May 3	- Sept 20	1949 Apl 24	- Nov 27	1968 Apl 28	- Oct 27
1926 May 2	- Sept 19	1950 Apl 30	- Nov 26	1969 Apl 27	- Oct 26
1927 May 1	- Sept 25	1951 Apl 29	- Sept 30	1970 Apl 26	- Oct 25
1928 Apl 29	- Sept 30	1952 Apl 27	- Sept 28	1971 Apl 25	- Oct 24
1929 Apl 28	- Sept 29	1953 Apl 26	- Sept 27	1972 Apl 30	- Oct 29
1930 Apl 27	- Sept 28	1954 Apl 25	- Sept 26	1973 Apl 29	- Oct 28
1931 Apl 26	- Sept 27	1955 Apl 24	- Sept 25	1974 Apl 28	- Oct 27
1932 May 1	- Sept 25	1956 Apl 29	- Sept 30	1975 Apl 27	- Oct 26
1933 Apl 30	- Oct 1	1957 Apl 28	- Oct 27	1976 Apl 25	- Oct 31
1934 Apl 29	- Sept 30	1958 Apl 27	- Oct 26	1977 Apl 24	- Oct 30
1935 Apl 28	- Sept 29	1959 Apl 26	- Oct 25	1978 Apl 30	- Oct 29
1936 Apl 26	- Sept 27	1960 Apl 24	- Oct 30	1979 Apl 29	- Oct 28
1937 Apl 25	- Sept 26	1961 Apl 30	- Oct 29		

Note: In 1919, the first change took effect at 11:00 PM, the second at 0 hour. In 1920, the first change took effect at 2:00 AM, the second at 0 hour. In 1929, 1947 and 1948 changes took effect at 12:01 AM.

Hamilton

1916 June 4 - Aug 13	1933 June 4 - Sept 17	1938 Apl 25 - Sept 12
1929 June 17- Sept 3	1934 May 6 - Sept 16	1939 May 1 - Sept 10
1930 June 9 - Sept 2	1935 May 5 - Sept 15	1940 Apl 29 -
1931 June 15- Sept 8	1936 May 3 - Sept 13	1946-79: see Toronto
1932 May 30 - Sept 18	1937 May 2 - Sept 12	

Note: From 1930 to 1940 and in 1949, changes took effect at 0 hour.

Ottawa

1920 May 2 - Oct 23	1925 May 3 - Sept 27	1946-49: see Toronto
1921 May 1 - Oct 2	1926 May 2 - Sept 26	1950 Apl 30 - Sept 24
1922 Apl 30 - Oct 1	1927-38: see Toronto	1951-79: see Toronto
1923 May 13 - Sept 30	1939 Apl 30 - Oct 1	
1924 May 18 - Sept 28	1940 Apl 28 -	

Note; Changes took effect at 0 hour in the years 1920-24, 1926, and 1932-40

Kingston

1932 May 2 - Sept 26	1939 May 8 - Sept 25	1951 Apl 29 - Sept 30
1933 May 8 - Sept 25	1940 May 6 -	1952 Apl 27 - Sept 28
1934 May 7 - Oct 1	1946 May 5 - Sept 30	1953 Apl 26 - Sept 27
1935 May 6 - Sept 30	1947 Apl 20 - Oct 4	1954 Apl 25 - Sept 26
1936 Apl 26 - Sept 28	1948 Apl 25 - Sept 26	1955 Apl 30 - Sept 24
1937 Apl 24 - Sept 27	1949 Apl 24 - Sept 25	1956-79: see Toronto
1938 May 2 - Sept 26	1950 Apl 30 - Sept 24	

Note: Changes from 1932 to 1940 and from 1947 to 1948 took effect at 0 hour.

Windsor

1947 Apl 27 - Sept 28	1950 Apl 30 - Sept 24
1948 Apl 25 - Sept 26	1968-79: see Toronto

Note: Changes in 1947 and 1948 took effect at 0 hour

PRINCE EDWARD ISLAND. DST has been observed province-wide since 1962.

1918 Apl 14 - Oct 31	1966 Apl 24 - Oct 30	1973 Apl 29 - Oct 28
1942 Feb 9 -	1967 Apl 30 - Oct 29	1974 Apl 28 - Oct 27
1945 - Sept 30	1968 Apl 28 - Oct 27	1975 Apl 27 - Oct 26
1962 Apl 29 - Oct 28	1969 Apl 27 - Oct 26	1976 Apl 25 - Oct 31
1963 Apl 28 - Oct 27	1970 Apl 26 - Oct 25	1977 Apl 24 - Oct 30
1964 Apl 26 - Oct 25	1971 Apl 25 - Oct 31	1978 Apl 30 - Oct 29
1965 Apl 25 - Oct 31	1971 Apl 30 - Oct 29	1979 Apl 29 - Oct 28

Charlottetown

1946 Apl 28 - Sept 29	1947 Apl 27 - Sept 28

QUEBEC. DST has been observed province-wide since 1968.

1918 Apl 14 - Oct 31	1970 Apl 26 - Oct 25	1975 Apl 27 - Oct 26
1940 Sept 29 -	1971 Apl 25 - Oct 31	1976 Apl 25 - Oct 31
1945 - Sept 30	1972 Apl 30 - Oct 29	1977 Apl 24 - Oct 30
1968 Apl 28 - Oct 27	1973 Apl 29 - Oct 28	1978 Apl 30 - Oct 29
1969 Apl 27 - Oct 26	1974 Apl 28 - Oct 27	1979 Apl 29 - Oct 28

Montreal

1917 Mar 25 - Apl 24	1934 Apl 29 - Sept 30	1954 Apl 25 - Sept 26
1919 Mar 31 - Oct 25	1935 Apl 28 - Sept 29	1955 Apl 24 - Sept 25
1920 May 2 - Oct 3	1936 Apl 26 - Oct 27	1956 Apl 29 - Sept 30
1921 May 1 - Oct 2	1937 Apl 25 - Sept 26	1957 Apl 28 - Oct 27
1922 Apl 30 - Oct 1	1938 Apl 24 - Sept 25	1958 Apl 27 - Oct 26
1924 May 17 - Sept 28	1939 Apl 30 - Sept 24	1959 Apl 26 - Oct 25
1925 May 3 - Sept 27	1940 Apl 28 -	1960 Apl 24 - Oct 30
1926 May 2 - Sept 26	1946 Apl 28 - Sept 29	1961 Apl 30 - Oct 29
1927 May 1 - Sept 25	1947 Apl 27 - Sept 28	1962 Apl 29 - Oct 28
1928 Apl 29 - Sept 30	1948 Apl 25 - Sept 26	1963 Apl 28 - Oct 27
1929 Apl 28 - Sept 29	1949 Apl 24 - Oct 30	1964 Apl 26 - Oct 25
1930 Apl 27 - Sept 28	1950 Apl 30 - Oct 29	1965 Apl 25 - Oct 31
1931 Apl 26 - Sept 27	1951 Apl 29 - Sept 30	1966 Apl 25 - Oct 30
1932 Apl 24 - Sept 25	1952 Apl 27 - Sept 28	1967 Apl 30 - Oct 29
1933 Apl 30 - Sept 24	1953 Apl 26 - Sept 27	

Note: In 1917 the first change took effect at 2:00 AM, the second at 0 hour.
Changes in 1919 and 1920 took effect at 2:30 AM. From 1921 to 1926, the first change took effect at 2:00 AM, the second at 2:30 AM. From 1927 through 1940, changes took effect at 0 hour.

Quebec City
    Except for War Time in 1918, Quebec City did not observe DST before 1928.
From 1928 onward, Quebec City changed on the same dates and at the same
times as Montreal.

Sherbrooke
    1919 Mar 29 - Oct 25   1924 May 4   - Sept 28   1928-49: see Montreal
    1920 May 1   - Oct 2   1925 May 3   - Sept 27   1950 Apl 30 - Sept 24
    1921 May 1   - Oct 2   1926 May 3   - Sept 26   1951-65: see Montreal
    1923 May 31 - Sept 30   1927 May 1   - Sept 25
Note: In 1919 the first change took effect at 11:00 PM, the second at 2:00 AM.
    From 1920 through 1940 changes took effect at 0 hour.

SASKATCHEWAN. Except for the War years, DST has only been observed
throughout Saskatchewan twice, in 1947 and 1959. Under 1966 legislation, the
boundary of the Central Time Zone was shifted from the Manitoba border to run
down the centre of the province. Communities in the eastern part of the province
stay on Central Time all year. Those communities in the western part of the
province that choose each year to adopt Mountain Standard Time during the
winter revert to Central Time during the summer months, in effect, adopting DST.
    1918 Apl 14 - Oct 31   1945   - Sept 30   1959 Apl 26   - Oct 25
    1942 Feb 9   -   1947 Apl 27 - Sept 28
Regina
    1930 May 5 - Oct 6   1940 Apl 15 - Oct 14   1952 Apl 27 - Sept 28
    1931 May 4 - Oct 5   1941 Apl 14 - Oct 13   1953 Apl 26 - Sept 27
    1932 May 2 - Oct 3   1946 Apl 14 - Oct 13   1954 Apl 25 - Sept 26
    1933 May 8 - Oct 2   1948 Apl 25 - Sept 26   1955 Apl 24 - Sept 25
    1934 May 7 - Oct 8   1949 Apl 24 - Sept 25   1956 Apl 29 - Sept 30
    1938 Apl 11 - Oct 10   1950 Apl 30 - Sept 24   1957 Apl 28 - Sept 29
    1939 Apl 10 - Oct 9   1951 Apl 24 - Sept 25   1961 All year
Note: Changes took effect at 0 hour in the years 1930-34 and 1938-41.

Saskatoon
    1921 June 3 - Sept 30   1947 Apl 27 - Sept 28   1954 Apl 25 - Sept 26
    1932 May 1   - Oct 2   1948 Apl 25 - Sept 26   1955 Apl 24 - Sept 25
    1933 May 7   - Oct 1   1949 Apl 24 - Sept 25   1956 Apl 29 - Sept 30
    1938 Apl 24 - Oct 2   1950 Apl 30 - Sept 24   1957 Apl 28 - Oct 27
    1939 Apl 30 - Oct 1   1951 Apl 24 - Sept 25   1960 Apl 24 - Sept 25
    1940 Apl 28 - Sept 30   1952 Apl 27 - Sept 28   1961 Apl 30 - Sept 24
    1946 Apl 28 - Oct 13   1953 Apl 26 - Sept 27
Note: In 1932 and 1933, changes took effect at 1:00 AM. From 1938 to 1940,
    changes took effect at 0 hour.

Tables of houses

These tables give House Cusp positions within a few degrees and are adequate
for most practical purposes for the major cities of Canada. For information about
other latitudes, consult tables of houses available from most astrological or
occult bookstores.

When in doubt as to the Ascending Sign, check the Ascendant Graph on page
83 for the closest appearance and temperament description.

Tables of houses for 43° 40′N

Suitable for Toronto, Windsor, Halifax and Kingston.

TABLES OF HOUSES FOR *Latitude* 43° 40′ N.

Sidereal Time. H. M. S.	10 ♎ °	11 ♎ °	12 ♏ °	Ascen ♐ °	′	2 ♑ °	3 ♒ °
12 0 0	0	28	21	9	12	13	23
12 3 40	1	29	21	9	56	14	24
12 7 20	2	♏	22	10	40	15	25
12 11 0	3	1	23	11	25	16	26
12 14 41	4	2	23	12	10	17	27
12 18 21	5	3	24	12	54	18	28
12 22 2	6	4	25	13	39	19	♓
12 25 42	7	4	26	14	24	20	1
12 29 23	8	5	27	15	10	21	2
12 33 4	9	6	27	15	56	22	3
12 36 45	10	7	28	16	42	23	4
12 40 26	11	8	29	17	28	24	5
12 44 8	12	9	30	18	14	25	6
12 47 50	13	9	♐	19	1	26	7
12 51 32	14	10	1	19	48	27	9
12 55 14	15	11	2	20	35	28	10
12 58 57	16	12	3	21	23	29	11
13 2 40	17	13	3	22	11	♒	12
13 6 23	18	14	4	23	0	1	13
13 10 7	19	15	5	23	48	2	14
13 13 51	20	15	6	24	37	3	15
13 17 35	21	16	7	25	26	4	17
13 21 20	22	17	7	26	16	5	18
13 25 6	23	18	8	27	6	6	19
13 28 52	24	19	9	27	57	7	20
13 32 38	25	20	10	28	48	9	21
13 36 25	26	20	10	29	40	10	22
13 40 12	27	21	11	0 ♑	32	11	24
13 44 0	28	22	12	1	25	12	25
13 47 48	29	23	13	2	18	13	26
13 51 37	30	24	14	3	12	14	27

Sidereal Time. H. M. S.	10 ♏ °	11 ♏ °	12 ♐ °	Ascen ♑ °	′	2 ♒ °	3 ♓ °
13 51 37	0	24	14	3	12	14	27
13 55 27	1	25	15	4	6	16	29
13 59 17	2	26	15	5	1	17	♈
14 3 8	3	27	16	5	57	18	1
14 6 59	4	27	17	6	54	19	2
14 10 51	5	28	18	7	51	21	3
14 14 44	6	29	19	8	49	22	5
14 18 37	7	♐	20	9	47	23	6
14 22 31	8	1	20	10	46	25	7
14 26 25	9	2	21	11	46	26	8
14 30 20	10	3	22	12	46	27	10
14 34 16	11	3	23	13	47	29	11
14 38 13	12	4	24	14	50	♓	12
14 42 10	13	5	25	15	53	1	13
14 46 8	14	6	26	16	58	3	14
14 50 7	15	7	27	18	3	4	16
14 54 7	16	8	27	19	10	5	17
14 58 7	17	9	28	20	17	7	18
15 2 8	18	10	29	21	25	8	19
15 6 9	19	11	♑	22	35	10	21
15 10 12	20	11	1	23	45	11	22
15 14 15	21	12	2	24	57	13	23
15 18 19	22	13	3	26	10	14	25
15 22 23	23	14	4	27	24	16	26
15 26 29	24	15	5	28	39	17	27
15 30 35	25	16	6	29	56	19	28
15 34 41	26	17	7	1 ♒	14	20	29
15 38 49	27	18	8	2	33	22	♉
15 42 57	28	19	9	3	54	24	2
15 47 6	29	20	10	5	16	25	3
15 51 15	30	21	11	6	39	27	4

Sidereal Time. H. M. S.	10 ♐ °	11 ♐ °	12 ♑ °	Ascen ♒ °	′	2 ♓ °	3 ♉ °
15 51 15	0	21	11	6	39	27	4
15 55 25	1	21	12	8	5	28	6
15 59 36	2	22	13	9	31	♈	7
16 3 48	3	23	14	11	0	1	8
16 8 0	4	24	15	12	30	3	9
16 12 13	5	25	16	14	1	5	10
16 16 26	6	26	17	15	34	6	12
16 20 40	7	27	18	17	9	8	13
16 24 55	8	28	19	18	45	9	14
16 29 10	9	29	20	20	23	11	15
16 33 26	10	♑	22	22	2	13	16
16 37 42	11	1	23	23	44	14	18
16 41 59	12	2	24	25	27	16	19
16 46 16	13	3	25	27	11	17	20
16 50 34	14	4	26	28	57	19	21
16 54 52	15	5	27	0 ♓	45	20	22
16 59 10	16	6	29	2	34	22	23
17 3 29	17	7	♒	4	25	24	25
17 7 49	18	8	1	6	17	25	26
17 12 9	19	9	2	8	10	27	27
17 16 29	20	10	4	10	4	28	28
17 20 49	21	11	5	12	1	♉	29
17 25 9	22	12	6	13	58	1	♊
17 29 30	23	13	7	15	56	3	2
17 33 51	24	14	9	17	55	4	3
17 38 12	25	15	10	19	54	6	4
17 42 34	26	16	11	21	55	7	5
17 46 55	27	18	13	23	55	9	6
17 51 17	28	19	14	25	57	10	7
17 55 38	29	20	16	27	58	12	8
18 0 0	30	21	17	30	0	13	9

Sidereal Time. H. M. S.	10 ♑ °	11 ♑ °	12 ♒ °	Ascen ♈ °	′	2 ♉ °	3 ♊ °
18 0 0	0	21	17	0	0	13	9
18 4 22	1	22	18	2	2	14	10
18 8 43	2	23	20	4	3	16	11
18 13 5	3	24	21	6	5	17	12
18 17 26	4	25	23	8	5	19	14
18 21 48	5	26	24	10	6	20	15
18 26 9	6	27	26	12	5	21	16
18 30 30	7	28	27	14	4	23	17
18 34 51	8	♒	28	16	2	24	18
18 39 11	9	1	♓	17	59	25	19
18 43 31	10	2	2	19	56	26	20
18 47 51	11	3	3	21	50	28	21
18 52 11	12	4	5	23	43	29	22
18 56 31	13	5	6	25	35	♊	23
19 0 50	14	7	8	27	26	1	24
19 5 8	15	8	10	29	15	3	25
19 9 26	16	9	11	1 ♉	3	4	26
19 13 44	17	10	13	2	49	5	27
19 18 1	18	11	14	4	33	6	28
19 22 18	19	12	16	6	16	7	29
19 26 34	20	14	17	7	58	8	♋
19 30 50	21	15	19	9	37	10	1
19 35 5	22	16	21	11	15	11	2
19 39 20	23	17	22	12	51	12	3
19 43 34	24	18	24	14	26	13	4
19 47 47	25	20	25	15	59	14	5
19 52 0	26	21	27	17	30	15	6
19 56 12	27	22	29	19	0	16	7
20 0 24	28	23	♈	20	29	17	8
20 4 35	29	24	2	21	55	18	9
20 8 45	30	26	3	23	21	19	9

Sidereal Time. H. M. S.	10 ♒ °	11 ♒ °	12 ♈ °	Ascen ♉ °	′	2 ♊ °	3 ♋ °
20 8 45	0	26	3	23	21	19	9
20 12 54	1	27	5	24	44	20	10
20 17 3	2	28	6	26	6	21	11
20 21 11	3	♓	8	27	27	22	12
20 25 19	4	1	10	28	46	23	13
20 29 26	5	2	11	0 ♊	4	24	14
20 33 31	6	3	13	1	21	25	15
20 37 37	7	4	14	2	36	26	16
20 41 41	8	5	16	3	50	27	17
20 45 45	9	7	17	5	3	28	18
20 49 48	10	8	19	6	15	29	19
20 53 51	11	9	20	7	25	♋	19
20 57 52	12	11	22	8	35	1	20
21 1 53	13	12	23	9	43	2	21
21 5 53	14	13	25	10	50	3	22
21 9 53	15	14	26	11	57	3	23
21 13 52	16	16	27	13	2	4	24
21 17 50	17	17	29	14	7	5	25
21 21 47	18	18	♉	15	10	6	26
21 25 44	19	19	1	16	13	7	27
21 29 40	20	20	3	17	14	8	27
21 33 35	21	22	4	18	14	9	28
21 37 29	22	23	5	19	14	10	29
21 41 23	23	24	7	20	13	10	♌
21 45 16	24	25	8	21	11	11	1
21 49 9	25	27	9	22	9	12	2
21 53 1	26	28	11	23	6	13	3
21 56 52	27	29	12	24	3	14	3
22 0 43	28	♈	13	24	59	15	4
22 4 33	29	1	14	25	54	15	5
22 8 23	30	3	16	26	48	16	6

Sidereal Time. H. M. S.	10 ♓ °	11 ♈ °	12 ♉ °	Ascen ♊ °	′	2 ♋ °	3 ♌ °
22 8 23	0	3	16	26	48	16	6
22 12 12	1	4	17	27	42	17	7
22 16 0	2	5	18	28	35	18	8
22 19 48	3	6	19	29	28	19	9
22 23 35	4	8	20	0 ♋	20	20	10
22 27 22	5	9	21	1	12	20	10
22 31 8	6	10	23	2	3	21	11
22 34 54	7	11	24	2	54	22	12
22 38 40	8	12	25	3	44	23	13
22 42 25	9	13	26	4	34	23	14
22 46 9	10	15	27	5	23	24	15
22 49 53	11	16	28	6	12	25	15
22 53 37	12	17	29	7	0	26	16
22 57 20	13	18	♊	7	49	27	17
23 1 3	14	19	1	8	37	27	18
23 4 46	15	20	2	9	25	28	19
23 8 28	16	21	3	10	12	29	20
23 12 10	17	23	4	10	59	30	21
23 15 52	18	24	5	11	46	♌	21
23 19 34	19	25	6	12	32	1	22
23 23 15	20	26	7	13	18	2	23
23 26 56	21	27	8	14	4	3	24
23 30 37	22	28	9	14	50	3	25
23 34 18	23	29	10	15	36	4	26
23 37 58	24	♉	11	16	21	5	26
23 41 39	25	2	12	17	6	6	27
23 45 19	26	3	13	17	50	7	28
23 49 0	27	4	14	18	35	7	29
23 52 40	28	5	15	19	20	8	♍
23 56 20	29	6	16	20	4	9	1
24 0 0	30	7	17	20	48	9	2

TABLES OF HOUSES FOR *Latitude* 43° 40′ N.

Sidereal Time. H. M. S.	10 ♈ °	11 ♉ °	12 ♊ °	Ascen ♋ °	′	2 ♌ °	3 ♍ °
0 0 0	0	7	17	20	48	9	2
0 3 40	1	8	18	21	32	10	2
0 7 20	2	9	19	22	16	11	3
0 11 0	3	10	20	23	0	12	4
0 14 41	4	11	21	23	43	13	5
0 18 21	5	12	21	24	27	13	6
0 22 2	6	13	22	25	11	14	7
0 25 42	7	14	23	25	55	15	8
0 29 23	8	15	24	26	38	16	8
0 33 4	9	16	25	27	21	16	9
0 36 45	10	17	26	28	4	17	10
0 40 26	11	18	27	28	47	18	11
0 44 8	12	19	28	29	30	19	12
0 47 50	13	20	28	0 ♌	14	19	13
0 51 32	14	21	29	0	57	20	14
0 55 14	15	22	♋	1	40	21	15
0 58 57	16	23	1	2	23	22	15
1 2 40	17	24	2	3	6	22	16
1 6 23	18	25	3	3	49	23	17
1 10 7	19	26	4	4	32	24	18
1 13 51	20	27	4	5	15	25	19
1 17 35	21	28	5	5	59	26	20
1 21 20	22	29	6	6	42	26	21
1 25 6	23	♊	7	7	25	27	22
1 28 52	24	1	8	8	8	28	23
1 32 38	25	2	8	8	52	29	23
1 36 25	26	3	9	9	35	30	24
1 40 12	27	4	10	10	18	♍	25
1 44 0	28	5	11	11	2	1	26
1 47 48	29	6	12	11	45	2	27
1 51 37	30	7	13	12	29	3	28

Sidereal Time. H. M. S.	10 ♉ °	11 ♊ °	12 ♋ °	Ascen ♌ °	′	2 ♍ °	3 ♍ °
1 51 37	0	7	13	12	29	3	28
1 55 27	1	8	14	13	13	4	29
1 59 17	2	9	14	13	57	4	♎
2 3 8	3	10	15	14	41	5	1
2 6 59	4	11	16	15	25	6	2
2 10 51	5	12	17	16	9	7	3
2 14 44	6	13	18	16	53	8	3
2 18 37	7	14	18	17	38	8	4
2 22 31	8	15	19	18	22	9	5
2 26 25	9	16	20	19	7	10	6
2 30 20	10	17	21	19	51	11	7
2 34 16	11	18	22	20	36	12	8
2 38 13	12	19	23	21	21	13	9
2 42 10	13	19	23	22	6	13	10
2 46 8	14	20	24	22	51	14	11
2 50 7	15	21	25	23	37	15	12
2 54 7	16	22	26	24	23	16	13
2 58 7	17	23	27	25	8	17	14
3 2 8	18	24	28	25	54	18	15
3 6 9	19	25	28	26	40	19	16
3 10 12	20	26	29	27	26	19	17
3 14 15	21	27	♌	28	13	20	18
3 18 19	22	28	1	28	59	21	19
3 22 23	23	29	2	29	46	22	19
3 26 29	24	♋	3	0 ♍	32	23	20
3 30 35	25	1	4	1	19	24	21
3 34 41	26	2	4	2	6	25	22
3 38 49	27	3	5	2	53	25	23
3 42 57	28	4	6	3	41	26	24
3 47 6	29	4	7	4	29	27	25
3 51 15	30	5	8	5	16	28	26

Sidereal Time. H. M. S.	10 ♊ °	11 ♋ °	12 ♌ °	Ascen ♍ °	′	2 ♍ °	3 ♎ °
3 51 15	0	5	8	5	16	28	26
3 55 25	1	6	9	6	4	29	27
3 59 36	2	7	9	6	52	♎	28
4 3 48	3	8	10	7	40	1	29
4 8 0	4	9	11	8	29	2	♏
4 12 13	5	10	12	9	17	3	1
4 16 26	6	11	13	10	5	3	2
4 20 40	7	12	14	10	54	4	3
4 24 55	8	13	15	11	42	5	4
4 29 10	9	14	16	12	31	6	5
4 33 26	10	15	16	13	21	7	6
4 37 42	11	16	17	14	10	8	7
4 41 59	12	17	18	14	59	9	8
4 46 16	13	18	19	15	48	10	9
4 50 34	14	19	20	16	38	11	10
4 54 52	15	20	21	17	28	12	11
4 59 10	16	21	22	18	18	13	12
5 3 29	17	22	23	19	7	14	13
5 7 49	18	23	24	19	57	15	14
5 12 9	19	24	24	20	47	15	15
5 16 29	20	25	25	21	37	16	16
5 20 49	21	25	26	22	27	17	17
5 25 9	22	26	27	23	17	18	18
5 29 30	23	27	28	24	7	19	19
5 33 51	24	28	29	24	58	20	20
5 38 12	25	29	♍	25	48	21	21
5 42 34	26	♌	1	26	38	22	22
5 46 55	27	1	2	27	29	23	23
5 51 17	28	2	3	28	19	24	24
5 55 38	29	3	4	29	10	25	25
6 0 0	30	4	4	30	0	26	26

Sidereal Time. H. M. S.	10 ♋ °	11 ♌ °	12 ♍ °	Ascen ♎ °	′	2 ♎ °	3 ♏ °
6 0 0	0	4	4	0	0	26	26
6 4 22	1	5	5	0	50	26	27
6 8 43	2	6	6	1	41	27	28
6 13 5	3	7	7	2	31	28	29
6 17 26	4	8	8	3	22	29	♐
6 21 48	5	9	9	4	12	♏	1
6 26 9	6	10	10	5	2	1	2
6 30 30	7	11	11	5	53	2	3
6 34 51	8	12	12	6	43	3	4
6 39 11	9	13	13	7	37	4	5
6 43 31	10	14	14	8	23	5	5
6 47 51	11	15	15	9	13	6	6
6 52 11	12	16	15	10	3	6	7
6 56 31	13	17	16	10	53	7	8
7 0 50	14	18	17	11	42	8	9
7 5 8	15	19	18	12	32	9	10
7 9 26	16	20	19	13	22	10	11
7 13 44	17	21	20	14	12	11	12
7 18 1	18	22	21	15	1	12	13
7 22 18	19	23	22	15	50	13	14
7 26 34	20	24	23	16	39	14	15
7 30 50	21	25	24	17	29	14	16
7 35 5	22	26	25	18	18	15	17
7 39 20	23	27	26	19	6	16	18
7 43 34	24	28	27	19	55	17	19
7 47 47	25	29	27	20	43	18	20
7 52 0	26	♍	28	21	31	19	21
7 56 12	27	1	29	22	20	20	22
8 0 24	28	2	♎	23	8	21	23
8 4 35	29	3	1	23	56	21	24
8 8 45	30	4	2	24	44	22	25

Sidereal Time. H. M. S.	10 ♌ °	11 ♍ °	12 ♎ °	Ascen ♎ °	′	2 ♏ °	3 ♐ °
8 8 45	0	4	2	24	44	22	25
8 12 54	1	5	3	25	31	23	26
8 17 3	2	6	4	26	19	24	26
8 21 11	3	7	5	27	7	25	27
8 25 19	4	8	5	27	54	26	28
8 29 26	5	9	6	28	41	26	29
8 33 31	6	10	7	29	28	27	♑
8 37 37	7	11	8	0 ♏	14	28	1
8 41 41	8	11	9	1	1	29	2
8 45 45	9	12	10	1	47	♐	3
8 49 48	10	13	11	2	34	1	4
8 53 51	11	14	11	3	20	2	5
8 57 52	12	15	12	4	6	2	6
9 1 53	13	16	13	4	52	3	7
9 5 53	14	17	14	5	37	4	8
9 9 53	15	18	15	6	23	5	9
9 13 52	16	19	16	7	9	6	10
9 17 50	17	20	17	7	54	7	11
9 21 47	18	21	17	8	39	7	11
9 25 44	19	22	18	9	24	8	12
9 29 40	20	23	19	10	9	9	13
9 33 35	21	24	20	10	53	10	14
9 37 29	22	25	21	11	38	11	15
9 41 23	23	26	22	12	22	12	16
9 45 16	24	27	22	13	7	12	17
9 49 9	25	27	23	13	51	13	18
9 53 1	26	28	24	14	35	14	19
9 56 52	27	29	25	15	19	15	20
10 0 42	28	♎	26	16	3	16	21
10 4 33	29	1	26	16	47	16	22
10 8 23	30	2	27	17	31	17	23

Sidereal Time. H. M. S.	10 ♍ °	11 ♎ °	12 ♎ °	Ascen ♏ °	′	2 ♐ °	3 ♑ °
10 8 23	0	2	27	17	31	17	23
10 12 12	1	3	28	18	15	18	24
10 16 0	2	4	29	18	58	19	25
10 19 48	3	5	30	19	42	20	26
10 23 35	4	6	♏	20	25	21	27
10 27 22	5	7	1	21	8	22	28
10 31 8	6	7	2	21	52	22	29
10 34 54	7	8	3	22	35	23	♒
10 38 40	8	9	4	23	18	24	1
10 42 25	9	10	4	24	1	25	2
10 46 9	10	11	5	24	45	26	3
10 49 53	11	12	6	25	28	26	4
10 53 37	12	13	7	26	11	27	5
10 57 20	13	14	8	26	54	28	6
11 1 3	14	15	8	27	37	29	7
11 4 46	15	15	9	28	20	♑	8
11 8 28	16	16	10	29	3	1	9
11 12 10	17	17	11	29	46	2	10
11 15 52	18	18	11	0 ♐	30	2	11
11 19 34	19	19	12	1	13	3	12
11 23 15	20	20	13	1	56	4	13
11 26 56	21	21	14	2	39	5	14
11 30 37	22	22	14	3	22	6	15
11 34 18	23	22	15	4	5	7	16
11 37 58	24	23	16	4	49	8	17
11 41 39	25	24	17	5	33	9	18
11 45 19	26	25	17	6	17	9	19
11 49 0	27	26	18	7	0	10	20
11 52 40	28	27	19	7	44	11	21
11 56 20	29	28	20	8	28	12	22
12 0 0	30	28	21	9	12	13	23

Tables of houses for 45° 30′N

Suitable for St. John, Fredericton, Moncton, Charlottetown, Quebec City, Montreal, Ottawa and Sudbury.

TABLES OF HOUSES FOR *Latitude* 45° 30′ N.

Sidereal Time H.	M.	S.	10 ♈ °	11 ♉ °	12 ♊ °	Ascen ♋ °	′	2 ♌ °	3 ♍ °
0	0	0	0	7	18	22	3	10	2
0	3	40	1	8	19	22	46	11	3
0	7	20	2	9	20	23	29	12	3
0	11	0	3	10	21	24	12	12	4
0	14	41	4	11	22	24	55	13	5
0	18	21	5	13	23	25	38	14	6
0	22	2	6	14	23	26	21	15	7
0	25	42	7	15	24	27	3	15	8
0	29	23	8	16	25	27	46	16	9
0	33	4	9	17	26	28	29	17	9
0	36	45	10	18	27	29	11	18	10
0	40	26	11	19	28	29	54	18	11
0	44	8	12	20	29	0 ♌	36	19	12
0	47	50	13	21	30	1	19	20	13
0	51	32	14	22	♋	2	1	21	14
0	55	14	15	23	1	2	43	22	15
0	58	57	16	24	2	3	26	22	16
1	2	40	17	25	3	4	8	23	16
1	6	23	18	26	4	4	50	24	17
1	10	7	19	27	5	5	33	25	18
1	13	51	20	28	5	6	15	25	19
1	17	35	21	29	6	6	57	26	20
1	21	20	22	♊	7	7	40	27	21
1	25	6	23	1	8	8	22	28	22
1	28	52	24	2	9	9	5	28	23
1	32	38	25	3	9	9	47	29	23
1	36	25	26	4	10	10	30	♍	24
1	40	12	27	5	11	11	13	1	25
1	44	0	28	6	12	11	56	1	26
1	47	48	29	7	13	12	38	2	27
1	51	37	30	8	14	13	21	3	28

Sidereal Time H.	M.	S.	10 ♉ °	11 ♊ °	12 ♋ °	Ascen ♌ °	′	2 ♍ °	3 ♍ °
1	51	37	0	8	14	13	21	3	28
1	55	27	1	9	14	14	4	4	29
1	59	17	2	10	15	14	47	5	♎
2	3	8	3	11	16	15	31	5	1
2	6	59	4	12	17	16	14	6	2
2	10	51	5	13	18	16	57	7	3
2	14	44	6	13	18	17	41	8	3
2	18	37	7	14	19	18	25	9	4
2	22	31	8	15	20	19	8	10	5
2	26	25	9	16	21	19	52	10	6
2	30	20	10	17	22	20	36	11	7
2	34	16	11	18	23	21	20	12	8
2	38	13	12	19	23	22	4	13	9
2	42	10	13	20	24	22	48	14	10
2	46	8	14	21	25	23	33	14	11
2	50	7	15	22	26	24	17	15	12
2	54	7	16	23	27	25	2	16	13
2	58	7	17	24	27	25	47	17	14
3	2	8	18	25	28	26	32	18	15
3	6	9	19	26	29	27	17	19	16
3	10	12	20	27	♌	28	3	20	17
3	14	15	21	28	1	28	48	20	17
3	18	19	22	28	2	29	33	21	18
3	22	23	23	29	3	0 ♍	19	22	19
3	26	29	24	♋	3	1	5	23	20
3	30	35	25	1	4	1	51	24	21
3	34	41	26	2	5	2	37	25	22
3	38	49	27	3	6	3	24	25	23
3	42	57	28	4	7	4	10	26	24
3	47	6	29	5	8	4	57	27	25
3	51	15	30	6	8	5	44	28	26

Sidereal Time H.	M.	S.	10 ♊ °	11 ♋ °	12 ♌ °	Ascen ♍ °	′	2 ♍ °	3 ♎ °
3	51	15	0	6	8	5	44	28	26
3	55	25	1	7	9	6	30	29	27
3	59	36	2	8	10	7	17	♎	28
4	3	48	3	9	11	8	5	1	29
4	8	0	4	10	12	8	52	2	♏
4	12	13	5	11	13	9	40	3	1
4	16	26	6	12	14	10	27	3	2
4	20	40	7	13	14	11	15	4	3
4	24	55	8	14	15	12	3	5	4
4	29	10	9	14	16	12	51	6	5
4	33	26	10	15	17	13	39	7	6
4	37	42	11	16	18	14	28	8	7
4	41	59	12	17	19	15	16	9	8
4	46	16	13	18	20	16	4	10	9
4	50	34	14	19	21	16	53	11	10
4	54	52	15	20	21	17	42	11	11
4	59	10	16	21	22	18	30	12	12
5	3	29	17	22	23	19	19	13	13
5	7	49	18	23	24	20	8	14	14
5	12	9	19	24	25	20	57	15	15
5	16	29	20	25	26	21	46	16	16
5	20	49	21	26	27	22	35	17	17
5	25	9	22	27	28	23	25	18	18
5	29	30	23	28	29	24	14	19	19
5	33	51	24	29	29	25	3	20	20
5	38	12	25	♌	♍	25	52	21	21
5	42	34	26	1	1	26	42	21	21
5	46	55	27	2	2	27	31	22	22
5	51	17	28	3	3	28	20	23	23
5	55	38	29	4	4	29	10	24	24
6	0	0	30	5	5	30	0	25	25

Sidereal Time H.	M.	S.	10 ♋ °	11 ♌ °	12 ♍ °	Ascen ♎ °	′	2 ♎ °	3 ♏ °
6	0	0	0	5	5	0	0	25	25
6	4	22	1	6	6	0	50	26	26
6	8	43	2	7	7	1	40	27	27
6	13	5	3	8	8	2	29	28	28
6	17	26	4	9	9	3	18	29	29
6	21	48	5	9	9	4	8	♏	♐
6	26	9	6	10	10	4	57	1	1
6	30	30	7	11	11	5	46	1	2
6	34	51	8	12	12	6	35	2	3
6	39	11	9	13	13	7	25	3	4
6	43	31	10	14	14	8	14	4	5
6	47	51	11	15	15	9	3	5	6
6	52	11	12	16	16	9	52	6	7
6	56	31	13	17	17	10	41	7	8
7	0	50	14	18	18	11	30	8	9
7	5	8	15	19	19	12	18	9	10
7	9	26	16	20	19	13	7	9	11
7	13	44	17	21	20	13	56	10	12
7	18	1	18	22	21	14	44	11	13
7	22	18	19	23	22	15	32	12	14
7	26	34	20	24	23	16	21	13	15
7	30	50	21	25	24	17	9	14	16
7	35	5	22	26	25	17	57	15	16
7	39	20	23	27	26	18	45	16	17
7	43	34	24	28	27	19	33	16	18
7	47	47	25	29	27	20	20	17	19
7	52	0	26	♍	28	21	8	18	20
7	56	12	27	1	29	21	55	19	21
8	0	24	28	2	♎	22	43	20	22
8	4	35	29	3	1	23	30	21	23
8	8	45	30	4	2	24	16	22	24

Sidereal Time H.	M.	S.	10 ♌ °	11 ♍ °	12 ♎ °	Ascen ♎ °	′	2 ♏ °	3 ♐ °
8	8	45	0	4	2	24	16	22	24
8	12	54	1	5	3	25	3	22	25
8	17	3	2	6	4	25	50	23	26
8	21	11	3	7	5	26	36	24	27
8	25	19	4	8	5	27	23	25	28
8	29	26	5	9	6	28	9	26	29
8	33	31	6	10	7	28	55	27	♑
8	37	37	7	11	8	29	41	27	1
8	41	41	8	12	9	0 ♏	27	28	2
8	45	45	9	13	10	1	12	29	2
8	49	48	10	13	10	1	57	♐	3
8	53	51	11	14	11	2	43	1	4
8	57	52	12	15	12	3	28	2	5
9	1	53	13	16	13	4	13	3	6
9	5	53	14	17	14	4	58	3	7
9	9	53	15	18	15	5	43	4	8
9	13	52	16	19	16	6	27	5	9
9	17	50	17	20	16	7	12	6	10
9	21	47	18	21	17	7	56	7	11
9	25	44	19	22	18	8	40	7	12
9	29	40	20	23	19	9	24	8	13
9	33	35	21	24	20	10	8	9	14
9	37	29	22	25	20	10	52	10	15
9	41	23	23	26	21	11	35	11	16
9	45	16	24	27	22	12	19	12	17
9	49	9	25	27	23	13	3	12	17
9	53	1	26	28	24	13	46	13	18
9	56	52	27	29	25	14	29	14	19
10	0	42	28	♎	25	15	13	15	20
10	4	33	29	1	26	15	56	16	21
10	8	23	30	2	27	16	39	16	22

Sidereal Time H.	M.	S.	10 ♍ °	11 ♎ °	12 ♎ °	Ascen ♏ °	′	2 ♐ °	3 ♑ °
10	8	23	0	2	27	16	39	16	22
10	12	12	1	3	28	17	22	17	23
10	16	0	2	4	29	18	4	18	24
10	19	48	3	5	29	18	47	19	25
10	23	35	4	6	♏	19	30	20	26
10	27	22	5	7	1	20	13	21	27
10	31	8	6	7	2	20	55	21	28
10	34	54	7	8	2	21	38	22	29
10	38	40	8	9	3	22	20	23	♒
10	42	25	9	10	4	23	3	24	1
10	46	9	10	11	5	23	45	25	2
10	49	53	11	12	5	24	27	25	3
10	53	37	12	13	6	25	10	26	4
10	57	20	13	14	7	25	52	27	5
11	1	3	14	14	8	26	34	28	6
11	4	46	15	15	8	27	17	29	7
11	8	28	16	16	9	27	59	♑	8
11	12	10	17	17	10	28	41	0	9
11	15	52	18	18	11	29	24	1	10
11	19	34	19	19	12	0 ♐	6	2	11
11	23	15	20	20	12	0	49	3	12
11	26	56	21	21	13	1	31	4	13
11	30	37	22	21	14	2	14	5	14
11	34	18	23	22	15	2	57	6	15
11	37	58	24	23	15	3	39	7	16
11	41	39	25	24	16	4	22	7	17
11	45	19	26	25	17	5	5	8	19
11	49	0	27	26	18	5	48	9	20
11	52	40	28	27	18	6	31	10	21
11	56	20	29	27	19	7	14	11	22
12	0	0	30	28	20	7	57	12	23

TABLES OF HOUSES FOR *Latitude* 45° 30′ N.

Sidereal Time H.	M.	S.	10 ♎ °	11 ♎ °	12 ♏ °	Ascen ♐ °	′	2 ♑ °	3 ♒ °
12	0	0	0	28	20	7	57	12	23
12	3	40	1	29	20	8	40	13	24
12	7	20	2	♏	21	9	24	14	25
12	11	0	3	1	22	10	8	15	26
12	14	41	4	2	23	10	52	16	27
12	18	21	5	2	23	11	36	17	28
12	22	2	6	3	24	12	20	17	29
12	25	42	7	4	25	13	5	18	♓
12	29	23	8	5	26	13	50	19	2
12	33	4	9	6	26	14	35	20	3
12	36	45	10	7	27	15	19	21	4
12	40	26	11	7	28	16	5	22	5
12	44	8	12	8	29	16	51	23	6
12	47	50	13	9	30	17	37	24	7
12	51	32	14	10	♐	18	22	25	8
12	55	14	15	11	1	19	9	26	9
12	58	57	16	12	2	19	56	27	11
13	2	40	17	12	3	20	43	28	12
13	6	23	18	13	3	21	31	♒	13
13	10	7	19	14	4	22	19	1	14
13	13	51	20	15	5	23	7	2	15
13	17	35	21	16	6	23	56	3	17
13	21	20	22	17	6	24	45	4	18
13	25	6	23	18	7	25	34	5	19
13	28	52	24	18	8	26	24	6	20
13	32	38	25	19	9	27	15	7	21
13	36	25	26	20	10	28	6	9	22
13	40	12	27	21	10	28	57	10	24
13	44	0	28	22	11	29	49	11	25
13	47	48	29	23	12	0 ♑	42	12	26
13	51	37	30	24	13	1	35	13	27

Sidereal Time H.	M.	S.	10 ♏ °	11 ♏ °	12 ♐ °	Ascen ♑ °	′	2 ♒ °	3 ♓ °
13	51	37	0	24	13	1	35	13	27
13	55	27	1	24	14	2	28	15	28
13	59	17	2	25	14	3	23	16	♈
14	3	8	3	26	15	4	18	17	1
14	6	59	4	27	16	5	14	18	2
14	10	51	5	28	17	6	10	20	3
14	14	44	6	29	18	7	7	21	5
14	18	37	7	30	19	8	4	22	6
14	22	31	8	♐	19	9	3	24	7
14	26	25	9	1	20	10	2	25	8
14	30	20	10	2	21	11	2	26	10
14	34	16	11	3	22	12	3	28	11
14	38	13	12	4	23	13	5	29	12
14	42	10	13	5	24	14	8	♓	13
14	46	8	14	6	25	15	12	2	15
14	50	7	15	6	25	16	17	4	16
14	54	7	16	7	26	17	22	5	17
14	58	7	17	8	27	18	29	7	18
15	2	8	18	9	28	19	37	8	20
15	6	9	19	10	29	20	46	9	21
15	10	12	20	11	♑	21	56	11	22
15	14	15	21	12	1	23	8	12	24
15	18	19	22	13	2	24	21	14	25
15	22	23	23	14	3	25	34	15	26
15	26	29	24	15	4	26	50	17	27
15	30	35	25	15	5	28	7	19	28
15	34	41	26	16	6	29	25	20	♉
15	38	49	27	17	7	0 ♒	45	22	1
15	42	57	28	18	8	2	6	23	2
15	47	6	29	19	9	3	28	25	3
15	51	15	30	20	10	4	53	27	5

Sidereal Time H.	M.	S.	10 ♐ °	11 ♐ °	12 ♑ °	Ascen ♒ °	′	2 ♓ °	3 ♉ °
15	51	15	0	20	10	4	53	27	5
15	55	25	1	21	11	6	19	28	6
15	59	36	2	22	12	7	47	♈	7
16	3	48	3	23	13	9	16	1	8
16	8	0	4	24	14	10	47	3	9
16	12	13	5	25	15	12	20	5	11
16	16	26	6	26	16	13	54	6	12
16	20	40	7	27	17	15	31	8	13
16	24	55	8	28	18	17	9	10	14
16	29	10	9	29	19	18	49	11	16
16	33	26	10	♑	20	20	31	13	17
16	37	42	11	1	22	22	14	15	18
16	41	59	12	2	23	24	0	16	19
16	46	16	13	3	24	25	48	18	20
16	50	34	14	4	25	27	37	19	22
16	54	52	15	5	26	29	28	21	23
16	59	10	16	6	28	1 ♓	21	23	24
17	3	29	17	7	29	3	16	24	25
17	7	49	18	8	♒	5	12	26	26
17	12	9	19	9	1	7	10	27	27
17	16	29	20	10	3	9	10	29	29
17	20	49	21	11	4	11	10	♉	♊
17	25	9	22	12	5	13	13	2	1
17	29	30	23	13	6	15	16	4	2
17	33	51	24	14	8	17	20	5	3
17	38	12	25	15	9	19	25	7	4
17	42	34	26	16	10	21	31	8	5
17	46	55	27	17	12	23	38	10	6
17	51	17	28	18	13	25	45	11	8
17	55	38	29	19	15	27	53	12	9
18	0	0	30	20	16	30	0	14	10

Sidereal Time H.	M.	S.	10 ♑ °	11 ♑ °	12 ♒ °	Ascen ♈ °	′	2 ♉ °	3 ♊ °
18	0	0	0	20	16	0	0	14	10
18	4	22	1	21	18	2	7	15	11
18	8	43	2	22	19	4	15	17	12
18	13	5	3	24	20	6	22	18	13
18	17	26	4	25	22	8	29	20	14
18	21	48	5	26	23	10	35	21	15
18	26	9	6	27	25	12	40	22	16
18	30	30	7	28	26	14	44	24	17
18	34	51	8	29	28	16	47	25	18
18	39	11	9	♒	♓	18	50	26	19
18	43	31	10	1	1	20	50	27	20
18	47	51	11	3	3	22	50	28	21
18	52	11	12	4	4	24	48	♊	22
18	56	31	13	5	6	26	44	1	23
19	0	50	14	6	7	28	39	2	24
19	5	8	15	7	9	0 ♉	32	4	25
19	9	26	16	8	11	2	23	5	26
19	13	44	17	10	12	4	12	6	27
19	18	1	18	11	14	6	0	7	28
19	22	18	19	12	15	7	46	8	29
19	26	34	20	13	17	9	29	10	♋
19	30	50	21	14	19	11	11	11	1
19	35	5	22	16	20	12	51	12	2
19	39	20	23	17	22	14	29	13	3
19	43	34	24	18	24	16	6	14	4
19	47	47	25	19	25	17	40	15	5
19	52	0	26	21	27	19	13	16	6
19	56	12	27	22	28	20	44	17	7
20	0	24	28	23	♈	22	13	18	8
20	4	35	29	24	2	23	41	19	9
20	8	45	30	25	8	25	7	20	10

Sidereal Time H.	M.	S.	10 ♒ °	11 ♒ °	12 ♈ °	Ascen ♉ °	′	2 ♊ °	3 ♋ °
20	8	45	0	25	3	25	7	20	10
20	12	54	1	27	5	26	32	21	11
20	17	3	2	28	7	27	54	22	12
20	21	11	3	29	8	29	15	23	13
20	25	19	4	♓	10	0 ♊	35	24	14
20	29	26	5	2	11	1	53	25	15
20	33	31	6	3	13	3	10	26	15
20	37	37	7	4	15	4	26	27	16
20	41	41	8	5	16	5	39	28	17
20	45	45	9	6	18	6	52	29	18
20	49	48	10	8	19	8	4	♋	19
20	53	51	11	9	21	9	14	1	20
20	57	52	12	10	22	10	23	2	21
21	1	53	13	12	23	11	31	3	22
21	5	53	14	13	25	12	38	4	23
21	9	53	15	14	26	13	43	5	24
21	13	52	16	15	28	14	48	5	24
21	17	50	17	17	♉	15	52	6	25
21	21	47	18	18	1	16	55	7	26
21	25	44	19	19	2	17	57	8	27
21	29	40	20	20	4	18	58	9	28
21	33	35	21	22	5	19	58	10	29
21	37	29	22	23	6	20	57	11	♌
21	41	23	23	24	8	21	56	11	0
21	45	16	24	25	9	22	53	12	1
21	49	9	25	27	10	23	50	13	2
21	53	1	26	28	12	24	46	14	3
21	56	52	27	29	13	25	42	15	4
22	0	43	28	♈	14	26	37	16	5
22	4	33	29	2	15	27	32	16	6
22	8	23	30	3	17	28	25	17	6

Sidereal Time H.	M.	S.	10 ♓ °	11 ♈ °	12 ♉ °	Ascen ♊ °	′	2 ♋ °	3 ♌ °
22	8	23	0	3	17	28	25	17	6
22	12	12	1	4	18	29	18	18	7
22	16	0	2	5	19	0 ♋	11	19	8
22	19	48	3	6	20	1	3	20	9
22	23	35	4	8	21	1	54	20	10
22	27	22	5	9	23	2	45	21	11
22	31	8	6	10	24	3	36	22	12
22	34	54	7	11	25	4	26	23	12
22	38	40	8	12	26	5	15	24	13
22	42	25	9	13	27	6	4	24	14
22	46	9	10	15	28	6	53	25	15
22	49	53	11	16	29	7	41	26	16
22	53	37	12	17	♊	8	29	27	17
22	57	20	13	18	2	9	17	27	18
23	1	3	14	19	3	10	4	28	18
23	4	46	15	21	4	10	51	29	19
23	8	28	16	22	5	11	38	♌	20
23	12	10	17	23	6	12	23	0	21
23	15	52	18	24	7	13	9	1	22
23	19	34	19	25	8	13	55	2	23
23	23	15	20	26	9	14	41	3	23
23	26	56	21	27	10	15	25	4	24
23	30	37	22	28	11	16	10	4	25
23	34	18	23	♉	12	16	55	5	26
23	37	58	24	1	13	17	40	6	27
23	41	39	25	2	13	18	24	7	28
23	45	19	26	3	14	19	8	7	28
23	49	0	27	4	15	19	52	8	29
23	52	40	28	5	16	20	36	9	♍
23	56	20	29	6	17	21	20	10	1
24	0	0	30	7	18	22	3	10	2

Tables of houses for 47° 29′ N

Suitable for St. John's, Thunder Bay and Victoria, B.C.

TABLES OF HOUSES FOR *Latitude* 47° 29′ N.

Sidereal Time H.	M.	S.	10 ♈ °	11 ♉ °	12 ♊ °	Ascen ♋ °	′	2 ♌ °	3 ♍ °
0	0	0	0	8	19	23	28	11	2
0	3	40	1	9	20	24	11	12	3
0	7	20	2	10	21	24	53	12	4
0	11	0	3	11	22	25	35	13	5
0	14	41	4	12	23	26	17	14	5
0	18	21	5	13	24	26	59	15	6
0	22	2	6	14	25	27	41	15	7
0	25	42	7	15	26	28	23	16	8
0	29	23	8	16	26	29	4	17	9
0	33	4	9	17	27	29	46	18	10
0	36	45	10	18	28	0 ♌	28	18	11
0	40	26	11	19	29	1	10	19	11
0	44	8	12	20	♋	1	51	20	12
0	47	50	13	21	1	2	32	21	13
0	51	32	14	22	2	3	14	21	14
0	55	14	15	23	2	3	56	22	15
0	58	57	16	24	3	4	37	23	16
1	2	40	17	25	4	5	18	24	17
1	6	23	18	26	5	6	0	24	17
1	10	7	19	27	6	6	41	25	18
1	13	51	20	28	7	7	23	26	19
1	17	35	21	29	7	8	4	27	20
1	21	20	22	♊	8	8	45	27	21
1	25	6	23	1	9	9	27	28	22
1	28	52	24	2	10	10	9	29	23
1	32	38	25	3	11	10	51	30	24
1	36	25	26	4	11	11	33	♍	24
1	40	12	27	5	12	12	14	1	25
1	44	0	28	6	13	12	56	2	26
1	47	48	29	7	14	13	38	3	27
1	51	37	30	8	15	14	20	3	28

Sidereal Time H.	M.	S.	10 ♉ °	11 ♊ °	12 ♋ °	Ascen ♌ °	′	2 ♍ °	3 ♍ °
1	51	37	0	8	15	14	20	3	28
1	55	27	1	9	16	15	2	4	29
1	59	17	2	10	16	15	44	5	♎
2	3	8	3	11	17	16	27	6	1
2	6	59	4	12	18	17	10	7	2
2	10	51	5	13	19	17	52	7	3
2	14	44	6	14	20	18	34	8	3
2	18	37	7	15	20	19	17	9	4
2	22	31	8	16	21	20	0	10	5
2	26	25	9	17	22	20	43	11	6
2	30	20	10	18	23	21	26	11	7
2	34	16	11	19	24	22	9	12	8
2	38	13	12	20	24	22	52	13	9
2	42	10	13	21	25	23	36	14	10
2	46	8	14	22	26	24	20	15	11
2	50	7	15	23	27	25	3	16	12
2	54	7	16	23	28	25	47	16	13
2	58	7	17	24	28	26	31	17	14
3	2	8	18	25	29	27	15	18	15
3	6	9	19	26	♌	27	59	19	15
3	10	12	20	27	1	28	43	20	16
3	14	15	21	28	2	29	28	21	17
3	18	19	22	29	3	0 ♍	13	21	18
3	22	23	23	♋	3	0	57	22	19
3	26	29	24	1	4	1	42	23	20
3	30	35	25	2	5	2	27	24	21
3	34	41	26	3	6	3	13	25	22
3	38	49	27	4	7	3	58	26	23
3	42	57	28	5	7	4	43	26	24
3	47	6	29	6	8	5	29	27	25
3	51	15	30	7	9	6	15	28	26

Sidereal Time H.	M.	S.	10 ♊ °	11 ♋ °	12 ♌ °	Ascen ♍ °	′	2 ♍ °	3 ♎ °
3	51	15	0	7	9	6	15	28	26
3	55	25	1	8	10	7	1	29	27
3	59	36	2	8	11	7	47	♎	28
4	3	48	3	9	12	8	33	1	29
4	8	0	4	10	13	9	20	2	♏
4	12	13	5	11	13	10	6	2	1
4	16	26	6	12	14	10	52	3	2
4	20	40	7	13	15	11	39	4	3
4	24	55	8	14	16	12	26	5	4
4	29	10	9	15	17	13	13	6	5
4	33	26	10	16	18	14	0	7	6
4	37	42	11	17	19	14	48	8	7
4	41	59	12	18	19	15	35	9	8
4	46	16	13	19	20	16	22	10	9
4	50	34	14	20	21	17	10	10	10
4	54	52	15	21	22	17	58	11	11
4	59	10	16	22	23	18	46	12	12
5	3	29	17	23	24	19	33	13	12
5	7	49	18	24	25	20	21	14	13
5	12	9	19	24	25	21	9	15	14
5	16	29	20	25	26	21	57	16	15
5	20	49	21	26	27	22	45	17	16
5	25	9	22	27	28	23	33	18	17
5	29	30	23	28	29	24	21	18	18
5	33	51	24	29	♍	25	9	19	19
5	38	12	25	♌	1	25	58	20	20
5	42	34	26	1	2	26	46	21	21
5	46	55	27	2	3	27	34	22	22
5	51	17	28	3	3	28	23	23	23
5	55	38	29	4	4	29	11	24	24
6	0	0	30	5	5	30	0	25	25

Sidereal Time H.	M.	S.	10 ♋ °	11 ♌ °	12 ♍ °	Ascen ♎ °	′	2 ♎ °	3 ♏ °
6	0	0	0	5	5	0	0	25	25
6	4	22	1	6	6	0	49	26	26
6	8	43	2	7	7	1	37	27	27
6	13	5	3	8	8	2	26	27	28
6	17	26	4	9	9	3	14	28	29
6	21	48	5	10	10	4	2	29	♐
6	26	9	6	11	11	4	51	♏	1
6	30	30	7	12	12	5	39	1	2
6	34	51	8	13	12	6	27	2	3
6	39	11	9	14	13	7	15	3	4
6	43	31	10	15	14	8	3	4	5
6	47	51	11	16	15	8	51	5	6
6	52	11	12	17	16	9	39	5	6
6	56	31	13	18	17	10	27	6	7
7	0	50	14	18	18	11	14	7	8
7	5	8	15	19	19	12	2	8	9
7	9	26	16	20	20	12	50	9	10
7	13	44	17	21	20	13	38	10	11
7	18	1	18	22	21	14	25	11	12
7	22	18	19	23	22	15	12	11	13
7	26	34	20	24	23	16	0	12	14
7	30	50	21	25	24	16	47	13	15
7	35	5	22	26	25	17	34	14	16
7	39	20	23	27	26	18	21	15	17
7	43	34	24	28	27	19	8	16	18
7	47	47	25	29	28	19	54	17	19
7	52	0	26	♍	28	20	40	17	20
7	56	12	27	1	29	21	27	18	21
8	0	24	28	2	♎	22	13	19	22
8	4	35	29	3	1	22	59	20	22
8	8	45	30	4	2	23	45	21	23

Sidereal Time H.	M.	S.	10 ♌ °	11 ♍ °	12 ♎ °	Ascen ♎ °	′	2 ♏ °	3 ♐ °
8	8	45	0	4	2	23	45	21	23
8	12	54	1	5	3	24	31	22	24
8	17	3	2	6	4	25	17	23	25
8	21	11	3	7	4	26	2	23	26
8	25	19	4	8	5	26	47	24	27
8	29	26	5	9	6	27	33	25	28
8	33	31	6	10	7	28	18	26	29
8	37	37	7	11	8	29	3	27	♑
8	41	41	8	12	9	29	47	27	1
8	45	45	9	13	9	0 ♏	32	28	2
8	49	48	10	14	10	1	17	29	3
8	53	51	11	15	11	2	1	♐	4
8	57	52	12	15	12	2	45	1	5
9	1	53	13	16	13	3	29	2	6
9	5	53	14	17	14	4	13	2	7
9	9	53	15	18	14	4	57	3	7
9	13	52	16	19	15	5	40	4	8
9	17	50	17	20	16	6	24	5	9
9	21	47	18	21	17	7	8	6	10
9	25	44	19	22	18	7	51	6	11
9	29	40	20	23	19	8	34	7	12
9	33	35	21	24	19	9	17	8	13
9	37	29	22	25	20	10	0	9	14
9	41	23	23	26	21	10	43	10	15
9	45	16	24	27	22	11	26	10	16
9	49	9	25	27	23	12	8	11	17
9	53	1	26	28	23	12	50	12	18
9	56	52	27	29	24	13	33	13	19
10	0	42	28	♎	25	14	16	14	20
10	4	33	29	1	26	14	58	14	21
10	8	23	30	2	27	15	40	15	22

Sidereal Time H.	M.	S.	10 ♍ °	11 ♎ °	12 ♎ °	Ascen ♏ °	′	2 ♐ °	3 ♑ °
10	8	23	0	2	27	15	40	15	22
10	12	12	1	3	27	16	22	16	23
10	16	0	2	4	28	17	4	17	24
10	19	48	3	5	29	17	46	18	25
10	23	35	4	6	30	18	27	19	26
10	27	22	5	6	♏	19	9	19	27
10	31	8	6	7	1	19	51	20	28
10	34	54	7	8	2	20	33	21	29
10	38	40	8	9	3	21	15	22	♒
10	42	25	9	10	3	21	56	23	1
10	46	9	10	11	4	22	37	23	2
10	49	53	11	12	5	23	19	24	3
10	53	37	12	13	6	24	0	25	4
10	57	20	13	13	6	24	42	26	5
11	1	3	14	14	7	25	23	27	6
11	4	46	15	15	8	26	4	28	7
11	8	28	16	16	9	26	46	28	8
11	12	10	17	17	9	27	28	29	9
11	15	52	18	18	10	28	9	♑	10
11	19	34	19	19	11	28	50	1	11
11	23	15	20	19	12	29	32	2	12
11	26	56	21	20	12	0 ♐	14	3	13
11	30	37	22	21	13	0	56	4	14
11	34	18	23	22	14	1	37	4	15
11	37	58	24	23	15	2	19	5	16
11	41	39	25	24	15	3	1	6	17
11	45	19	26	25	16	3	43	7	18
11	49	0	27	25	17	4	25	8	19
11	52	40	28	26	18	5	7	9	20
11	56	20	29	27	18	5	49	10	21
12	0	0	30	28	19	6	32	11	22

TABLES OF HOUSES FOR *Latitude* 47° 29′ N.

Sidereal Time H.	M.	S.	10 ♎ °	11 ♎ °	12 ♏ °	Ascen ♐ °	′	2 ♑ °	3 ♒ °
12	0	0	0	28	19	6	32	11	22
12	3	40	1	29	20	7	15	12	23
12	7	20	2	♏	21	7	57	12	24
12	11	0	3	1	21	8	40	13	26
12	14	41	4	1	22	9	23	14	27
12	18	21	5	2	23	10	6	15	28
12	22	2	6	3	24	10	49	16	29
12	25	42	7	4	24	11	33	17	♓
12	29	23	8	5	25	12	17	18	1
12	33	4	9	6	26	13	2	19	2
12	36	45	10	6	26	13	45	20	3
12	40	26	11	7	27	14	29	21	5
12	44	8	12	8	28	15	14	22	6
12	47	50	13	9	29	16	0	23	7
12	51	32	14	10	29	16	45	24	8
12	55	14	15	11	♐	17	30	25	9
12	58	57	16	11	1	18	16	26	10
13	2	40	17	12	2	19	2	27	12
13	6	23	18	13	2	19	48	28	13
13	10	7	19	14	3	20	36	29	14
13	13	51	20	15	4	21	23	♒	15
13	17	35	21	16	5	22	11	2	16
13	21	20	22	16	6	22	59	3	18
13	25	6	23	17	6	23	48	4	19
13	28	52	24	18	7	24	37	5	20
13	32	38	25	19	8	25	26	6	21
13	36	25	26	20	9	26	16	7	22
13	40	12	27	21	9	27	6	9	24
13	44	0	28	22	10	27	57	10	25
13	47	48	29	22	11	28	49	11	26
13	51	37	30	23	12	29	41	12	27

Sidereal Time H.	M.	S.	10 ♏ °	11 ♏ °	12 ♐ °	Ascen ♐ °	′	2 ♒ °	3 ♓ °
13	51	37	0	23	12	29	41	13	27
13	55	27	1	24	13	0 ♑	34	14	28
13	59	17	2	25	13	1	27	15	♈
14	3	8	3	26	14	2	21	16	1
14	6	59	4	27	15	3	16	18	2
14	10	51	5	27	16	4	11	19	4
14	14	44	6	28	17	5	7	20	5
14	18	37	7	29	17	6	4	21	6
14	22	31	8	♐	18	7	1	23	7
14	26	25	9	1	19	8	0	24	9
14	30	20	10	2	20	8	59	26	10
14	34	16	11	3	21	9	59	27	11
14	38	13	12	3	22	11	0	29	12
14	42	10	13	4	23	12	2	♓	14
14	46	8	14	5	23	13	5	1	15
14	50	7	15	6	24	14	9	3	16
14	54	7	16	7	25	15	14	4	17
14	58	7	17	8	26	16	21	6	19
15	2	8	18	9	27	17	28	7	20
15	6	9	19	10	28	18	36	9	21
15	10	12	20	10	29	19	46	10	23
15	14	15	21	11	♑	20	57	12	24
15	18	19	22	12	1	22	10	13	25
15	22	23	23	13	2	23	24	15	26
15	26	29	24	14	3	24	39	17	27
15	30	35	25	15	4	25	56	18	29
15	34	41	26	16	4	27	14	20	♉
15	38	49	27	17	5	28	33	22	1
15	42	57	28	18	6	29	55	23	3
15	47	6	29	19	7	1 ♒	18	25	4
15	51	15	30	20	8	2	43	26	5

Sidereal Time H.	M.	S.	10 ♐ °	11 ♐ °	12 ♑ °	Ascen ♒ °	′	2 ♓ °	3 ♉ °
15	51	15	0	20	8	2	43	26	5
15	55	25	1	20	9	4	9	28	6
15	59	36	2	21	10	5	38	♈	7
16	3	48	3	22	11	7	8	1	9
16	8	0	4	23	13	8	41	3	10
16	12	13	5	24	14	10	15	5	11
16	16	26	6	25	15	11	51	7	12
16	20	40	7	26	16	13	29	8	14
16	24	55	8	27	17	15	9	10	15
16	29	10	9	28	18	16	52	12	16
16	33	26	10	29	19	18	37	13	17
16	37	42	11	♑	20	20	23	15	18
16	41	59	12	1	21	22	12	17	20
16	46	16	13	2	23	24	3	18	21
16	50	34	14	3	24	25	56	20	22
16	54	52	15	4	25	27	52	22	23
16	59	10	16	5	26	29	49	23	25
17	3	29	17	6	27	1 ♓	49	25	26
17	7	49	18	7	29	3	50	26	27
17	12	9	19	8	♒	5	54	28	28
17	16	29	20	9	1	7	58	♉	29
17	20	49	21	10	2	10	6	1	♊
17	25	9	22	11	4	12	14	3	1
17	29	30	23	12	5	14	24	4	3
17	33	51	24	13	6	16	35	6	4
17	38	12	25	14	8	18	47	8	5
17	42	34	26	15	9	21	1	9	6
17	46	55	27	16	11	23	15	11	7
17	51	17	28	17	12	25	30	12	8
17	55	38	29	19	14	27	45	13	9
18	0	0	30	20	15	30	0	15	10

Sidereal Time H.	M.	S.	10 ♑ °	11 ♑ °	12 ♒ °	Ascen ♈ °	′	2 ♉ °	3 ♊ °
18	0	0	0	20	15	0	0	15	10
18	4	22	1	21	17	2	15	16	11
18	8	43	2	22	18	4	30	18	13
18	13	5	3	23	19	6	45	19	14
18	17	26	4	24	21	8	59	21	15
18	21	48	5	25	22	11	13	22	16
18	26	9	6	26	24	13	25	24	17
18	30	30	7	27	26	15	36	25	18
18	34	51	8	29	27	17	46	26	19
18	39	11	9	♒	29	19	54	28	20
18	43	31	10	1	♓	22	2	29	21
18	47	51	11	2	2	24	6	♊	22
18	52	11	12	3	4	26	10	1	23
18	56	31	13	4	5	28	11	3	24
19	0	50	14	5	7	0 ♉	11	4	25
19	5	8	15	7	8	2	8	5	26
19	9	26	16	8	10	4	4	6	27
19	13	44	17	9	12	5	57	7	28
19	18	1	18	10	13	7	48	9	29
19	22	18	19	12	15	9	37	10	♋
19	26	34	20	13	17	11	23	11	1
19	30	50	21	14	18	13	8	12	2
19	35	5	22	15	20	14	51	13	3
19	39	20	23	16	22	16	31	14	4
19	43	34	24	18	23	18	9	15	5
19	47	47	25	19	25	19	45	16	6
19	52	0	26	20	27	21	19	17	7
19	56	12	27	21	29	22	52	19	8
20	0	24	28	23	♈	24	22	20	9
20	4	35	29	24	2	25	51	21	10
20	8	45	30	25	4	27	17	22	10

Sidereal Time H.	M.	S.	10 ♒ °	11 ♒ °	12 ♈ °	Ascen ♉ °	′	2 ♊ °	3 ♋ °
20	8	45	0	25	4	27	17	22	10
20	12	54	1	26	5	28	42	23	11
20	17	3	2	27	7	0 ♊	5	24	12
20	21	11	3	29	9	1	27	25	13
20	25	19	4	♓	10	2	46	26	14
20	29	26	5	1	12	4	4	26	15
20	33	31	6	3	13	5	21	27	16
20	37	37	7	4	15	6	36	28	17
20	41	41	8	5	17	7	50	29	18
20	45	45	9	6	18	9	3	♋	19
20	49	48	10	7	20	10	14	1	20
20	53	51	11	9	21	11	24	2	20
20	57	52	12	10	23	12	32	3	21
21	1	53	13	11	24	13	39	4	22
21	5	53	14	13	26	14	46	5	23
21	9	53	15	14	27	15	51	6	24
21	13	52	16	15	29	16	55	7	25
21	17	50	17	16	♉	17	58	7	26
21	21	47	18	18	1	19	0	8	27
21	25	44	19	19	3	20	1	9	27
21	29	40	20	20	4	21	1	10	28
21	33	35	21	21	6	22	0	11	29
21	37	29	22	23	7	22	59	12	♌
21	41	23	23	24	9	23	56	13	1
21	45	16	24	25	10	24	53	13	2
21	49	9	25	26	11	25	49	14	3
21	53	1	26	28	12	26	44	15	3
21	56	52	27	29	14	27	39	16	4
22	0	43	28	♈	15	28	33	17	5
22	4	33	29	2	16	29	26	17	6
22	8	23	30	3	18	0 ♋	19	18	7

Sidereal Time H.	M.	S.	10 ♓ °	11 ♈ °	12 ♉ °	Ascen ♋ °	′	2 ♋ °	3 ♌ °
22	8	23	0	3	18	0	19	18	7
22	12	12	1	4	19	1	11	19	8
22	16	0	2	5	20	2	3	20	8
22	19	48	3	6	21	2	54	21	9
22	23	35	4	8	23	3	44	21	10
22	27	22	5	9	24	4	34	22	11
22	31	8	6	10	25	5	23	23	12
22	34	54	7	11	26	6	12	24	13
22	38	40	8	12	27	7	1	24	14
22	42	25	9	14	28	7	49	25	14
22	46	9	10	15	♊	8	37	26	15
22	49	53	11	16	1	9	24	27	16
22	53	37	12	17	2	10	12	28	17
22	57	20	13	18	3	10	58	28	18
23	1	3	14	20	4	11	44	29	19
23	4	46	15	21	5	12	30	♌	19
23	8	28	16	22	6	13	15	1	20
23	12	10	17	23	7	14	0	1	21
23	15	52	18	24	8	14	46	2	22
23	19	34	19	25	9	15	31	3	23
23	23	15	20	27	10	16	15	4	24
23	26	56	21	28	11	16	58	4	24
23	30	37	22	29	12	17	43	5	25
23	34	18	23	♉	13	18	27	6	26
23	37	58	24	1	14	19	11	6	27
23	41	39	25	2	15	19	54	7	28
23	45	19	26	3	16	20	37	8	29
23	49	0	27	4	17	21	20	9	29
23	52	40	28	6	18	22	3	9	♍
23	56	20	29	7	18	22	45	10	1
24	0	0	30	8	19	23	28	11	2

Tables of houses for 48° 50′ N

Suitable for Winnipeg, Brandon, Lethbridge, Vancouver and New Westminster.

TABLES OF HOUSES FOR *Latitude* 48° 50′ N.

Sidereal Time H.	M.	S.	10 ♈ °	11 ♉ °	12 ♊ °	Ascen ♋ °	′	2 ♌ °	3 ♍ °
0	0	0	0	8	20	24	28	12	2
0	3	40	1	9	21	25	10	12	3
0	7	20	2	10	22	25	52	13	4
0	11	0	3	12	23	26	33	14	5
0	14	41	4	13	24	27	15	15	6
0	18	21	5	14	25	27	56	15	7
0	22	2	6	15	26	28	37	16	7
0	25	42	7	16	27	29	19	17	8
0	29	23	8	17	27	0 ♌	0	18	9
0	33	4	9	18	28	0	41	18	10
0	36	45	10	19	29	1	22	19	11
0	40	26	11	20	♋	2	3	20	12
0	44	8	12	21	1	2	44	20	12
0	47	50	13	22	2	3	25	21	13
0	51	32	14	23	2	4	5	22	14
0	55	14	15	24	3	4	46	23	15
0	58	57	16	25	4	5	27	23	16
1	2	40	17	26	5	6	8	24	17
1	6	23	18	27	6	6	49	25	18
1	10	7	19	28	7	7	30	26	18
1	13	51	20	29	7	8	11	26	19
1	17	35	21	♊	8	8	51	27	20
1	21	20	22	1	9	9	32	28	21
1	25	6	23	2	10	10	13	29	22
1	28	52	24	3	11	10	54	29	23
1	32	38	25	4	12	11	35	♍	24
1	36	25	26	5	12	12	17	1	25
1	40	12	27	6	13	12	58	2	25
1	44	0	28	7	14	13	39	2	26
1	47	48	29	8	15	14	20	3	27
1	51	37	30	9	16	15	2	4	28

Sidereal Time H.	M.	S.	10 ♉ °	11 ♊ °	12 ♋ °	Ascen ♌ °	′	2 ♍ °	3 ♍ °
1	51	37	0	9	16	15	2	4	28
1	55	27	1	10	16	15	43	5	29
1	59	17	2	11	17	16	25	6	♎
2	3	8	3	12	18	17	6	6	1
2	6	59	4	13	19	17	48	7	2
2	10	51	5	14	20	18	30	8	3
2	14	44	6	15	20	19	12	9	3
2	18	37	7	16	21	19	54	9	4
2	22	31	8	17	22	20	36	10	5
2	26	25	9	18	23	21	18	11	6
2	30	20	10	18	24	22	1	12	7
2	34	16	11	19	24	22	43	13	8
2	38	13	12	20	25	23	26	13	9
2	42	10	13	21	26	24	9	14	10
2	46	8	14	22	27	24	52	15	11
2	50	7	15	23	28	25	35	16	12
2	54	7	16	24	28	26	18	17	13
2	58	7	17	25	29	27	1	17	13
3	2	8	18	26	♌	27	45	18	14
3	6	9	19	27	1	28	28	19	15
3	10	12	20	28	2	29	12	20	16
3	14	15	21	29	2	29	56	21	17
3	18	19	22	♋	3	0 ♍	40	22	18
3	22	23	23	1	4	1	24	22	19
3	26	29	24	2	5	2	8	23	20
3	30	35	25	3	6	2	53	24	21
3	34	41	26	4	7	3	37	25	22
3	38	49	27	4	7	4	22	26	23
3	42	57	28	5	8	5	7	27	24
3	47	6	29	6	9	5	52	27	25
3	51	15	30	7	10	6	37	28	26

Sidereal Time H.	M.	S.	10 ♊ °	11 ♋ °	12 ♌ °	Ascen ♍ °	′	2 ♍ °	3 ♎ °
3	51	15	0	7	10	6	37	28	26
3	55	25	1	8	11	7	22	29	27
3	59	36	2	9	12	8	7	♎	28
4	3	48	3	10	12	8	53	1	28
4	8	0	4	11	13	9	39	2	29
4	12	13	5	12	14	10	24	2	♏
4	16	26	6	13	15	11	10	3	1
4	20	40	7	14	16	11	56	4	2
4	24	55	8	15	17	12	43	5	3
4	29	10	9	16	17	13	29	6	4
4	33	26	10	17	18	14	15	7	5
4	37	42	11	18	19	15	2	8	6
4	41	59	12	18	20	15	48	9	7
4	46	16	13	19	21	16	35	9	8
4	50	34	14	20	22	17	22	10	9
4	54	52	15	21	23	18	9	11	10
4	59	10	16	22	23	18	56	12	11
5	3	29	17	23	24	19	43	13	12
5	7	49	18	24	25	20	30	14	13
5	12	9	19	25	26	21	17	15	14
5	16	29	20	26	27	22	5	16	15
5	20	49	21	27	28	22	52	16	16
5	25	9	22	28	29	23	39	17	17
5	29	30	23	29	30	24	27	18	18
5	33	51	24	♌	♏	25	14	19	19
5	38	12	25	1	1	26	2	20	20
5	42	34	26	2	2	26	49	21	21
5	46	55	27	3	3	27	37	22	22
5	51	17	28	4	4	28	25	23	22
5	55	38	29	5	5	29	12	23	23
6	0	0	30	6	5	30	0	24	24

Sidereal Time H.	M.	S.	10 ♋ °	11 ♌ °	12 ♍ °	Ascen ♎ °	′	2 ♎ °	3 ♏ °
6	0	0	0	6	6	0	0	24	24
6	4	22	1	7	7	0	48	25	25
6	8	43	2	8	7	1	35	26	26
6	13	5	3	8	8	2	23	27	27
6	17	26	4	9	9	3	11	28	28
6	21	48	5	10	10	3	58	29	29
6	26	9	6	11	11	4	46	30	♐
6	30	30	7	12	12	5	33	♏	1
6	34	51	8	13	13	6	21	1	2
6	39	11	9	14	14	7	8	2	3
6	43	31	10	15	14	7	55	3	4
6	47	51	11	16	15	8	43	4	5
6	52	11	12	17	16	9	30	5	6
6	56	31	13	18	17	10	17	6	7
7	0	50	14	19	18	11	4	7	8
7	5	8	15	20	19	11	51	7	9
7	9	26	16	21	20	12	38	8	10
7	13	44	17	22	21	13	25	9	11
7	18	1	18	23	21	14	12	10	12
7	22	18	19	24	22	14	58	11	13
7	26	34	20	25	23	15	45	12	13
7	30	50	21	26	24	16	31	13	14
7	35	5	22	27	25	17	17	13	15
7	39	20	23	28	26	18	4	14	16
7	43	34	24	29	27	18	50	15	17
7	47	47	25	♍	28	19	36	16	18
7	52	0	26	1	28	20	21	17	19
7	56	12	27	2	29	21	7	18	20
8	0	24	28	3	♎	21	53	18	21
8	4	35	29	3	1	22	38	19	22
8	8	45	30	4	2	23	23	20	23

Sidereal Time H.	M.	S.	10 ♌ °	11 ♍ °	12 ♎ °	Ascen ♎ °	′	2 ♏ °	3 ♐ °
8	8	45	0	4	2	23	23	20	23
8	12	54	1	5	3	24	8	21	24
8	17	3	2	6	3	24	53	22	25
8	21	11	3	7	4	25	38	23	26
8	25	19	4	8	5	26	23	23	27
8	29	26	5	9	6	27	7	24	27
8	33	31	6	10	7	27	52	25	28
8	37	37	7	11	8	28	36	26	29
8	41	41	8	12	8	29	20	27	♑
8	45	45	9	13	9	0 ♏	4	28	1
8	49	48	10	14	10	0	48	28	2
8	53	51	11	15	11	1	32	29	3
8	57	52	12	16	12	2	15	♐	4
9	1	53	13	17	13	2	59	1	5
9	5	53	14	17	13	3	42	2	6
9	9	53	15	18	14	4	25	2	7
9	13	52	16	19	15	5	8	3	8
9	17	50	17	20	16	5	51	4	9
9	21	47	18	21	17	6	34	5	10
9	25	44	19	22	17	7	17	6	11
9	29	40	20	23	18	7	59	6	12
9	33	35	21	24	19	8	42	7	13
9	37	29	22	25	20	9	24	8	13
9	41	23	23	26	21	10	6	9	14
9	45	16	24	27	21	10	48	10	15
9	49	9	25	27	22	11	30	10	16
9	53	1	26	28	23	12	12	11	17
9	56	52	27	29	24	12	54	12	18
10	0	42	28	♎	24	13	35	13	19
10	4	33	29	1	25	14	17	14	20
10	8	23	30	2	26	14	58	14	21

Sidereal Time H.	M.	S.	10 ♍ °	11 ♎ °	12 ♎ °	Ascen ♏ °	′	2 ♐ °	3 ♑ °
10	8	23	0	2	26	14	58	14	21
10	12	12	1	3	27	15	40	15	22
10	16	0	2	4	28	16	21	16	23
10	19	48	3	5	28	17	2	17	24
10	23	35	4	5	29	17	43	18	25
10	27	22	5	6	♏	18	25	19	26
10	31	8	6	7	1	19	6	19	27
10	34	54	7	8	1	19	47	20	28
10	38	40	8	9	2	20	28	21	29
10	42	25	9	10	3	21	9	22	♒
10	46	9	10	11	4	21	50	23	1
10	49	53	11	12	4	22	30	23	2
10	53	37	12	12	5	23	11	24	3
10	57	20	13	13	6	23	52	25	4
11	1	3	14	14	7	24	33	26	5
11	4	46	15	15	7	25	14	27	6
11	8	28	16	16	8	25	55	28	7
11	12	10	17	17	9	26	36	28	8
11	15	52	18	18	9	27	16	29	9
11	19	34	19	18	10	27	57	♑	10
11	23	15	20	19	11	28	38	1	11
11	26	56	21	20	12	29	19	2	12
11	30	37	22	21	12	0 ♐	0	3	13
11	34	18	23	22	13	0	41	3	14
11	37	58	24	23	14	1	23	4	15
11	41	39	25	23	15	2	4	5	16
11	45	19	26	24	15	2	45	6	17
11	49	0	27	25	16	3	27	7	18
11	52	40	28	26	17	4	8	8	20
11	56	20	29	27	18	4	50	9	21
12	0	0	30	28	18	5	32	10	22

TABLES OF HOUSES FOR *Latitude* 48° 50′ N.

Sidereal Time H.	M.	S.	10 ♎ °	11 ♎ °	12 ♏ °	Ascen ♐ °	′	2 ♑ °	3 ♒ °
12	0	0	0	28	18	5	32	10	22
12	3	40	1	28	19	6	13	11	23
12	7	20	2	29	20	6	55	11	24
12	11	0	3	♏	21	7	38	12	25
12	14	41	4	1	21	8	20	13	26
12	18	21	5	2	22	9	3	14	27
12	22	2	6	3	23	9	45	15	28
12	25	42	7	3	24	10	28	16	29
12	29	23	8	4	24	11	11	17	♓
12	33	4	9	5	25	11	55	18	2
12	36	45	10	6	26	12	38	19	3
12	40	26	11	7	27	13	22	20	4
12	44	8	12	8	27	14	6	21	5
12	47	50	13	8	28	14	50	22	6
12	51	32	14	9	29	15	35	23	8
12	55	14	15	10	29	16	20	24	9
12	58	57	16	11	♐	17	5	25	10
13	2	40	17	12	1	17	50	26	11
13	6	23	18	13	2	18	37	27	12
13	10	7	19	13	2	19	23	28	14
13	13	51	20	14	3	20	9	29	15
13	17	35	21	15	4	20	56	♒	16
13	21	20	22	16	5	21	44	2	17
13	25	6	23	17	5	22	31	3	18
13	28	52	24	18	6	23	20	4	20
13	32	38	25	18	7	24	8	5	21
13	36	25	26	19	8	24	58	6	22
13	40	12	27	20	9	25	47	8	23
13	44	0	28	21	9	26	38	9	25
13	47	48	29	22	10	27	28	10	26
13	51	37	30	23	11	28	20	11	27

Sidereal Time H.	M.	S.	10 ♏ °	11 ♏ °	12 ♐ °	Ascen ♐ °	′	2 ♒ °	3 ♓ °
13	51	37	0	23	11	28	20	11	27
13	55	27	1	23	12	29	12	12	28
13	59	17	2	24	13	0 ♑	4	14	♈
14	3	8	3	25	13	0	57	15	1
14	6	59	4	26	14	1	51	16	2
14	10	51	5	27	15	2	46	18	4
14	14	44	6	28	16	3	41	19	5
14	18	37	7	29	17	4	37	20	6
14	22	31	8	29	17	5	34	22	7
14	26	25	9	♐	18	6	32	23	9
14	30	20	10	1	19	7	30	25	10
14	34	16	11	2	20	8	30	26	11
14	38	13	12	3	21	9	30	27	13
14	42	10	13	4	22	10	32	29	14
14	46	8	14	5	23	11	34	♓	15
14	50	7	15	5	23	12	37	2	16
14	54	7	16	6	24	13	42	3	18
14	58	7	17	7	25	14	47	5	19
15	2	8	18	8	26	15	54	7	20
15	6	9	19	9	27	17	2	8	22
15	10	12	20	10	28	18	11	10	23
15	14	15	21	11	29	19	22	11	24
15	18	19	22	12	♑	20	34	13	25
15	22	23	23	13	1	21	47	15	27
15	26	29	24	13	2	23	2	16	28
15	30	35	25	14	3	24	19	18	29
15	34	41	26	15	4	25	37	20	♉
15	38	49	27	16	4	26	56	21	2
15	42	57	28	17	5	28	18	23	3
15	47	6	29	18	6	29	41	25	4
15	51	15	30	19	7	1 ♒	6	26	6

Sidereal Time H.	M.	S.	10 ♐ °	11 ♐ °	12 ♑ °	Ascen ♒ °	′	2 ♓ °	3 ♉ °
15	51	15	0	19	7	1	6	26	6
15	55	25	1	20	8	2	33	28	7
15	59	36	2	21	9	4	1	♈	8
16	3	48	3	22	11	5	32	2	9
16	8	0	4	23	12	7	5	3	11
16	12	13	5	24	13	8	40	5	12
16	16	26	6	25	14	10	17	7	13
16	20	40	7	25	15	11	57	9	14
16	24	55	8	26	16	13	39	10	15
16	29	10	9	27	17	15	23	12	17
16	33	26	10	28	18	17	9	14	18
16	37	42	11	29	19	18	58	15	19
16	41	59	12	♑	20	20	49	17	20
16	46	16	13	1	22	22	43	19	22
16	50	34	14	2	23	24	38	21	23
16	54	52	15	3	24	26	37	22	24
16	59	10	16	4	25	28	38	24	25
17	3	29	17	5	26	0 ♓	41	26	26
17	7	49	18	6	28	2	46	27	28
17	12	9	19	7	29	4	53	29	29
17	16	29	20	8	♒	7	3	♉	♊
17	20	49	21	9	2	9	14	2	1
17	25	9	22	10	3	11	28	4	2
17	29	30	23	11	4	13	43	5	3
17	33	51	24	13	6	16	0	7	4
17	38	12	25	14	7	18	17	8	6
17	42	34	26	15	8	20	37	10	7
17	46	55	27	16	10	22	57	11	8
17	51	17	28	17	11	25	17	13	9
17	55	38	29	18	13	27	39	14	10
18	0	0	30	19	14	30	0	16	11

Sidereal Time H.	M.	S.	10 ♑ °	11 ♑ °	12 ♒ °	Ascen ♈ °	′	2 ♉ °	3 ♊ °
18	0	0	0	19	14	0	0	16	11
18	4	22	1	20	15	2	21	17	12
18	8	43	2	21	17	4	43	19	13
18	13	5	3	22	18	7	3	20	14
18	17	26	4	23	20	9	23	22	15
18	21	48	5	24	22	11	43	23	16
18	26	9	6	26	23	14	0	24	17
18	30	30	7	27	25	16	17	26	18
18	34	51	8	28	26	18	32	27	20
18	39	11	9	29	28	20	46	28	21
18	43	31	10	♒	29	22	57	♊	22
18	47	51	11	1	♓	25	7	1	23
18	52	11	12	2	3	27	14	2	24
18	56	31	13	4	4	29	19	4	25
19	0	50	14	5	6	1 ♉	22	5	26
19	5	8	15	6	8	3	23	6	27
19	9	26	16	7	9	5	22	7	28
19	13	44	17	8	11	7	17	8	29
19	18	1	18	10	13	9	11	10	♋
19	22	18	19	11	15	11	2	11	1
19	26	34	20	12	16	12	51	12	2
19	30	50	21	13	18	14	37	13	3
19	35	5	22	14	20	16	21	14	4
19	39	20	23	16	22	18	3	15	5
19	43	34	24	17	23	19	43	16	5
19	47	47	25	18	25	21	20	17	6
19	52	0	26	19	27	22	55	18	7
19	56	12	27	21	28	24	28	19	8
20	0	24	28	22	♈	25	59	20	9
20	4	35	29	23	2	27	27	21	10
20	8	45	30	24	4	28	54	22	11

Sidereal Time H.	M.	S.	10 ♒ °	11 ♒ °	12 ♈ °	Ascen ♉ °	′	2 ♊ °	3 ♋ °
20	8	45	0	24	4	28	54	22	11
20	12	54	1	26	5	0 ♊	19	23	12
20	17	3	2	27	7	1	42	24	13
20	21	11	3	28	9	3	4	25	14
20	25	19	4	29	10	4	23	26	15
20	29	26	5	♓	12	5	41	27	16
20	33	31	6	2	14	6	58	28	17
20	37	37	7	3	15	8	13	29	18
20	41	41	8	5	17	9	26	♋	18
20	45	45	9	6	19	10	38	1	19
20	49	48	10	7	20	11	49	2	20
20	53	51	11	8	22	12	58	3	21
20	57	52	12	10	23	14	6	4	22
21	1	53	13	11	25	15	13	5	23
21	5	53	14	12	27	16	18	6	24
21	9	53	15	14	28	17	23	7	25
21	13	52	16	15	♉	18	26	7	25
21	17	50	17	16	1	19	29	8	26
21	21	47	18	17	3	20	30	9	27
21	25	44	19	19	4	21	30	10	28
21	29	40	20	20	5	22	30	11	29
21	33	35	21	21	7	23	28	12	♌
21	37	29	22	23	8	24	26	13	1
21	41	23	23	24	10	25	23	13	2
21	45	16	24	25	11	26	19	14	2
21	49	9	25	26	12	27	14	15	3
21	53	1	26	28	14	28	9	16	4
21	56	52	27	29	15	29	3	17	5
22	0	43	28	♈	16	29	56	17	6
22	4	33	29	2	18	0 ♋	48	18	7
22	8	23	30	3	19	1	40	19	7

Sidereal Time H.	M.	S.	10 ♓ °	11 ♈ °	12 ♉ °	Ascen ♋ °	′	2 ♋ °	3 ♌ °
22	8	23	0	3	19	1	40	19	7
22	12	12	1	4	20	2	32	20	8
22	16	0	2	5	21	3	22	21	9
22	19	48	3	7	22	4	13	21	10
22	23	35	4	8	24	5	2	22	11
22	27	22	5	9	25	5	52	23	12
22	31	8	6	10	26	6	40	24	12
22	34	54	7	12	27	7	29	25	13
22	38	40	8	13	28	8	16	25	14
22	42	25	9	14	29	9	4	26	15
22	46	9	10	15	♊	9	51	27	16
22	49	53	11	16	2	10	37	28	17
22	53	37	12	18	3	11	23	28	17
22	57	20	13	19	4	12	10	29	18
23	1	3	14	20	5	12	55	♌	19
23	4	46	15	21	6	13	40	1	20
23	8	28	16	22	7	14	25	1	21
23	12	10	17	24	8	15	10	2	22
23	15	52	18	25	9	15	54	3	22
23	19	34	19	26	10	16	38	4	23
23	23	15	20	27	11	17	22	4	24
23	26	56	21	28	12	18	5	5	25
23	30	37	22	29	13	18	49	6	26
23	34	18	23	♉	14	19	32	7	27
23	37	58	24	2	15	20	15	7	27
23	41	39	25	3	16	20	57	8	28
23	45	19	26	4	17	21	40	9	29
23	49	0	27	5	18	22	22	9	♍
23	52	40	28	6	19	23	5	10	1
23	56	20	29	7	19	23	47	11	2
24	0	0	30	8	20	24	28	12	2

Tables of houses for 50° 22′ N

Suitable for Regina, Calgary, Banff and Kamloops.

TABLES OF HOUSES FOR — *Latitude 50° 22′ N.*

Sidereal Time H.	M.	S.	10 ♈ °	11 ♉ °	12 ♊ °	Ascen ♋ °	Ascen ′	2 ♌ °	3 ♍ °
0	0	0	0	8	22	25	40	12	2
0	3	40	1	9	23	26	21	13	3
0	7	20	2	11	23	27	2	14	4
0	11	1	3	12	24	27	42	14	5
0	14	41	4	13	25	28	23	15	6
0	18	21	5	14	26	29	3	16	7
0	22	2	6	15	27	29	44	17	7
0	25	42	7	16	28	0 ♌	24	17	8
0	29	23	8	17	29	1	5	18	9
0	33	4	9	18	29	1	45	19	10
0	36	45	10	19	♋	2	25	19	11
0	40	27	11	20	1	3	5	20	12
0	44	8	12	21	2	3	46	21	12
0	47	50	13	22	3	4	26	22	13
0	51	32	14	23	4	5	6	22	14
0	55	14	15	24	4	5	46	23	15
0	58	57	16	25	5	6	26	24	16
1	2	40	17	26	6	7	6	25	17
1	6	24	18	27	7	7	46	25	18
1	10	7	19	28	8	8	26	26	18
1	13	51	20	29	9	9	6	27	19
1	17	36	21	♊	9	9	47	27	20
1	21	21	22	1	10	10	27	28	21
1	25	6	23	2	11	11	7	29	22
1	28	52	24	3	12	11	47	♍	23
1	32	38	25	4	13	12	28	0	24
1	36	25	26	5	13	13	8	1	25
1	40	13	27	6	14	13	48	2	25
1	44	1	28	7	15	14	29	3	26
1	47	49	29	8	16	15	10	3	27
1	51	38	30	9	17	15	50	4	28

Sidereal Time H.	M.	S.	10 ♉ °	11 ♊ °	12 ♋ °	Ascen ♌ °	Ascen ′	2 ♍ °	3 ♍ °
1	51	38	0	9	17	15	50	4	28
1	55	28	1	10	17	16	31	5	29
1	59	18	2	11	18	17	12	6	♎
2	3	8	3	12	19	17	53	7	1
2	7	0	4	13	20	18	34	7	2
2	10	52	5	14	20	19	15	8	3
2	14	44	6	15	21	19	56	9	3
2	18	37	7	16	22	20	37	10	4
2	22	31	8	17	23	21	19	10	5
2	26	26	9	18	24	22	0	11	6
2	30	21	10	19	24	22	42	12	7
2	34	17	11	20	25	23	24	13	8
2	38	14	12	21	26	24	5	14	9
2	42	11	13	22	27	24	47	14	10
2	46	9	14	23	28	25	30	15	11
2	50	9	15	24	28	26	12	16	12
2	54	7	16	25	29	26	54	17	13
2	58	8	17	25	♌	27	37	18	13
3	2	8	18	26	1	28	19	18	14
3	6	10	19	27	2	29	2	19	15
3	10	12	20	28	2	29	45	20	16
3	14	16	21	29	3	0 ♍	28	21	17
3	18	19	22	♋	4	1	11	22	18
3	22	24	23	1	5	1	55	22	19
3	26	29	24	2	6	2	38	23	20
3	30	35	25	3	6	3	22	24	21
3	34	42	26	4	7	4	6	25	22
3	38	49	27	5	8	4	50	26	23
3	42	57	28	6	9	5	34	27	24
3	47	6	29	7	10	6	18	27	25
3	51	16	30	8	10	7	2	28	26

Sidereal Time H.	M.	S.	10 ♊ °	11 ♋ °	12 ♌ °	Ascen ♍ °	Ascen ′	2 ♍ °	3 ♎ °
3	51	16	0	8	10	7	2	28	26
3	55	26	1	9	11	7	47	29	27
3	59	37	2	9	12	8	31	♎	28
4	3	48	3	10	13	9	16	1	28
4	8	1	4	11	14	10	1	2	29
4	12	13	5	12	15	10	46	2	♏
4	16	27	6	13	15	11	31	3	1
4	20	41	7	14	16	12	16	4	2
4	24	55	8	15	17	13	1	5	3
4	29	11	9	16	18	13	47	6	4
4	33	26	10	17	19	14	32	7	5
4	37	42	11	18	20	15	18	8	6
4	41	59	12	19	20	16	4	8	7
4	46	17	13	20	21	16	50	9	8
4	50	34	14	21	22	17	36	10	9
4	54	52	15	22	23	18	22	11	10
4	59	11	16	23	24	19	8	12	11
5	3	30	17	23	25	19	54	13	12
5	7	49	18	24	26	20	40	14	13
5	12	9	19	25	26	21	27	15	14
5	16	29	20	26	27	22	13	15	15
5	20	49	21	27	28	23	0	16	16
5	25	10	22	28	29	23	46	17	17
5	29	30	23	29	♍	24	33	18	18
5	33	51	24	♌	1	25	20	19	19
5	38	13	25	1	2	26	6	20	19
5	42	34	26	2	2	26	53	21	20
5	46	55	27	3	3	27	40	21	21
5	51	17	28	4	4	28	26	22	22
5	55	38	29	5	5	29	13	23	23
6	0	0	30	6	6	30	0	24	24

Sidereal Time H.	M.	S.	10 ♋ °	11 ♌ °	12 ♍ °	Ascen ♎ °	Ascen ′	2 ♎ °	3 ♏ °
6	0	0	0	6	6	0	0	24	24
6	4	22	1	7	7	0	47	25	25
6	8	43	2	8	8	1	34	26	26
6	13	5	3	9	9	2	20	27	27
6	17	26	4	10	9	3	7	28	28
6	21	47	5	11	10	3	54	28	29
6	26	9	6	11	11	4	40	29	♐
6	30	30	7	12	12	5	27	♏	1
6	34	50	8	13	13	6	14	1	2
6	39	11	9	14	14	7	0	2	3
6	43	31	10	15	15	7	47	3	4
6	47	51	11	16	15	8	33	4	5
6	52	11	12	17	16	9	20	4	6
6	56	30	13	18	17	10	6	5	7
7	0	49	14	19	18	10	52	6	7
7	5	8	15	20	19	11	38	7	8
7	9	26	16	21	20	12	24	8	9
7	13	43	17	22	21	13	10	9	10
7	18	1	18	23	22	13	56	10	11
7	22	18	19	24	22	14	42	10	12
7	26	34	20	25	23	15	28	11	13
7	30	49	21	26	24	16	13	12	14
7	35	5	22	27	25	16	59	13	15
7	39	19	23	28	26	17	44	14	16
7	43	33	24	29	27	18	29	15	17
7	47	47	25	♍	28	19	14	15	18
7	51	59	26	1	28	19	59	16	19
7	56	12	27	2	29	20	44	17	20
8	0	23	28	2	♎	21	29	18	21
8	4	34	29	3	1	22	13	19	21
8	8	44	30	4	2	22	58	20	22

Sidereal Time H.	M.	S.	10 ♌ °	11 ♍ °	12 ♎ °	Ascen ♎ °	Ascen ′	2 ♏ °	3 ♐ °
8	8	44	0	4	2	22	58	20	22
8	12	54	1	5	3	23	42	20	23
8	17	3	2	6	3	24	26	21	24
8	21	11	3	7	4	25	10	22	25
8	25	19	4	8	5	25	54	23	26
8	29	25	5	9	6	26	38	24	27
8	33	31	6	10	7	27	22	24	28
8	37	36	7	11	8	28	5	25	29
8	41	41	8	12	8	28	49	26	♑
8	45	44	9	13	9	29	32	27	1
8	49	48	10	14	10	0 ♏	15	28	2
8	53	50	11	15	11	0	58	28	3
8	57	52	12	16	12	1	41	29	4
9	1	52	13	17	12	2	23	♐	5
9	5	53	14	17	13	3	6	1	5
9	9	51	15	18	14	3	48	2	6
9	13	51	16	19	15	4	30	2	7
9	17	49	17	20	16	5	13	3	8
9	21	46	18	21	16	5	55	4	9
9	25	43	19	22	17	6	36	5	10
9	29	39	20	23	18	7	18	6	11
9	33	34	21	24	19	8	0	6	12
9	37	29	22	25	20	8	41	7	13
9	41	23	23	26	20	9	23	8	14
9	45	16	24	27	21	10	4	9	15
9	49	8	25	27	22	10	45	10	16
9	53	0	26	28	23	11	26	10	17
9	56	52	27	29	23	12	7	11	18
10	0	42	28	♎	24	12	48	12	19
10	4	32	29	1	25	13	29	13	20
10	8	22	30	2	26	14	10	13	21

Sidereal Time H.	M.	S.	10 ♍ °	11 ♎ °	12 ♎ °	Ascen ♏ °	Ascen ′	2 ♐ °	3 ♑ °
10	8	22	0	2	26	14	10	13	21
10	12	11	1	3	27	14	50	14	22
10	15	59	2	4	27	15	31	15	23
10	19	47	3	5	28	16	12	16	24
10	23	35	4	5	29	16	52	17	25
10	27	22	5	6	♏	17	32	17	26
10	31	8	6	7	0	18	13	18	27
10	34	54	7	8	1	18	53	19	28
10	38	39	8	9	2	19	33	20	29
10	42	24	9	10	3	20	13	21	♒
10	46	9	10	11	3	20	54	21	1
10	49	53	11	12	4	21	34	22	2
10	53	36	12	12	5	22	14	23	3
10	57	20	13	13	5	22	54	24	4
11	1	3	14	14	6	23	34	25	5
11	4	46	15	15	7	24	14	26	6
11	8	28	16	16	8	24	54	26	7
11	12	10	17	17	8	25	34	27	8
11	15	52	18	18	9	26	14	28	9
11	19	33	19	18	10	26	55	29	10
11	23	15	20	19	11	27	35	♑	11
11	26	56	21	20	11	28	15	1	12
11	30	37	22	21	12	28	55	1	13
11	34	18	23	22	13	29	36	2	14
11	37	58	24	23	13	0 ♐	16	3	15
11	41	39	25	23	14	0	57	4	16
11	45	19	26	24	15	1	37	5	17
11	48	59	27	25	16	2	18	6	18
11	52	40	28	26	16	2	58	7	19
11	56	20	29	27	17	3	39	7	21
12	0	0	30	28	18	4	20	8	22

TABLES OF HOUSES FOR — *Latitude 50° 22′. N.*

Sidereal Time H.	M.	S.	10 ♎ °	11 ♎ °	12 ♏ °	Ascen ♐ °	Ascen ′	2 ♑ °	3 ♒ °
12	0	0	0	28	18	4	20	8	22
12	3	40	1	28	19	5	1	9	23
12	7	20	2	29	19	5	43	10	24
12	11	1	3	♏	20	6	24	11	25
12	14	41	4	1	21	7	5	12	26
12	18	21	5	2	21	7	47	13	27
12	22	2	6	3	22	8	29	14	28
12	25	42	7	3	23	9	11	15	29
12	29	23	8	4	24	9	53	16	♓
12	33	4	9	5	24	10	36	17	2
12	36	45	10	6	25	11	18	18	3
12	40	27	11	7	26	12	1	19	4
12	44	8	12	8	27	12	45	20	5
12	47	50	13	8	27	13	28	21	6
12	51	32	14	9	28	14	12	22	8
12	55	14	15	10	29	14	56	23	9
12	58	57	16	11	29	15	40	24	10
13	2	40	17	12	♐	16	25	25	11
13	6	24	18	12	1	17	10	26	12
13	10	7	19	13	2	17	55	27	14
13	13	51	20	14	2	18	41	28	15
13	17	36	21	15	3	19	27	♒	16
13	21	21	22	16	4	20	13	1	17
13	25	6	23	17	5	21	0	2	19
13	28	52	24	17	5	21	47	3	20
13	32	38	25	18	6	22	35	4	21
13	36	25	26	19	7	23	23	5	22
13	40	13	27	20	8	24	12	7	23
13	44	1	28	21	8	25	1	8	25
13	47	49	29	22	9	25	51	9	26
13	51	38	30	22	10	26	42	10	27

Sidereal Time H.	M.	S.	10 ♏ °	11 ♏ °	12 ♐ °	Ascen ♐ °	Ascen ′	2 ♒ °	3 ♓ °
13	51	38	0	22	10	26	42	10	27
13	55	28	1	23	11	27	33	12	28
13	59	18	2	24	12	28	24	13	♈
14	3	8	3	25	12	29	16	14	1
14	7	0	4	26	13	0 ♑	9	16	2
14	10	52	5	27	14	1	3	17	4
14	14	44	6	27	15	1	57	18	5
14	18	37	7	28	16	2	52	20	6
14	22	31	8	29	16	3	48	21	7
14	26	26	9	♐	17	4	45	22	9
14	30	21	10	1	18	5	42	24	10
14	34	17	11	2	19	6	41	25	11
14	38	14	12	3	20	7	40	27	13
14	42	11	13	3	21	8	40	28	14
14	46	9	14	4	21	9	42	♓	15
14	50	9	15	5	22	10	44	1	16
14	54	7	16	6	23	11	48	3	18
14	58	8	17	7	24	12	52	5	19
15	2	8	18	8	25	13	58	6	20
15	6	10	19	9	26	15	5	8	22
15	10	12	20	10	27	16	14	9	23
15	14	16	21	10	28	17	24	11	24
15	18	19	22	11	29	18	35	13	26
15	22	24	23	12	29	19	48	14	27
15	26	29	24	13	♑	21	2	16	28
15	30	35	25	14	1	22	18	18	29
15	34	42	26	15	2	23	35	19	♉
15	38	49	27	16	3	24	54	21	2
15	42	57	28	17	4	26	15	23	3
15	47	6	29	18	5	27	39	25	4
15	51	16	30	19	6	29	4	26	6

Sidereal Time H.	M.	S.	10 ♐ °	11 ♐ °	12 ♑ °	Ascen ♑ °	Ascen ′	2 ♓ °	3 ♉ °
15	51	16	0	19	6	29	4	26	6
15	55	26	1	19	7	0 ♒	31	28	7
15	59	37	2	20	8	2	0	♈	8
16	3	48	3	21	9	3	31	2	10
16	8	1	4	22	10	5	4	3	11
16	12	13	5	23	11	6	40	5	12
16	16	27	6	24	13	8	18	7	13
16	20	41	7	25	14	9	59	9	15
16	24	55	8	26	15	11	42	10	16
16	29	11	9	27	16	13	28	12	17
16	33	26	10	28	17	15	16	14	18
16	37	42	11	29	18	17	7	16	19
16	41	59	12	♑	19	19	1	17	21
16	46	17	13	1	20	20	58	19	22
16	50	34	14	2	22	22	57	21	23
16	54	52	15	3	23	24	59	23	24
16	59	11	16	4	24	27	4	24	25
17	3	30	17	5	25	29	11	26	27
17	7	49	18	6	27	1 ♓	21	28	28
17	12	9	19	7	28	3	34	29	29
17	16	29	20	8	29	5	49	♉	♊
17	20	49	21	9	♒	8	7	3	1
17	25	10	22	10	2	10	27	4	3
17	29	30	23	11	3	12	49	6	4
17	33	51	24	12	5	15	13	8	5
17	38	13	25	13	6	17	38	9	6
17	42	34	26	14	7	20	4	11	7
17	46	55	27	15	9	22	32	12	8
17	51	17	28	16	10	25	1	14	9
17	55	38	29	17	12	27	30	15	10
18	0	0	30	19	13	30	0	17	11

Sidereal Time H.	M.	S.	10 ♑ °	11 ♑ °	12 ♒ °	Ascen ♈ °	Ascen ′	2 ♉ °	3 ♊ °
18	0	0	0	19	13	0	0	17	11
18	4	22	1	20	15	2	30	18	13
18	8	43	2	21	16	4	59	20	14
18	13	5	3	22	18	7	28	21	15
18	17	26	4	23	19	9	56	23	16
18	21	47	5	24	21	12	22	24	17
18	26	9	6	25	22	14	47	25	18
18	30	30	7	26	24	17	11	27	19
18	34	50	8	28	26	19	33	28	20
18	39	11	9	29	27	21	53	♊	21
18	43	31	10	♒	29	24	11	1	22
18	47	51	11	1	♓	26	26	2	23
18	52	11	12	2	2	28	39	3	24
18	56	30	13	3	4	0 ♉	49	5	25
19	0	49	14	5	6	2	56	6	26
19	5	8	15	6	7	5	1	7	27
19	9	26	16	7	9	7	3	8	28
19	13	43	17	8	11	9	2	10	29
19	18	1	18	9	13	10	59	11	♋
19	22	18	19	11	14	12	53	12	1
19	26	34	20	12	16	14	44	13	2
19	30	49	21	13	18	16	32	14	3
19	35	5	22	14	20	18	18	15	4
19	39	10	23	15	21	20	1	16	5
19	43	33	24	17	23	21	42	17	6
19	47	47	25	18	25	23	20	19	7
19	51	59	26	19	27	24	56	20	8
19	56	12	27	20	28	26	29	21	9
20	0	23	28	22	♈	28	0	22	10
20	4	34	29	23	2	29	29	23	11
20	8	44	30	24	4	0 ♊	56	24	11

Sidereal Time H.	M.	S.	10 ♒ °	11 ♒ °	12 ♈ °	Ascen ♊ °	Ascen ′	2 ♊ °	3 ♋ °
20	8	44	0	24	4	0	56	24	11
20	12	54	1	26	5	2	21	25	12
20	17	3	2	27	7	3	45	26	13
20	21	11	3	28	9	5	6	27	14
20	25	18	4	29	11	6	25	28	15
20	29	25	5	♓	12	7	42	29	16
20	33	31	6	2	14	8	58	♋	17
20	37	36	7	3	16	10	12	1	18
20	41	41	8	4	17	11	25	1	19
20	45	44	9	6	19	12	36	2	20
20	49	48	10	7	21	13	46	3	20
20	53	50	11	8	22	14	55	4	21
20	57	52	12	10	24	16	2	5	22
21	1	52	13	11	25	17	8	6	23
21	5	53	14	12	27	18	12	7	24
21	9	51	15	14	29	19	16	8	25
21	13	51	16	15	♉	20	18	9	26
21	17	49	17	16	2	21	20	9	27
21	21	46	18	17	3	22	20	10	27
21	25	43	19	19	5	23	19	11	28
21	29	39	20	20	6	24	18	12	29
21	33	34	21	21	8	25	15	13	♌
21	37	29	22	22	9	26	12	14	1
21	41	23	23	24	10	27	8	14	2
21	45	16	24	25	12	28	3	15	3
21	49	8	25	26	13	28	57	16	3
21	53	0	26	28	14	29	51	17	4
21	56	52	27	29	16	0 ♋	44	18	5
22	0	42	28	♈	17	1	36	18	6
22	4	32	29	2	18	2	27	19	7
22	8	22	30	3	20	3	18	20	8

Sidereal Time H.	M.	S.	10 ♓ °	11 ♈ °	12 ♉ °	Ascen ♋ °	Ascen ′	2 ♋ °	3 ♌ °
22	8	22	0	3	20	3	18	20	8
22	12	11	1	4	21	4	9	21	8
22	15	59	2	5	22	4	59	22	9
22	19	47	3	7	23	5	48	22	10
22	23	35	4	8	25	6	37	23	11
22	27	22	5	9	26	7	25	24	12
22	31	8	6	10	27	8	13	25	13
22	34	54	7	11	28	9	0	25	13
22	38	39	8	13	29	9	47	26	14
22	42	24	9	14	♊	10	33	27	15
22	46	9	10	15	2	11	19	28	16
22	49	53	11	16	3	12	5	28	17
22	53	36	12	18	4	12	50	29	18
22	57	20	13	19	5	13	35	♌	18
23	1	3	14	20	6	14	20	1	19
23	4	46	15	21	7	15	4	1	20
23	8	28	16	22	8	15	48	2	21
23	12	10	17	24	9	16	32	3	22
23	15	52	18	25	10	17	15	3	22
23	19	33	19	26	11	17	59	4	23
23	23	15	20	27	12	18	42	5	24
23	26	56	21	28	13	19	24	6	25
23	30	37	22	29	14	20	7	6	26
23	34	18	23	♉	15	20	49	7	27
23	37	58	24	2	16	21	31	8	27
23	41	39	25	3	17	22	13	9	28
23	45	19	26	4	18	22	55	9	29
23	48	59	27	5	19	23	36	10	♍
23	52	40	28	6	20	24	17	11	1
23	56	20	29	7	21	24	59	11	2
24	0	0	30	8	22	25	40	12	2

Tables of houses for 53° 45′ N
Suitable for Edmonton and Prince Rupert.

TABLES OF HOUSES FOR *Latitude 53° 45′ N.*

H.	M.	S.	10 ♈ °	11 ♉ °	12 ♊ °	Ascen ♋ °	′	2 ♌ °	3 ♍ °
0	0	0	0	10	25	28	29	14	3
0	3	40	1	11	26	29	8	15	4
0	7	20	2	12	27	29	47	16	5
0	11	1	3	13	28	0 ♌	26	16	6
0	14	41	4	14	29	1	5	17	6
0	18	21	5	15	29	1	43	18	7
0	22	2	6	16	♋	2	22	18	8
0	25	42	7	18	1	3	0	19	9
0	29	23	8	19	2	3	39	20	10
0	33	4	9	20	3	4	17	21	11
0	36	45	10	21	4	4	55	21	11
0	40	27	11	22	4	5	34	22	12
0	44	8	12	23	5	6	12	23	13
0	47	50	13	24	6	6	50	23	14
0	51	32	14	25	7	7	28	24	15
0	55	14	15	26	8	8	7	25	15
0	58	57	16	27	8	8	45	25	16
1	2	40	17	28	9	9	23	26	17
1	6	24	18	29	10	10	1	27	18
1	10	7	19	♊	11	10	40	28	19
1	13	51	20	1	12	11	18	28	20
1	17	36	21	2	12	11	56	29	20
1	21	21	22	3	13	12	35	30	21
1	25	6	23	4	14	13	13	♍	22
1	28	52	24	5	15	13	52	1	23
1	32	38	25	6	16	14	30	2	24
1	36	25	26	7	16	15	9	3	25
1	40	13	27	8	17	15	47	3	26
1	44	1	28	9	18	16	26	4	26
1	47	49	29	10	19	17	5	5	27
1	51	38	30	11	19	17	44	5	28

H.	M.	S.	10 ♉ °	11 ♊ °	12 ♋ °	Ascen ♌ °	′	2 ♍ °	3 ♍ °
1	51	38	0	11	19	17	44	5	28
1	55	28	1	12	20	18	23	6	29
1	59	18	2	13	21	19	2	7	♎
2	3	8	3	14	22	19	41	8	1
2	7	0	4	15	22	20	20	8	2
2	10	52	5	16	23	20	59	9	2
2	14	44	6	17	24	21	39	10	3
2	18	37	7	18	25	22	18	11	4
2	22	31	8	19	26	22	58	11	5
2	26	26	9	20	26	23	38	12	6
2	30	21	10	20	27	24	17	13	7
2	34	17	11	21	28	24	57	14	8
2	38	14	12	22	29	25	37	15	9
2	42	11	13	23	29	26	18	15	9
2	46	9	14	24	♌	26	58	16	10
2	50	9	15	25	1	27	38	17	11
2	54	7	16	26	2	28	19	18	12
2	58	8	17	27	2	29	0	18	13
3	2	8	18	28	3	29	40	19	14
3	6	10	19	29	4	0 ♍	21	20	15
3	10	12	20	♋	5	1	2	20	16
3	14	16	21	1	6	1	44	21	17
3	18	19	22	2	6	2	25	22	18
3	22	24	23	3	7	3	7	23	18
3	26	29	24	4	8	3	48	24	19
3	30	35	25	4	9	4	30	24	20
3	34	42	26	5	9	5	12	25	21
3	38	49	27	6	10	5	54	26	22
3	42	57	28	7	11	6	36	27	23
3	47	6	29	8	12	7	18	28	24
3	51	16	30	9	13	8	1	28	25

H.	M.	S.	10 ♊ °	11 ♋ °	12 ♌ °	Ascen ♍ °	′	2 ♍ °	3 ♎ °
3	51	16	0	9	13	8	1	28	25
3	55	26	1	10	13	8	43	29	26
3	59	37	2	11	14	9	26	♎	27
4	3	48	3	12	15	10	9	1	28
4	8	1	4	13	16	10	52	2	28
4	12	13	5	14	17	11	35	2	29
4	16	27	6	15	17	12	18	3	♏
4	20	41	7	16	18	13	1	4	1
4	24	55	8	16	19	13	45	5	2
4	29	11	9	17	20	14	28	6	3
4	33	26	10	18	21	15	12	6	4
4	37	42	11	19	21	15	56	7	5
4	41	59	12	20	22	16	39	8	6
4	46	17	13	21	23	17	23	9	7
4	50	34	14	22	24	18	7	10	8
4	54	52	15	23	25	18	51	11	9
4	59	11	16	24	25	19	36	11	10
5	3	30	17	25	26	20	20	12	11
5	7	49	18	26	27	21	4	13	12
5	12	9	19	27	28	21	49	14	13
5	16	29	20	28	29	22	33	15	14
5	20	49	21	29	30	23	18	16	15
5	25	10	22	29	♍	24	2	16	15
5	29	30	23	♌	1	24	47	17	16
5	33	51	24	1	2	25	31	18	17
5	38	13	25	2	3	26	16	19	18
5	42	34	26	3	4	27	1	20	19
5	46	55	27	4	5	27	46	21	20
5	51	17	28	5	5	28	30	21	21
5	55	38	29	6	6	29	15	22	22
6	0	0	30	7	7	30	0	23	23

H.	M.	S.	10 ♋ °	11 ♌ °	12 ♍ °	Ascen ♎ °	′	2 ♎ °	3 ♏ °
6	0	0	0	7	7	0	0	23	23
6	4	22	1	8	8	0	45	24	24
6	8	43	2	9	9	1	30	25	25
6	13	5	3	10	10	2	14	25	26
6	17	26	4	11	10	2	59	26	27
6	21	47	5	12	11	3	44	27	28
6	26	9	6	13	12	4	29	28	29
6	30	30	7	14	13	5	13	29	♐
6	34	50	8	15	14	5	58	30	1
6	39	11	9	15	15	6	42	♏	1
6	43	31	10	16	15	7	27	1	2
6	47	51	11	17	16	8	11	2	3
6	52	11	12	18	17	8	56	3	4
6	56	30	13	19	18	9	40	4	5
7	0	49	14	20	19	10	24	5	6
7	5	8	15	21	20	11	9	5	7
7	9	26	16	22	20	11	53	6	8
7	13	43	17	23	21	12	37	7	9
7	18	1	18	24	22	13	21	8	10
7	22	18	19	25	23	14	4	9	11
7	26	34	20	26	24	14	48	9	12
7	30	49	21	27	24	15	32	10	13
7	35	5	22	28	25	16	15	11	14
7	39	19	23	29	26	16	59	12	14
7	43	33	24	30	27	17	42	13	15
7	47	47	25	♍	28	18	25	13	16
7	51	59	26	1	28	19	8	14	17
7	56	12	27	2	29	19	51	15	18
8	0	23	28	3	♎	20	34	16	19
8	4	34	29	4	1	21	17	17	20
8	8	44	30	5	2	21	59	17	21

H.	M.	S.	10 ♌ °	11 ♍ °	12 ♎ °	Ascen ♎ °	′	2 ♏ °	3 ♐ °
8	8	44	0	5	2	21	59	17	21
8	12	54	1	6	2	22	42	18	22
8	17	3	2	7	3	23	24	19	23
8	21	11	3	8	4	24	6	20	24
8	25	19	4	9	5	24	48	21	25
8	29	25	5	10	6	25	30	21	26
8	33	31	6	11	6	26	12	22	27
8	37	36	7	12	7	26	53	23	27
8	41	41	8	12	8	27	35	24	28
8	45	44	9	13	9	28	16	24	29
8	49	48	10	14	10	28	58	25	♑
8	53	50	11	15	10	29	39	26	1
8	57	52	12	16	11	0 ♏	20	27	2
9	1	52	13	17	12	1	0	28	3
9	5	53	14	18	13	1	41	28	4
9	9	51	15	19	13	2	22	29	5
9	13	51	16	20	14	3	2	♐	6
9	17	49	17	21	15	3	42	1	7
9	21	46	18	21	16	4	23	2	8
9	25	43	19	22	16	5	3	2	9
9	29	39	20	23	17	5	43	3	10
9	33	34	21	24	18	6	22	4	11
9	37	29	22	25	19	7	2	4	11
9	41	23	23	26	19	7	42	5	12
9	45	16	24	27	20	8	21	6	13
9	49	8	25	28	21	9	1	7	14
9	53	0	26	28	22	9	40	8	15
9	56	52	27	29	22	10	19	8	16
10	0	42	28	♎	23	10	58	9	17
10	4	32	29	1	24	11	37	10	18
10	8	22	30	2	25	12	16	11	19

H.	M.	S.	10 ♍ °	11 ♎ °	12 ♎ °	Ascen ♏ °	′	2 ♐ °	3 ♑ °
10	8	22	0	2	25	12	16	11	19
10	12	11	1	3	25	12	55	11	20
10	15	59	2	4	26	13	34	12	21
10	19	47	3	4	27	14	13	13	22
10	23	35	4	5	27	14	51	14	23
10	27	22	5	6	28	15	30	14	24
10	31	8	6	7	29	16	8	15	25
10	34	54	7	8	30	16	47	16	26
10	38	39	8	9	♏	17	25	17	27
10	42	24	9	10	1	18	4	18	28
10	46	9	10	10	2	18	42	18	29
10	49	53	11	11	3	19	20	19	♒
10	53	36	12	12	3	19	59	20	1
10	57	20	13	13	4	20	37	21	2
11	1	3	14	14	5	21	15	22	3
11	4	46	15	15	5	21	53	22	4
11	8	28	16	15	6	22	32	23	5
11	12	10	17	16	7	23	10	24	6
11	15	52	18	17	7	23	48	25	7
11	19	33	19	18	8	24	26	26	8
11	23	15	20	19	9	25	5	26	9
11	26	56	21	19	9	25	43	27	10
11	30	37	22	20	10	26	21	28	11
11	34	18	23	21	11	27	0	29	12
11	37	58	24	22	12	27	38	♑	14
11	41	39	25	23	12	28	17	1	15
11	45	19	26	24	13	28	55	1	16
11	48	59	27	24	14	29	34	2	17
11	52	40	28	25	14	0 ♐	13	3	18
11	56	20	29	26	15	0	52	4	19
12	0	0	30	27	16	1	31	5	20

TABLES OF HOUSES FOR *Latitude 53° 45′ N.*

H.	M.	S.	10 ♎ °	11 ♎ °	12 ♏ °	Ascen ♐ °	′	2 ♑ °	3 ♒ °
12	0	0	0	27	16	1	31	5	20
12	3	40	1	28	16	2	10	6	21
12	7	20	2	28	17	2	49	7	22
12	11	1	3	29	18	3	28	8	24
12	14	41	4	♏	19	4	8	8	25
12	18	21	5	1	19	4	47	9	26
12	22	2	6	2	20	5	27	10	27
12	25	42	7	2	21	6	7	11	28
12	29	23	8	3	21	6	47	12	29
12	33	4	9	4	22	7	27	13	♓
12	36	45	10	5	23	8	7	14	2
12	40	27	11	6	23	8	48	15	3
12	44	8	12	7	24	9	29	16	4
12	47	50	13	7	25	10	11	17	5
12	51	32	14	8	26	10	52	18	7
12	55	14	15	9	26	11	34	19	8
12	58	57	16	10	27	12	16	20	9
13	2	40	17	11	28	12	58	21	10
13	6	24	18	11	28	13	41	22	12
13	10	7	19	12	29	14	24	23	13
13	13	51	20	13	♐	15	7	24	14
13	17	36	21	14	1	15	50	26	15
13	21	21	22	15	1	16	34	27	17
13	25	6	23	15	2	17	19	28	18
13	28	52	24	16	3	18	3	29	19
13	32	38	25	17	3	18	48	♒	21
13	36	25	26	18	4	19	34	1	22
13	40	13	27	19	5	20	20	3	23
13	44	1	28	20	6	21	7	4	24
13	47	49	29	20	7	21	54	5	26
13	51	38	30	21	7	22	42	6	27

H.	M.	S.	10 ♏ °	11 ♏ °	12 ♐ °	Ascen ♐ °	′	2 ♒ °	3 ♓ °
13	51	38	0	21	7	22	42	6	27
13	55	28	1	22	8	23	30	8	28
13	59	18	2	23	9	24	18	9	♈
14	3	8	3	24	10	25	8	10	1
14	7	0	4	24	10	25	58	12	2
14	10	52	5	25	11	26	49	13	4
14	14	44	6	26	12	27	40	15	5
14	18	37	7	27	13	28	32	16	6
14	22	31	8	28	13	29	25	18	8
14	26	26	9	29	14	0 ♑	19	19	9
14	30	21	10	30	15	1	13	20	10
14	34	17	11	♐	16	2	9	22	12
14	38	14	12	1	17	3	5	23	13
14	42	11	13	2	18	4	2	25	15
14	46	9	14	3	18	5	1	26	16
14	50	9	15	4	19	6	0	28	17
14	54	7	16	5	20	7	0	♓	19
14	58	8	17	5	21	8	2	2	20
15	2	8	18	6	22	9	5	4	21
15	6	10	19	7	23	10	9	5	23
15	10	12	20	8	23	11	15	7	24
15	14	16	21	9	24	12	22	9	25
15	18	19	22	10	25	13	30	11	27
15	22	24	23	11	26	14	40	13	28
15	26	29	24	12	27	15	52	14	29
15	30	35	25	13	28	17	6	16	♉
15	34	42	26	13	29	18	21	18	2
15	38	49	27	14	♑	19	38	20	3
15	42	57	28	15	1	20	57	22	4
15	47	6	29	16	2	22	18	24	6
15	51	16	30	17	3	23	41	26	7

H.	M.	S.	10 ♐ °	11 ♐ °	12 ♑ °	Ascen ♑ °	′	2 ♓ °	3 ♉ °
15	51	16	0	17	3	23	41	26	7
15	55	26	1	18	4	25	7	28	8
15	59	37	2	19	5	26	35	♈	10
16	3	48	3	20	6	28	6	2	11
16	8	1	4	21	7	29	39	4	12
16	12	13	5	22	8	1 ♒	16	6	14
16	16	27	6	23	9	2	55	8	15
16	20	41	7	24	10	4	37	10	16
16	24	55	8	25	11	6	22	12	17
16	29	11	9	25	12	8	11	14	19
16	33	26	10	26	13	10	3	16	20
16	37	42	11	27	14	11	59	17	21
16	41	59	12	28	16	13	58	19	22
16	46	17	13	29	17	16	1	21	23
16	50	34	14	♑	18	18	8	23	25
16	54	52	15	1	19	20	19	25	26
16	59	11	16	2	20	22	34	27	27
17	3	30	17	3	21	24	52	29	28
17	7	49	18	4	23	27	15	♉	29
17	12	9	19	5	24	29	42	2	♊
17	16	29	20	6	25	2 ♓	13	4	2
17	20	49	21	7	27	4	47	6	3
17	25	10	22	8	28	7	25	8	4
17	29	30	23	9	29	10	6	9	5
17	33	51	24	11	♒	12	51	11	6
17	38	13	25	12	2	15	38	13	7
17	42	34	26	13	3	18	27	14	9
17	46	55	27	14	5	21	19	16	10
17	51	17	28	15	6	24	12	18	11
17	55	38	29	16	8	27	6	19	12
18	0	0	30	17	9	30	0	21	13

H.	M.	S.	10 ♑ °	11 ♑ °	12 ♒ °	Ascen ♈ °	′	2 ♉ °	3 ♊ °
18	0	0	0	17	9	0	0	21	13
18	4	22	1	18	11	2	54	22	14
18	8	43	2	19	12	5	48	24	15
18	13	5	3	20	14	8	41	25	16
18	17	26	4	21	16	11	33	27	17
18	21	47	5	22	17	14	22	28	18
18	26	9	6	24	19	17	9	♊	19
18	30	30	7	25	21	19	54	1	21
18	34	50	8	26	22	22	35	2	22
18	39	11	9	27	24	25	13	3	23
18	43	31	10	28	26	27	47	5	24
18	47	51	11	29	28	0 ♉	18	6	25
18	52	11	12	♒	♓	2	45	7	26
18	56	30	13	2	1	5	8	9	27
19	0	49	14	3	3	7	26	10	28
19	5	8	15	4	5	9	41	11	29
19	9	26	16	5	7	11	52	12	♋
19	13	43	17	7	9	13	59	13	1
19	18	1	18	8	11	16	2	15	2
19	22	18	19	9	13	18	1	16	3
19	26	34	20	10	14	19	57	17	4
19	30	49	21	11	16	21	49	18	5
19	35	5	22	13	18	23	38	19	5
19	39	19	23	14	20	25	23	20	6
19	43	33	24	15	22	27	5	21	7
19	47	47	25	16	24	28	44	22	8
19	51	59	26	18	26	0 ♊	21	23	9
19	56	12	27	19	28	1	54	24	10
20	0	23	28	20	♈	3	25	25	11
20	4	34	29	22	2	4	53	26	12
20	8	44	30	23	4	6	19	27	13

H.	M.	S.	10 ♒ °	11 ♒ °	12 ♈ °	Ascen ♊ °	′	2 ♊ °	3 ♋ °
20	8	44	0	23	4	6	19	27	13
20	12	54	1	24	6	7	42	28	14
20	17	3	2	25	8	9	3	29	15
20	21	11	3	27	10	10	22	♋	16
20	25	18	4	28	12	11	39	1	17
20	29	25	5	29	14	12	54	2	17
20	33	31	6	♓	16	14	8	3	18
20	37	36	7	2	17	15	20	4	19
20	41	41	8	3	19	16	30	5	20
20	45	44	9	5	21	17	38	6	21
20	49	48	10	6	23	18	45	7	22
20	53	50	11	7	25	19	51	7	23
20	57	52	12	9	26	20	55	8	24
21	1	52	13	10	28	21	58	9	25
21	5	53	14	11	♉	23	0	10	25
21	9	51	15	13	2	24	0	11	26
21	13	51	16	14	3	24	59	12	27
21	17	49	17	16	5	25	58	12	28
21	21	46	18	17	6	26	55	13	29
21	25	43	19	18	8	27	51	14	♌
21	29	39	20	20	10	28	47	15	1
21	33	34	21	21	11	29	41	16	1
21	37	29	22	22	13	0 ♋	35	17	2
21	41	23	23	24	14	1	28	17	3
21	45	16	24	25	15	2	20	18	4
21	49	8	25	26	17	3	11	19	5
21	53	0	26	28	18	4	2	20	5
21	56	52	27	29	20	4	52	20	6
22	0	42	28	♈	21	5	42	21	7
22	4	32	29	2	22	6	30	22	8
22	8	22	30	3	24	7	18	23	9

H.	M.	S.	10 ♓ °	11 ♈ °	12 ♉ °	Ascen ♋ °	′	2 ♋ °	3 ♌ °
22	8	22	0	3	24	7	18	23	9
22	12	11	1	4	25	8	6	24	10
22	15	59	2	6	26	8	53	24	10
22	19	47	3	7	27	9	40	25	11
22	23	35	4	8	29	10	26	26	12
22	27	22	5	9	♊	11	12	26	13
22	31	8	6	11	1	11	57	27	14
22	34	54	7	12	2	12	41	28	15
22	38	39	8	13	3	13	26	29	15
22	42	24	9	15	4	14	10	29	16
22	46	9	10	16	6	14	53	♌	17
22	49	53	11	17	7	15	36	1	18
22	53	36	12	18	8	16	19	2	19
22	57	20	13	20	9	17	2	2	19
23	1	3	14	21	10	17	44	3	20
23	4	46	15	22	11	18	26	4	21
23	8	28	16	23	12	19	8	4	22
23	12	10	17	25	13	19	49	5	23
23	15	52	18	26	14	20	31	6	23
23	19	33	19	27	15	21	12	7	24
23	23	15	20	29	16	21	53	7	25
23	26	56	21	♉	17	22	33	8	26
23	30	37	22	1	18	23	13	9	27
23	34	18	23	2	19	23	53	9	28
23	37	58	24	3	20	24	33	10	28
23	41	39	25	4	21	25	13	11	29
23	45	19	26	5	22	25	52	11	♍
23	48	59	27	6	22	26	32	12	1
23	52	40	28	8	23	27	11	13	2
23	56	20	29	9	24	27	50	14	2
24	0	0	30	10	25	28	29	14	3

Computer calculating services for astrologers

The easiest and most accurate way of obtaining a horoscope is to contact a computer calculating service. Obtain fee information first. Then send all relevant birth information, including: Place, Day, Month, Year, and Time (specify AM or PM).

Among the services are:

ASTROLOGICAL BUREAU OF IDEAS, Box 521, Wethersfield, Conn. 06109

ASTRONOMICAL COMPUTATIONS FOR ASTROLOGERS, P.O. Box 395, Weston, Mass. 02193

ASTRO NUMERIC SERVICE, Box 512, El Cerrito, Calif. 94530

ASTRO COMPUTING SERVICES, 129 Secor Lane, Pelham, N.Y. 10803

THE THIRTEENTH MANSION, INC., P.O. Box 9924, Fort Lauderdale, Fla. 33310

ATLANTA CHART SERVICE, P.O. Box 52861, Atlanta, Georgia 30355

For the most satisfactory results, the author recommends the Tropical Zodiac and the Placidus House System.

Mini-computers for astrologers

If you have access to a home or office mini-computer such as the Commodore PET, TRS-80 (Level II) or Apple II, then you can use an astrological cassette tape program to calculate your natal birth chart. Such tapes are available from:

MATRIX, 1041 North Main Street, Ann Arbor, Michigan 48104

MICROTRONIX, P.O. Box Q, Philadelphia, Pa. 19105

Specify the manufacturer and memory size of your computer.